BEER LAW

What Brewers Need to Know

By John Szymankiewicz Esq, PE

Copyright © 2017 by John Szymankiewicz

All rights reserved. No part of this publication may be reproduced, distributed, or transmitted in any form or by any means, including photocopying, recording, or other electronic or mechanical methods, without the prior written permission of the publisher, except in the case of brief quotations embodied in critical reviews and certain other noncommercial uses permitted by copyright law. For permission requests, write to the publisher, addressed "Attention: Permissions Coordinator," at the address below.

Beer Law Center

16 West Martin Street

Suite 501

Raleigh NC 27601

www.mathesonlawoffice.com

www.beerlawcenter.com

Ordering Information:

Quantity sales. Special discounts are available on quantity purchases by corporations, associations, and others. For details, contact the publisher at the address above.

Orders by U.S. trade bookstores and wholesalers. Please contact Beer Law Center:

Tel: (919) 335-5291; Fax: (919) 516-0686; or visit www.beerlawcenter.com.

Printed in the United States of America

First Printing, 2017

Szymankiewicz, John.

Beer Law: What Brewers Need to Know / John Szymankiewicz.

ISBN 978-1542730884

CONTENTS

Dedication	v
Foreword	vii
Introduction	1
Chapter One: Forming a Company	5
Chapter Two: Liability and Insurance	43
Chapter Three: Fundraising	65
Chapter Four: Contracts and Agreements	85
Chapter Five: Intellectual Property	121
Chapter Six: Trademark	145
Chapter Seven: The Three-Tier System	181
Chapter Eight: Federal Licensing	197
Chapter Nine: State Licensing	229
Chapter Ten: Labeling	249
Chapter Eleven: Distribution Agreements and Franchise Law	277
Chapter Twelve: Taxes	299
Chapter Thirteen: Buying and Selling a Brewery	315
Chapter Fourteen: Human Resources and Employment Law for Brewers	331
Supplemental Material. Legal Basics: How the Law Really Works	369
Supplemental Material. Zoning and Land Use	377
Supplemental Material. Glossary	387
Index	399

DEDICATION

This book is dedicated to two people: M. Moseley Matheson, my law partner, and Heather Szymankiewicz, my life partner.

To Moseley—

Thanks for believing that this "beer" thing is actually a thing and for supporting all the work that's gone into this book and the practice. Beer Law Center wouldn't be what it is without you.

To Heather—

Thanks for the patience, the understanding, and well … for everything. I wouldn't be who I am without you. With this done, it's one less thing you have to hear me stress about. So … what enormous, time-sucking project can I take on next?

FOREWORD

I've been lucky to have known John for a few years now, both in a work environment and a personal one. Besides being the type of guy whos check always clears, John has a knack for distilling complex legal phrases crafted by practitioners of the Dark Arts (you know…lawyers) and putting them into words that mortal humans like yourselves can understand. He covers everything with ease - from which type of corporate person to create, to the small stuff you would forget about when talking liability for your business. In short, John will save your butt from … well, your head. Which we can all use a little bit of.

As a homebrewer, I've often had dreams of opening my own brewery. This seems to be a fairly common fantasy that tends to manifest itself within this particular hobby. Seeing rows and rows of shiny stainless tanks (or if you are a masochist, copper jackets), sliding that freshly poured pint of beer across the bar top to the uberist of uber beer nerds who waited in line for 2 days for this moment - my perfect pint of beer. If I squint hard and rub my eyes I can just make out his online review: "Best pint I've ever had in my life, 1/ 5"…

The reality is much more stark and requires a myriad of Local, State, and Federal hoops to jump through before you get to that beer-sliding bit above. Over the past 12 years of interviewing professional brewers, one common thread appears in the grand Sweater of Life: the law is stupid. Nearly everyone I have spoken to who has gone through the rough patches of getting their brewery up and running has mentioned the need for a guide to help them through some of these basic tenets that

John covers here. The internet seems to be more of a bucket of information rather than an actual resource. A giant catch-all for every thought, idea, or experience that anyone with a library card and a bus pass can contribute to. Don't get me wrong, it's great for some things, but when it comes down to putting your entire financial future at risk opening up a brewery, you don't want to do it based in part on the advice that "BigJilm6969" gave you in some random forum. Trust me, a book written by a professional is the better option.

No matter how much research you do, you will miss something. Why? Because there is a lot of information out there, and you have an actual life to live in addition to trying to sort out the pro's and con's of crowdfunding, or splitting equity amongst your partners, or thinking about adding shelf-life clauses into your contracts. John has no life, so he's well-suited for doing this sort of research and boiling it down for you to use to make an informed decision. He's lonely like that.

Opening a brewery is the hot thing - you know that, and banks know that. However, while it seems like a no-brainer as far as an ROI goes, if you aren't set up mentally and legally before entering into any sort of business agreement with anyone, you just might find yourself in some pretty hot water. Lawsuits are becoming more and more common in the beer world, many are the result of Intellectual Property Rights - specifically over names of beers. Some are brought by competing breweries, some by B-list celebrities. I hear you asking, "Jason, the beer world is chock full of friends just crafting the best beer they can, right? They have no concern as to what I call my beers or my actual brewery. Stop being a jerk about it!" Don't let the chummy attitude of the craft beer world fool you, those brands sitting next to you are your competition, and they will protect their IP at all costs. As should you. However, the name of the game is to never get to that point in the first place, and that's where this book can help. From covering trademarks to trade secrets, John gives some great insight into not only protecting your brand from others, but making sure you don't get the hops sued off of you for an honest mistake.

Got all that? Good. Now listen to John, get your ducks in a row, and get your beer out there! Also, please consider brewing a lager or two. The last thing the world needs is another IPA…

Jason "JP" Petros
The Brewing Network

INTRODUCTION

So, uh, I needed to write an introduction to this final destination of scribbling I've been journeying toward for several years now. So, this is, uh… it.

The issue for me, as far as an introduction, is that I wanted to give folks background and insight on how I want/hope this book will be used, and to elaborate on what this book is and what it isn't.

Let's start with the easy stuff: what it isn't. This book is not a replacement for a lawyer or specific legal advice for your situation. This book is not a means to make you an expert on all things legal-y for alcohol law. This book is not exhaustive or comprehensive for all the legal issues that a brewer or brewery might ever face. This book is not specific to your state's laws. And, this book is not the final authority—especially as laws and practices constantly change.

"In that case," I hear you begin, "why the hell should I buy this damn thing?" Well, thanks for that poignant, if maybe a little over assertive, segue. This book is a few things. This book is an attempt at a solid overview of the most common legal issues brewers and new breweries face in startup, growth, and managing their business. This book is a strong introduction not only in what the law is, but why the law is that way. "If you want to get where you're going, you've got to know where you've been," said somebody, somewhere. Understanding the genesis of things like "blue" laws, trademark rights, and distribution trade practices, helps us to be in a better position to make good arguments to regulators—or even ourselves—about why things should change or how we can assuage the fears of regulators and lawmakers to let us do what we do best: brew and sell beer.

I'll digress for a second here. I spend a lot of time with clients to make sure that they understand not only what they need to do, but why they need to do it. Blind obedience—even to a lawyer! —leads to misunderstandings and the wrong kind of legalism ("You said I 'shouldn't!' You didn't say I 'couldn't!'"). Building understanding for what you're doing gives you better tools to manage the issues in the future. "Why can I do this, but not that?" Well, if you understand how the ABC, TTB, or other regulators or law enforcement view these things, maybe the distinction between the two will be even more clear. So my philosophy is that, yes, you pay me for advice but you also pay me for education. After all, maybe the next time it comes up, you won't need me to make that same decision, and isn't that a "win?" Also, I believe that I do not bring value to my clients by hoarding information. I build value by sharing knowledge; not by charging you for access to that experience. Don't get me wrong, I still gotta make a living! But, let me work on the special problems where my expertise is needed, not when it's a simple "turn the crank" operation—you can probably do those for yourself, right?

Anyway, back to the introduction bit.

I want people to be able to use this book to get more familiar with the issues, understand the players, and educate themselves about how general principles and regulations impact their specific situation. I want Beer Law: What Brewers Need to Know to help people become conversant in the language of the law as it applies to beer and be able to ask informed questions rather than feel they're struggling in the dark with an amoebic blob called "the law."

Beer Law: What Brewers Need to Know was never intended to be a panacea for brewers. I merely want it to be some fundamental acetylsalicylic acid ("aspirin") for the headaches that you're likely to face on your own journey chasing beer-y dreams. I also didn't want it to be a legal textbook where every third word was italicized Latin for an obscure legal concept that just makes the lawyer sound uppity.

I hope we've hit the mark for something that's readable and useful. Let me know how we did, and feel free to drop me a line at john@beerlawcenter.com.

Cheers!
John

CHAPTER ONE: FORMING A COMPANY

"So," you may be asking, "I think I should be a corporation of some kind, but why? And, which one?" Well, first, let's take a step back. The idea of forming a corporation centers on the fact that a corporation is a legal entity.

What do we mean by a "legal entity?" A legal entity has an identity of its own; it's its own thing, a "legal fiction" that's treated like something it isn't. Really confused now? Here's the bottom line: a corporation is a fake person. A corporation has most of the rights of any real person, but no actual body with guts, bones, etc.

One other quick note: forming a company and really most "company-type" law is state law. Registration of a legal entity is a state function. Generally speaking, you register the company with the state's Office of the Secretary of State (or its equivalent) and the requirements for the entity are state specific. There are a couple of federal law interactions with "state" companies. We'll cover those interactions in this section as well.

 TOPICS TO CONSIDER

"Great. So it's a fake person. Why do we care?" Well, we care because of two special issues regarding "people" (here, "people" includes corporations). People are liable for crimes and civil wrongs (damages), and people have to pay taxes.

TOPICS: LIABILITY

Let's say that you run over your neighbor's fence with your car. Is it the car's fault? No. You did it. You're liable for the damages (compensation for the injury to their property).

John Says: "We'll talk a lot about liability, so buckle in. This is an important topic all around."

Another hypothetical: you're a brewer and you sell someone a beer, but it's really about 50% caustic cleaning solution. The person is rushed to the hospital and quickly racks up a couple hundred thousand dollars in medical bills and promptly sues you. Who's liable for this person's medical bills? Initially, they may pay the hospital, but I assure you they're going to come after someone for compensation. Who owes them the $200,000? Is it the brewery? Or is it you?

Well, essentially, only a "person" can cause something to

happen (your chair isn't responsible for burning your dinner on the stove, right?), so only a "person" can be liable for the damages. Here's where the corporation thing comes in. If it's the company-person that did the thing, then the company-person is liable—not the person-person. Make sense?

> *For example, let's say that you're Bill Brewer. And you own Bill's Beer. One day, during a brewery tour, Vicky Visitor trips over a transfer hose, falls, and sustains a serious head injury. (We'll set aside the tragedy of the situation and focus for now on the issue of liability). So, who's liable for the medical bills and ongoing care of Vicky?*

> *Well, if you're not a company (i.e. if there's no company-person), that means that you—Bill Brewer—may be personally liable for all the expenses, injuries, and forever care for Vicky.*

> *But if your brewery is set up as a company, then Bill's Beer Inc. is more likely to be responsible for everything, and not Bill Brewer.*

Being a company or some sort of legal entity means placing a shield between your personal liability (i.e. your home, retirement account, life savings, etc.) and your business. That shield takes the form of a fake-person ("legal fiction") as a corporation.

Knowing, and carefully choosing, what form of business you're running is an important part of understanding your legal and financial risk. It can also be a means to minimize or mitigate risk that you cannot avoid altogether.

TOPIC: TAXES

Time for honesty—this book is not a primer on taxes, tax law, or how to pay the least you possibly can. What we do know, and want to communicate, is that there are tax consequences for being (or being responsible for) a company. After all, a company is a "person" right? And if the "person" makes money (i.e. income), you can bet that someone somewhere is going to want to tax that income.

So what do you do? Make sure you have a relationship with a Certified Public Accountant (CPA) or tax specialist. Make sure and review with them the operating structure of the business (whatever it is). Also, on an ongoing basis, be sure to review with your tax specialist:

- Major (capital) purchases
- Employee/payroll
- Equity in the business
- How/when owner of the company get paid
- How/when to take money out of the business

All sorts of transactions can have tax consequences. And those consequences can vary for you personally or corporately depending on how you're legally structured. We recommend that clients choose a legal form based on guarding their liability or reducing personal risk, then confirm with a CPA that the tax consequences also make sense for your situation.

One last quick word on taxes, and that's the so-called "double taxation" bit. If you're a corporation (a "fake person"), the corporation gets taxed on the money it makes (remember, it's a person, if it makes money, that's income, which means somebody is going to pay income tax). And then, as an owner of a corporation you (personally) have to pay tax *again* on the money that the corporation pays to you. So, the same money is taxed *twice*; once as it comes to the corporation, and once as it comes to you. Yuck.

John Says: "I'm not a tax expert; you'll need to talk to a CPA."

But some forms of legal entities allow the money to "pass through" the company so you only pay income tax on it once— when *you* receive it. More on this later as it may be a serious factor in choosing the form of legal entity you want your business to be.

CORPORATION BASICS

Corporations have been around for a very long time. The earliest "corporations" date back to the Roman era and were principally public in nature, such as colleges, towns, or churches. The earliest known private corporation appears to be the Stora Kopparberg mine (or "Great Copper Mountain") in Sweden whose charter (i.e. status) was granted by King Magnus Erikkson in 1347. Each of the miners owned "shares" of the mine, with no one person owning the company's property or its assets/liabilities.

Some of the earliest corporations, that we in the U.S. would recognize as such, were chartered by the King of England. Some that we might recognize would include the famous/infamous East India Company (chartered in 1600) and the

Virginia Company (chartered in 1606). These were some of the first companies that were corporate (from the Latin *corpus*—meaning "body") in nature and did not a have a single person or persons liable for the losses or injuries of the company. You could invest in the company and you'd get a share of the profits. But if the company lost money, the creditors couldn't come back and get more money from you personally.

This sounds like routine stuff for us today, but during the Renaissance, this was the cutting edge of finance and law. Up until then, if you started a business, you were responsible for everything that the business did or didn't do—including paying debts. And this was back when they had debtor's prison!

The idea was that you could have a separate entity (that fake-person, remember) responsible, so that you could have some control over the entity (say, through owning shares), and that *your liability was limited* to what you had invested. This opened the floodgates to investment and economic growth globally, particularly for the colonization of the New World.

There's a catch. There's always a catch. Even a fake-person needs maintenance. Just like real people eat, breathe, and need shelter, companies have certain needs too. They act through agents (i.e. real people), so they need people and records of what people have done for the company. Let's see if an analogy works here:

	Real Person	Company
Birth	Birth Certificate	Certificate of Formation
Rules	Education or examples	Bylaws or Operating Agreement
Sustenance	Food or drink	Income
Reward/Incentive	Pleasure or survival	Profit
Decisions	Mental/emotional	Owner's Direction (Meetings)
Protection from Outside	Shelter	Capitalization
Cessation	Death Certificate	Certificate of Dissolution

Okay, so some of these aren't perfect fits, but you get the idea. The bottom line is that there are practices required for the "care and feeding" of your company. It's not just an "I've filed my piece of paper, now I'm a company!" sort of thing. Just like any other "person," if you don't feed them and make sure their needs are met, then they're not going to perform very well when you need their special talents.

 ## TYPES OF COMPANIES

As you might expect, there are different types of "legal entities" that your business can be. Way back in 1606 and right up until the recent past, there were relatively few types, but now there are many ways to set up a business, each with its advantages and disadvantages.

Prior to 1987, the general rule was that you could either be a Sole Practitioner, a General Partnership, or a Corporation. Now, there are LPs, LLCs, LLPs, PAs, PCs—a regular alphabet soup of choices. So, do you just dunk your spoon and see what you come up with? No, you need to understand what you choose and why—you want to make sure it fits your goals and business plan.

We'll look at each of these with a short overview/description and then try to hit the major advantages and disadvantages.

SOLE PROPRIETORSHIP

A Sole Proprietorship (SP) is probably the oldest form of business entity and the easiest to establish. An SP is essentially you, just you, doing business. You can still have employees and be an SP, but when push comes to shove, you're on the hook. When your eight-year-old opens up a lemonade stand, congratulations! They've just (technically) formed a Sole Proprietorship. An SP is mind-boggling, easy to form, but even more mind-bogglingly useless in protecting you personally from risk. As an SP, you are personally on the hook for everything the business does.

> *For example, let's say you're Larry Landscaper who just started a landscaping business. One day, you're mowing a particularly nice home's front lawn. A bolt comes loose on your 12 horsepower riding lawnmower and the grass cutting blade is ejected at high speed and embeds itself in the side of the homeowner's new Bugatti Veyron (Manufacturer's Suggested Retail Price (MSRP): just north of $2.2 MILLION), damaging the engine block. Estimated repair cost: $500,000. Your business insurance (you have some, right?) only covers $100,000; you never thought you'd need more than that for a landscaping business. That leaves you to absorb the other $400,000. The liability doesn't stop with the business; it goes right through to you personally. Filing for personal bankruptcy protection starts sounding not-so-bad.*

Now let's look at the advantages/disadvantages:

Sole Partnership	
Advantages	Disadvantages
• Super easy to form/start	• No persoanl liability protecton
• Taxes pass through	• Only one owner

GENERAL PARTNERSHIP

A General Partnership is sort of like an SP, but for really friendly people. A GP is also stupidly easy to form, but is *even worse* for the individual than an SP.

John Says: "This is generally a bad idea."

Specifically, a General Partnership is a partnership where all partners have an equal right to control the business, to commit or bind the business, or to dispose of or purchase assets of the business. In a GP, you are all 100% owners of the company. That sounds not too bad, right?

Here's the bit that will make your hair stand on end. Not only are you personally responsible for the debts and liabilities of the business, you are also personally responsible for the debts and liabilities of the business that are caused by one of the other partners.

> *For example, let's say you and Ned Nefarious decide to open an auto mechanic shop to repair very expensive cars. One day, as Ned is going through a particularly nasty divorce, he pulls a Bugatti Veyron (lawnmower blade still sticking out of the fender) into the main work bay. He then proceeds to crush the car with the inspection lift, totaling the car. When you go to confront Ned about it, you find him curled up in the fetal*

position sucking his thumb and mumbling something about Carol Channing.

After the psychiatric hospital has taken Ned away, the owner of the Veyron (who was formerly just weeping) is now screaming at you and pulling sizable chunks of his own hair out of his head. The owner's attorney explains to you that, because you're a General Partnership, you're on the hook for Ned's breakdown and the resulting destruction of his client's car. Unfortunately, he's probably right.

So, the moral of the story here is that, if you're going to form a General Partnership, you have to be very very VERY sure about the person and have a very very VERY large amount of trust in them. People (mostly lawyers probably) have said that it is often easier to get out of a marriage than it is to get out of a General Partnership.

John Says: *"This too, is generally a bad idea."*

It's surprising that a GP is so easy to form, and yet can expose you to that much risk. The general formula for forming a GP is "an agreement between two or more persons to conduct a business for profit." Depending on the kind of person you are, you could accidentally do that over a pint at the bar. So be careful!

Now let's look at the advantages/disadvantages:

General Partnership	
Advantages	Disadvantages
• Super easy to form/start	• No persoanl liability protecton
• Taxes pass through	• Only one owner

LIMITED PARTNERSHIP

"These all sound unbelievably bad," I hear you say, "Why would I want to do any of these?" Well, you probably don't want to do any of the ones we've discussed. It does get better as we move along, and it helps to look at each of these as adding layers to the ones beneath.

For example, we're going to talk about Limited Partnerships, which are better for the individual than either SPs or GPs, but do have some disadvantages.

As you might guess, history has a lot of SPs and GPs in it. Then we come along to folks who say, "Hey, I've got this pile of money here that I'd like to invest. But I'm not willing to go on the hook for everything if you screw this up." The Limited Partnership (LP) was made for this.

An LP is a partnership where one or more of the partners has limited liability, but also has limited rights. The upside: you can't lose more than you invest. The downside: you may not get to make a lot of decisions about the business or what the business does. Now, because there are Limited Partners, with limited rights, there has to be at least one General Partner, with unlimited rights (and unlimited liability). In an LP, it's normally the General Partner who gets to dictate the day-to-day operations of the business and make the business decisions.

> *Let's go back to Ned's nervous breakdown from before. If the partnership were formed as a Limited Partnership, maybe you wouldn't be on the hook for a new Veyron if you were the Limited Partner. But if you were the General Partner, you'd still be on the hook.*

So, just like in a GP, in an LP, there's at least one General Partner who has unlimited liability. In that sense they are very similar. But, with an LP you can have Limited Partners who have limited liability. We're starting to make the move to more and more limitation on the liability of the individual in business. This makes sense because generally we want to encourage investment and economic growth—and a major way of doing that is minimize the risk the investor is exposed to.

John Says: "Not great but getting better."

Now let's look at the advantages/disadvantages:

Limited Partnership	
Advantages	Disadvantages
• Limited Partners have limited liabilit	• No personal liability protection for general partnersn
• Taxes pass through	• Partnership Agreement requiredr

CORPORATION

A corporation is the standard/traditional "Inc." that we all know and love. The ownership of a corporation is based on the ownership of shares (or "stock") of the corporation. The percent ownership of the corporation is proportional to the number of shares owned. The ownership rights (and voting) of the owner of the shares is also proportional to the number of shares owned.

> *For example, if there are 100 shares of stock available at Billy Beer Co., and Billy Brewer owns sixty shares and Ivan Investor owns forty shares, then Billy Brewer owns 60% of the corporation. Additionally, for corporate votes (on matters like major purchases, sales, of the company) Billy has sixty votes to Ivan's forty.*

A corporation is the first entity we've discussed here that doesn't require a natural person (i.e. a "real" person) to be an owner. Companies or other corporations can be owners of corporations.

For example, continuing the example above, Ivan Investor could just as easily be Investico Inc. And, Investico Inc. (or its duly designated representative) holds the ownership interest and can cast the votes.

You've probably heard the terms S-Corp and C-Corp. A corporation is a creature of state law and, generally, upon registration (formation), the state doesn't really care what type of corporation you are. In fact, for most states, there is only one type of corporation. The distinction between S-Corp and C-Corp is a federal IRS designation and primarily relates to tax issues.

We'll talk about S-Corps and C-Corps separately because the distinction plays a big role in choosing what type of legal entity you want to be.

The S-Corp is the IRS's way to allow small businesses the advantages of being a corporation, without penalizing them with additional administrative burdens. Those burdens aren't a big deal to large corporations but could be traumatic for small businesses. To be an S-Corp, you have to meet certain requirements. These include:

- Be a domestic corporation (meaning that you can't be a foreign corporation registering in the U.S. to do business)
- Shareholders must be "allowable" shareholders—for our purposes this means only "real" people can be shareholders. There are exceptions for certain trusts, but shareholders of an S-Corp cannot be another corporation, partnership, or non-resident aliens.
- Have a hundred or fewer shareholders
- Have only one class of stock
- And it can't be an ineligible corporation (such as an insurance company or financial institution)—not a big deal for our purposes.

If your company meets the above requirements, the IRS will allow you to be treated as an S-Corp for tax purposes. So what does that mean? Well, for S-Corps, income taxes are passed through the corporation to the shareholders. Meaning that S-Corps avoid the "double-taxation" bit we talked about earlier. So, S-Corps are a good option for many small businesses, especially if you want to distribute "control" or "ownership" among many people and have those ownership rights fairly fluid or sellable.

C-Corp Corporations are much more like traditional corporations (like IBM or Sears). C-Corps don't have to meet the requirements listed above for S-Corps. That allows them to have multiple classes of stock, foreign ownership, ownership by other corporations, or many shareholders (think "publicly traded"). Unfortunately, C-Corps are squarely in the "double tax" crosshairs. Think of it as being a penalty for being too big or being owned by someone/something other than a "real" person.

Something worth mentioning is the issue of classes of stock (this will be discussed later in the chapter in more detail). If you have different classes of stock, you can have shareholders with different rights. In the corporate bylaws, the stock types can be defined in lots of creative ways such as different voting rights, different dividend rights, different sales rights, etc.

> *For example, if Billy Beer Co., Inc. is a C-Corp, there could be two classes of stock, Class A and Class B. Billy Brewer could own all of the Class A stock, while Ivan owns Class B stock. Class A stock could have two votes to every one vote of Class B stock, but Class B stock might have preference in getting paid dividends, or Class B gets paid first in the event of the sale of the company.*

As you can see, a C-Corp has some significant flexibility, but you pay for it with the tax issues. Additionally, the law relating to corporations has been around for hundreds of years, so there are parts of case law and statutes that will override whatever agreement you might have. Particularly, the law has special protections for "minority shareholders" to ensure that they're not unfairly treated by shareholders with more apparent control. Some of these issues may have a bearing on what you do with your corporation, but probably aren't determinative when selecting what kind of company to be.

S-Corp	
Advantages	Disadvantages
• Limited Liability for all owners and Board of Directors	• Business must meet several IRS requirements
• Taxes pass through	• Partnership Agreement Required
	• Corps have some established case law that may "overwrite" bylaws of shareholder agreementst

C-Corp	
Advantages	Disadvantages
• Limited Liability for all owners and Board of Directors	• Corp pays income tax on its income, then owners pay income tax AGAIN on money they receive from the Corp
• Very flexible ownership structures and options	• Corps have some established case law that may "overwrite" bylaws or shareholder agreements

LIMITED LIABILITY COMPANY

A Limited Liability Company, or LLC is a partnership at heart. It's in this portion of the list because it marked a substantial departure from almost everything that had ever gone before.

Back in 1977, Wyoming of all places, issued the very first Limited Liability Company act. The act was based on the German GmbH (or *Gesellschaft mit beschränkter Haftung*, meaning "company with limited liability") and allowed a company to behave like a corporation with all the liability shield, etc., but with more flexibility in how it would be run since it wasn't a "corporation." And, it didn't really catch on until the IRS issued a ruling indicating that an LLC would be taxed like a partnership rather than like a corporation. Then things took off.

An LLC is a company that can be owned by "members" that are not restricted to the kinds of owners required by an S-Corp. The taxes are "passed through" like a partnership. In addition, because it's not a corporation, there is less "settled law" on the subject. That means that generally the law of contracts governs the LLC as between the members and as to how the business will be run, i.e., what the rules are. As a result, there's a lot of flexibility in how LLCs can be organized, how they're run, and how they operate. This flexibility makes an LLC a super attractive option for small companies that are looking to grow. The agreement between the members as to how the LLC will be run is called an Operating Agreement. Think of the Operating Agreement for an LLC as

John Says: "This is probably where you want to look."

the same function bylaws serve in a corporation.

But there are a few other things to think about. First, even though it's called a "company," it's really based on the idea of a partnership. So, most of the statutes—and the case law supports this—are designed for a small number of owners ("members") and the members are real people. The members don't *have* to be real people, but that's the way it's designed. Also, the members are generally all treated equally—no member has more authority or ownership than any of the others. Because of the flexibility of the LLC, all of these can be tweaked or adjusted based on whatever the members agree to in the Operating Agreement. So, you can do almost anything with an LLC, but it's sometimes a little awkward.

> *For example, unless the Operating Agreement says otherwise, each member has an equal share in the company. If there are four members in Billy Beer LLC, then each member owns 25% equally.*

Alternately, the Operating Agreement can specify different types of members—some with more control or rights than others. So that, for Billy Beer LLC, Billy Brewer could be the only Class A member where Class A members control 60% of the company, and other members are Class B members (investors, for example).

There are endless permutations and tweaks to how the company "rules" can be structured. This flexibility makes it really attractive to companies that need to be quick and supple in their market.

BEER LAW: WHAT BREWERS NEED TO KNOW

Limited Liability Company LLC	
Advantages	Disadvantages
• Limited Liability for all owners and Managers	• Operating Agreement required to solidify ownership rights and responsibilities
• Very flexible ownership structures and options	
• Operating Agreement drafting lets owners "write the rules" of the LLC	
• Taxes pass through	•

For the vast majority of small businesses, an LLC is a great option for a company in the startup phase. It's almost become the "default setting" for new companies.

John Says: "This is also probably where you want to look."

LIMITED LIABILITY PARTNERSHIP

The Limited Liability Partnership (LLP) is really just an extension of partnership law to accommodate the "limited liability" aspect of LLCs. As we discussed before, an LLP allows all the partners in a partnership to have limited liability without the need to have a General Partner. However, the LLP goes back to a "general partnership" model of ownership, meaning that all partners are treated equally in terms of control, assets, and ownership rights. No one partner has more rights/control than another.

LLP	
Advantages	Disadvantages
• Limited Liability for all owners and Managers	• Partnership Agreement required to solidify ownership rights and responsibilities
• Partnership Agreement drafting lets owners "write the rules" of the LLP	• Partners generally need to be natural persons

LLLP, CO-OPS, NON-PROFITS, AND BEYOND...

As you might expect, some people out there want to be a partnership where all the partners have limited liability AND some partners are limited in their rights. So, some states have enacted a new type of partnership—the Limited Liability Limited Partnership (LLLP). As of this writing, only a few states have established this type of entity, and many states are trying to figure out how this works or whether it's needed.

"What about a Co-Op?" you might ask. Well, a Co-Op, or Cooperative Ownership, is a method of ownership, not a specific legal entity. Co-Ops must generally be registered as a C-Corp. C-Corp registration is generally preferred simply based on the number of owners (typically more than a hundred) and that means that, unfortunately, the corporation is open to the double-taxation of "income." However for Co-Ops, income to the shareholders is typically not the basis or reason for the investment, but it is something to be aware of.

Also, we should talk a little about non-profits. There's a lot of talk about breweries as Co-Ops and non-profits to give back to the community. We've already discussed Co-Ops. There are questions as to whether a brewery, brewpub, or bar can be a non-profit organization. Generally speaking, "non-profit" is an IRS designation, not a corporate/state recognition. Many states have "non-profit corporation" as an option, meaning that you can register your company that way, but the state will only "presume" that you're a legitimate non-profit until the IRS makes its determination (most states simply follow the IRS determination if there would ordinarily be state income tax). It's a way of saying, "Hey, this is what we think we're gonna do, so don't charge us right away." But, regardless of the "non-profit" moniker at the state level, non-profits generally have to be registered as a corporation, then apply for non-profit status through the IRS using Form 1023. Can a place that serves/manufactures alcohol be a non-profit business? Specifically, a non-profit business must be run to provide a public benefit and is generally prohibited from engaging in certain types of activities (like gambling or lobbying). For most non-profits, the "business" is providing the public benefit (like an educational foundation), while the fundraising or selling of a product (like a thrift store) is the ancillary or "necessary evil" that supports the public benefit part. It's an open question on whether or not a brewery could overcome the hurdles/obstacles necessary to get non-profit status.

 ## ONE MORE THING ... PIERCING THE CORPORATE VEIL

"Piercing the Corporate Veil" (PCV) is a legal doctrine and a fancy way of saying, "just because you're a corporation, we can still get to you personally." The idea is that a corporation (including LLCs, LLPs, etc.—anything with limited liability) has a "liability shield" between the owners and the company.

Generally, with limited liability, or a "liability shield" in place, you can sue the corporation, but that's where the liability ends. If you sue the corporation and win, you can get at the assets of the corporation, but you CANNOT get at the assets of the individual owners of the corporation.

But, there are certain instances where the court will push aside the liability shield and let the plaintiff (the person suing) get at the individual owners directly. Anytime you hear someone say "piercing the corporate veil," you should think one of two things:

John Says: "*Legal mumbo jumbo. Some people try to intimidate others. They are bozos.*"

- "This person has read a book once in his life and is completely full of manure, and is just trying to bully or impress me." OR
- "I may be in serious trouble."

Far and away the first choice is the more common. But in case you may be facing the "I may be in serious trouble" option, there are some things that you should know. First, the idea of pushing aside the liability shield comes from a desire to do equity (i.e. justice). If you're using a corporate structure just to avoid liability and you're trying to "get away with something," you're a prime target for PCV. If you're a legitimate corporation doing legitimate corporation things/actions, you're not very likely a target and if *you* are a target, you can likely defeat anyone wanting to assert a PCV against you.

So, how do you prove that you're a legitimate corporation doing legitimate corporation things? The answer is that you follow what's called "corporate formalities." It sounds like corporate formalities equals superficial administration, but that's not really the case. Corporate formalities are the evidence that the corporation is run as a business for a legitimate purpose and that the corporation is not the "mere instrument" of one of the owners. What are the corporate formalities you need to follow? We'll discuss that in the next section, but be aware the reason you do those things is to strengthen your liability shield to be able to show to someone that you, as an owner, should not be held liable for the corporation's actions.

WHAT ELSE DO I NEED TO DO?

There are two basic areas of "what's next?" Generally speaking, you need to complete (1) Registration/Filing and (2) Corporate Formalities. We'll touch on the registration and filing bit first, then the remainder of this section will be on the various corporate formalities.

REGISTRATION/FILING

When we talk about registration or filing we're talking about the corporation or company that you're forming. This doesn't have to do with the TTB (Tax and Trade Bureau), ABC (Alcohol Beverage Control), or any other regulatory agency or with alcohol at all. This part applies just as well as if you were opening a hotdog stand or a car dealership.

As we said earlier, corporations and companies—LLCs, LLPs, LPs, etc.—are all creatures of state law. You need to register your company in your state. Generally, corporations are registered and tracked through your state's Office of the Secretary of State (or equivalent). Most states have simple forms that you can fill out and send back with your appropriate filing fee and the office will complete the entity registration. However, you may want to consult with an attorney in your state to make sure you understand the nuances of the forms.

> *For example, the form in North Carolina is very simple, but there's a very important designation on one of the forms that's easy to miss. Specifically, you have to know the difference between a member-managed LLC and manager-managed LLC. This sounds like it's not a big deal, but it may have a huge impact on your working relationship if you and your partner "disagree" on something in the future.*

After you've registered, the Secretary of State (or equivalent) will send you a copy of your certificate of registration/formation/incorporation/whatever. Keep this certificate in a safe place at your principle place of business (wherever that is). At this point, if not previous to this, you now have "important corporate records" (this'll come up later). You should keep all your important corporate records in order and in a single location at your principle place of business. It's okay to have backups, electronic copies, or whatever, but your corporate records should be easily accessible from your place of business and should be in some logical order.

Additionally, after you've registered your company/entity, the state will likely require an Annual Report (or something like that) to verify that you're still in business and that the state's information is correct—they'll probably charge you a filing fee too. For most states the Annual Report is a simple one or two-page form that just indicates you're still in business and that your address info is the same—it's not an Annual Shareholder's Report that we've seen from large companies like International Paper Inc. or Home Depot Inc.; it's relatively painless to generate and file. However, if you fail to file your Annual Report, the state may revoke your registration. If you lose your registration, you're not a corporation anymore. No corporation equals no liability shield. Failing to file your Annual Report is probably the easiest way to lose your limited liability. Look into your state laws on annual filings to be sure you know what's due and when.

AGREEMENTS/BYLAWS

The single most important bit of corporate formality you need to have is some sort of agreement that specifies the rules you'll use to run the business. For corporations, these rules are called bylaws. For LLCs, they're called Operating Agreements, for partnerships, they're called Partnership Agreements. For this discussion, and the remainder of this section, we'll use "Operating Agreement" to cover both of these.

The idea is that the agreement spells out who owns what, how new owners buy into the company, how owners get out of the company (sell their share), who has what authority, who has what rights, and how disputes are resolved. Depending on the form of your business, there are different requirements for what needs to be and can't be included in the "rules."

> *For example, for corporations, minority shareholders are given special protections because of their status, notwithstanding any other agreement or direction in the bylaws.*

Generally, you should contact a lawyer for help in drafting your Operating Agreements. There are a lot of free templates available online, and they're probably worth what you pay for them. These agreements are state specific and can seriously affect your ability to run the company if they're not done correctly.

> *For example, say Billy Brewer and Ivan Investor start Billy Beer LLC. They have a badly drafted Operating Agreement (or worse, nothing at all), and then they have an argument. Well, without any specifics about who's entitled to do what, Ivan has equal access to the LLC and can clear out the accounts whenever or however he feels like it. And what can Billy do about it? Not much really. Billy could sue Ivan for Breach of Fiduciary Duty, but that's going to be tough after the money is gone. If they had had a properly drafted Operating Agreement, it would state which owner had the right to access company funds, or who had the right to bind the company, or who had the right to open (or close) an account in the company's name.* and much more

Which brings up another good point: if you have an Operating Agreement, follow it. If you consistently ignore your Operating

Agreement, the court will ignore it too. If you have something in place that doesn't fit your business, change it so that it does reflect what you're doing (within reason, of course). Again, a lawyer can help you figure out "yes, you can do that," or "no, that's a bad idea," or "well, you can, but you probably shouldn't." Consistency is key in your corporate formalities, and it starts with a set of rules that you follow for running the business, yet you must consistently follow those rules.

John Says: "This is really important."

OFFICERS/BOARD OF DIRECTORS

Any legal entity (like an LLC or corporation) acts through its agents. Can the corporation sign a piece of paper? No—it's not a "real" person. The corporation signs an agreement *through* an agent. An agent is someone authorized to act for the company.

You need to identify your first line of agents (i.e. the company officers). The initial identification of officers is typically listed in your Operating Agreement and any subsequent changes are listed in the corporate records. These are approved by whatever process is specified in your Operating Agreement.

> *For example, sometimes you'll see a signature space/title that says something like "Billy Brewer, President for Billy Beer LLC." This is the corporation designating that Billy is the agent through whom the company is acting to sign, accept, bind themselves, or take some action.*

Officers are the basis of agency for most companies. There should always be individuals designated as:

- President—is generally responsible for the company
- Vice-President—is responsible in the absence of the President
- Treasurer—is responsible for the company's finances
- Secretary—is responsible for the corporate records of the company

As generally indicated here, each of these officer positions (or their equivalent) has a basic set of recognized agency authority.

For example, when suing a company, you must serve a copy of the lawsuit to either the President, Secretary, or the company's Registered Agent (name and address on file with the Secretary of State). Handing a copy to the Treasurer does nothing. It has to go to someone with knowledge and responsibility for the corporate records. The President, Secretary, and Registered Agent all have a position which allows them to accept responsibility for receiving the lawsuit. The position of Registered Agent is specifically for receipt of legal service and has the duty to provide the service to the Secretary. The Secretary has overall responsibility for the corporate records and has the duty to inform the appropriate persons. The President has the overall responsibility for operating the company, as does the Secretary.

Agency (the ability to act for the company) follows along the generally accepted guidelines of responsibility. Generally only the Treasurer or the President can sign a binding contract for the company, unless they've specifically delegated that authority to a different agent. In most cases, only the Secretary has the authority to call a shareholder meeting. And, for the most part, only the Treasurer or President can sign checks for the company (again, unless they've delegated that authority).

It should be noted that often, especially in small and startup companies, one person may hold more than one office. The President and the Treasurer may be the same person. Or the Secretary and Treasurer may be the same person. If this is the way you're going to go, be sure to address it in your Operating Agreement.

In the vast majority of companies, officers report to the President. The President then reports to some sort of oversight body. For corporations, that oversight is generally done by a Board of Directors. The Board of Directors is elected by the shareholders of the corporation. In an LLC or the other limited liability entities, the Operating Agreement defines who the President or the Officers report to—typically some sort of management committee made up of owners/members.

Also, don't feel you're tied too closely to the names of the officer positions. The "C" level names have been gaining popularity in the last ten to twenty years. For the most part, President equals Chief Executive Officer (CEO); Treasurer equals Chief Financial Officer (CFO). But even in companies that use the "C" level designation, you will likely still find a position labeled Secretary or Corporate Secretary—that gives you some idea of how important the job really is (if you can't guess, it's pretty darned important).

MEETINGS

Next on the "must haves" for corporate formalities are meetings. Not meetings where you discuss the production schedule or how many coffee cups to order, but meetings of the owners to report on and discuss the critical decisions and direction of the company. For corporations, these are typically called "shareholder meetings." For other kinds of entities, they can be different names like "member meetings," "managing member meetings," "partner (or equity partner) meetings," etc. The idea is that those who "own" the company have to come together and do two things: (1) be informed about the company and its operations/status, and (2) make decisions.

Regular meetings should be held. For corporations, meetings should be held not less than once per year. For LLCs and other limited liability entities, the Operating Agreement should specify how often owner meetings are held, but annually is a good place to start. For most small businesses, especially during startup, it's often a good idea to hold meetings more frequently, say every six months or so.

The meetings should inform the owners about the financial condition of the business and address any major operational concerns or financial transactions—anything that would substantially impact how "risky" investment in the company is.

Certain kinds of decisions can only be made at meetings. The Operating Agreement should specify what types of decisions must be made at the meetings, but generally, these should include:

- Buying a new business (for example, a competitor or a new brand)

- Selling a/the business
- "Major" capital purchases—the Operating Agreement should define what's "major"
- Elections (of officers or Board of Directors members)

How often meetings are scheduled is really up to the owners and should be spelled out in the Operating Agreement. Failure to meet at least annually starts to look like the owners don't take their corporate responsibilities (and corporate formalities) seriously.

MEETING MINUTES

Now that you've had periodic meetings, you need to be sure and document the meeting. Meeting minutes should include:

- Name of the company
- Date, time, and location of the meeting
- Individuals in attendance and their title/role in the company, if appropriate
- Individuals not in attendance as well as some notation about whether they received notice of the meeting. It must be indicated if they were not able to attend, or if they sent a proxy (if that's allowed in the Operating Agreement)
- Name and title of the person chairing the meeting
- Major points of discussion, including financial reports, operations status update, major decisions made or discussed, and any action items from the meeting
- Decisions and the vote (if necessary) on those decisions

John Says: *"If it's not in writing it's sometimes hard to prove that it happened."*

The Secretary is responsible for putting together the meeting minutes and distributing copies to the owners. Meeting minutes should be published within thirty days of the meeting and should be distributed to all the owners (regardless of whether they were present at the meeting).

The meeting minutes (preferably an original, but if not available a copy is sufficient) should be included in the corporate records.

A best practice for meeting minutes is to create a template with the major points to be filled in. Use this template each time a meeting is held. When completing the meeting minutes, place a calendar reminder for the next meeting per the Operating Agreement.

On request, the Secretary should be able to produce meeting minutes for each meeting that *should have* taken place from the time the Operating Agreement was adopted until the present. Not being able to produce the meeting minutes leads to an inference that the meetings didn't happen. That inference seriously weakens your argument that the business is adhering to corporate formalities.

BOOKS AND RECORDS

When referring to "books" in the corporate sense, there are two broad categories: (1) financial records and (2) corporate records. We've already discussed corporate records that should at least include:

- Certificate of formation from the state

- Any filings or correspondence from the state about the corporation (such as annual reports)
- Operating Agreement (including the current version and all the valid previous versions)
- Corporate meeting minutes
- Corporate reports or attachments to meeting minutes (other than financial records/reports)
- Current list of owners/shareholders with their name, address, telephone number and "interest" (such as how many shares they own, are they a member? A partner?)
- Any legally significant/official correspondence to or from the company
- Any express delegation of authority or agency within the company or to someone outside the company (a sales agent who can bind the company is a common example; another common example would be the President delegating purchasing authority to a purchasing agent or someone else in the company)
- Personnel files (kept in conjunction with the Human Resources function)
- Company policies and procedures.

Corporate records are a major issue for corporate security. With them you can demonstrate corporate formalities, and be able to show control in the case of due diligence during a buyout or merger.

The Secretary is responsible overall for the records of the company; that includes financial records after they're used. Specifically, the Treasurer is responsible for the company finances, financial reports, taxes, and any additional necessary financial filings. The Treasurer generates and uses these "books" and then archives those records. The Secretary is responsible for maintaining those archived books and information.

> For example, if you want to know what your current bank and cash flow situation is, you go to your Treasurer. If the IRS wants to see your tax returns from two years ago, they should go through the Secretary (who will, no doubt, be assisted by the Treasurer as they sweat it out together).

So what financial records need to be kept? Generally speaking, any financial records or reports which support any reports, filings, or information provided to any regulatory agency, tax authority, or the owners should be retained and catalogued. These reports should include items such as:

- General Ledger
- Profit & Loss statements
- Balance Sheets
- Cash Flow statements
- Tax returns (or the appropriate schedules if passed through for tax purposes)
- Asset lists
- Sales and Cost of Goods Sold calculations and projections (at least as far as they pertain to the banking or credit of the organization)
- Credit or debt statements associated with the business
- Equity/loss of the owners/shareholders in the business

Again, this book isn't meant to be an all-inclusive treatise on taxes and bookkeeping. Be sure to consult with your CPA, bookkeeper, or tax specialist to determine precisely what makes sense for your company to keep and for how long.

The idea for the financial records, just like the corporate records, is that the Secretary—with the assistance of the Treasurer—can fulfill a request for certain records within a reasonable time. "So what's a reasonable time?" you ask. Well, it's easier to say what it isn't. It is unreasonable for it to take three months to put together all your records if you've only been in business for six months. Or, it's unreasonable for it to take four weeks to get a copy of your Operating Agreement—you should have that readily accessible. It would be considered lame if your one part-time intern is working on the records request even though you have a full time accountant and administrative staff. A "reasonable time" is really the time a reasonable person would expect for you to take to complete the task given the extent of the request. Is it all records? Some? Just a few? What about the nature of the records? Are the records paper only? And archived off site? Or are they electronic and easily searchable?

Also, bear in mind that regardless of your Operating Agreement's language, courts are generally going to hold that any owner has the right to examine the books and records of the company at the company's principal place of business as long as they give reasonable notice. There are exceptions to this, to be sure (just because you own one share of IBM stock, doesn't mean you can sally up to their corporate headquarters and look at everyone's paystubs). But, generally, owners—especially when the company is "closely held," meaning it has just a few owners—

should be easily able to review the books and records of the company on request.

POLICIES

Many people start their own business to get away from the bureaucracy of large corporations, procedures, policies, and paperwork. Yet, there is a critical purpose to some of those trappings of corporate America.

> *For example, as a business owner, if Billy Brewer or one of his employees discriminates against a minority or sexually harasses an employee, Billy and the company could be on the hook for a lawsuit from the employee and/or action by the government for violating someone's civil rights.*

How do you protect yourself and your business from these types of issues? How do you prove that something didn't happen or couldn't have happened? It's hard to prove a negative. You have to show that you've taken reasonable steps to ensure that these sorts of violations do not take place in your business. Documented policies, procedures, and training go a long way toward showing a court that you (or the business) didn't condone the behavior and therefore are not at fault.

Company policies should prescribe specific behavior that you either want OR don't want. They should spell out the behavior as well as the consequences of the behavior (such as termination). Each and every employee should be trained on the policy or policies and the training should be documented and kept in your employee files.

So what policies should you have? You should have a company policy against, at a minimum:

- Discrimination (race, gender, or national origin)
- Sexual harassment
- Workplace violence
- Substance abuse
- Theft

You should also consider policies that you want to have for convenience and consistency. Policies like attendance, vacation or paid time off, or your discipline process (prior to firing).

Consider having the employee fill out, sign, and date a form indicating that they received a copy of the policies. That way, if you or your employee(s) are accused of, for example, sexual harassment, you can point to your company policies and training to show that this conduct was specifically prohibited by the company and the responsibility is on the individual employee, not the business.

Also, you can't just "have" policies. You need to make sure that you're following and enforcing them. When you learn of an issue, you should immediately address it and document the violation as well as the consequences of the violation.

John Says: "If you have policies, FOLLOW THEM!"

Last, make sure that as policies change or are updated, you update and train your employees on the changes. Protecting yourself and your business isn't a one-time thing; it's an ongoing process.

CONSISTENCY

Whether it's policies, your Operating Agreement, or your meetings, consistency is key. Think of these things as promises to do something. If you promise and then don't do it—it looks really bad for your trustworthiness overall. If you're not following through on your promises on these things, look at why. Did you make the promise too hard to live up to? Is it a bad fit for your business?

Identify the issues that keep you and the company from being consistent and address those issues—even if it means changing the rules or the promise. The Operating Agreement is probably the most "sacred" of the documents you'll generate. And even that is a living document. Your Operating Agreement can change over time to reflect new issues, new owners, and new methods of doing business. Typically, all it takes to revise an Operating Agreement is for the owners to agree that it needs to be revised.

John Says: "We'll tie back to the HR and employment part of this stuff later."

Make sure you develop something you can live with (whether it's an Operating Agreement or policies or whatever). Always be sure to include the minimum requirements, but other than those, you can always add complexity later. Focus on what's achievable and what you can commit to do year after year.

CHAPTER TWO: LIABILITY AND INSURANCE

LIABILITY

There are many types of liability the savvy business owner should keep tabs on, the most important being criminal and civil liability.

To complicate matters for brewery owners, U.S. alcohol regulations make brewery ownerships much different from the rest of the American legal system. For the vast majority of the U.S. legal system, the law is one of prohibition; i.e., if it doesn't say you can't do it, then you can do it. But for alcohol, the law is one of permission: i.e. you can only do what the law says you can do. Suffice it to say that, when it comes deciphering the nuances and meaning of most alcohol statutes, everything that you think you know is wrong.

CRIMINAL LIABILITY

John Says: "Hopefully criminal charges aren't a real risk. But it depends how stupid you are. Wait, I mean...how high your risk tolerance is."

Criminal liability is perhaps better thought of as culpability or "guilt" for breaking the law. As an alcohol business owner, your primary concern in this regard is ensuring that you don't run afoul of the applicable federal and state laws and regulations. Federal law is pretty clear on most issues; state law varies wildly. Some of the intricacies of state and federal law will be discussed later on.

The critical part about criminal liability is that it can get you sent to jail. In many cases, regulations and alcohol laws do carry some criminal penalties, along with civil liability.

CIVIL LIABILITY

On the other hand, civil liability is generally limited to a concept called "money damages." Money damages are essentially the amount of money that one party suffered in being wronged, or injured, by the other party. In some cases, if you breach a contract or something, a court can order you to take specific action. But, generally, a court will only order the payment of money for civil liability. That is, the court will order the person found liable to pay money damages to the person who was wronged.

Within civil liability, there are different ways that civil liability can be acquired sometimes without even knowing it.

Specific issues of liability to be aware of for alcohol businesses, as opposed to many other businesses, include:

- Dram shop liability—what is the liability for the business if its employee over-serves a customer and the customer then harms himself or another?
- Premises liability—what is the liability for the business if the business invites individuals onto the premises to consume alcohol? For example, in a tap room located at a brewery:
    - Are all personnel appropriately trained in alcohol serving?
    - Are there production area tours where members of the general public might be exposed to cleaning chemicals, trip hazards, etc.?
    - Is alcohol served during the tour?
    - Are there adequate protections in place to prevent the general public (or employees for that matter) from getting injured? A brewery or distillery utilizes heated tanks, high pressure pumps, pressure vessels, and rotating equipment.
    - What about outside-the-normal-business premises use? What is the business's liability when the business holds a festival or party on their own property, but outside the production facility?
- Remote location liability—what is the liability of the business when the product is being served (perhaps by business personnel) at an offsite festival?

LIABILITY VERSUS BUSINESS STRUCTURE

When asked about how their business is structured, brewery owners often answer, "Oh, I'm just a Sole Proprietorship right now. I've thought about doing something else, but I really hadn't gotten around to it." Most folks looking at starting a brewery are somewhat more sophisticated than that, but as a business owner, do you know why this is important?

First, if nothing else, understand that being a Sole Proprietorship in any business that deals with the general public might be a really bad idea.

Here's the thing; being a defined "company" such as a Limited Liability Company (LLC), Limited Liability Partnership (LLP), or a corporation (Inc.) installs a "liability shield" between you and the business. "What," you may ask, "does that mean?" Here is where we apply the different types of business entities we covered back in Chapter One. The best way to answer that is with some examples:

> Let's say that you're a Sole Proprietorship. If you get sued (even by one of your own employees or clients), and they win, they could come after (and take) your personal assets to satisfy the judgment. "But, that's why I have business insurance. That'll pay for anything I get sued for, right?" Maybe not.

> Let's go deeper into that example. You get sued (and they win) for $1,000,000, but you only have $750,000 in insurance coverage. Who do you think gets to pay the other $250,000? That's right, it's you. "Aha! But, I don't have anything worth that much money. I don't own a house or anything, so I'm

safe, right?" Maybe not. A judgment is typically good for ten years or more and can be renewed after that. Then, the person who sued you can choose when to come after you for the judgment. That means they can take whatever you have now, AND maybe whatever you EVER have. Imagine if you closed the business, got a really good job working for someone else, and bought a house—that house is now on the chopping block for the judgment creditor. Not a good situation.

John Says: "Remember last chapter when I said a Sole Proprietorship was a bad idea?"

LIABILITY SHIELD

The personal liability shield is a big deal. It protects you and your fellow business owners from litigation (personally) for something that the business did or didn't do. It's a way to manage and mitigate your personal risk and your business. Given the sue-happy society here in America, you'd have to have a pretty gosh-darn good reason for a sole proprietorship to make sense. And, yes, "gosh-darn" is a legal term, as far as you know. In fact, it's not clear that there is a good enough reason (outside of some bizarre law school hypothetical) for someone to be a sole proprietorship instead of an LLC or a corporation.

Let's spin the example around; this time you're a corporation and you get sued. So long as you meet certain requirements, i.e., they can't sue you personally, they can only sue the corporation. What're they gonna get? A desk and a couple of chairs? Maybe as much as the equipment and the brewery. Certainly less than your personal home, car, bank accounts, etc.

"Wait a minute. What was that bit about 'as long as you meet certain requirements'?" Ah, good catch—you're a pretty sharp reader! Well, to become an LLC or a corporation, all you really have to do is file some paperwork at the Secretary of State's office. So, let's say that your liability shield is actually made up of all the paperwork you have about your legal structure and the rules established for running the business. If that shield is just the two-page document you filed with the state, that's a pretty flimsy shield, and that's essentially how the court will see it too. "Whaddya mean?" Well, let's say that you and your company get sued. You go to the judge:

You: Pointing to your state filing and triumphantly stating, "They can't sue me personally, the business is a corporation!"

Judge: "Is that it?"

You: "Uhm, yeah." (sheepishly)

Judge: "So you expect that because you filed a piece of paper with the state, and paid a small fee, you can never be sued personally for doing something stupid in the name of the business?"

You: "I'm guessing that 'yes' is not the right answer here…"

Judge: "Nope. You're on the hook personally as is the corporation. Good luck. NEXT!"

The point here is that you have to go beyond the state filing to show that you're more than just a person with a piece of paper at the state. You have to have rules, practices, policies and structure to show how you run the business in that it's not just "you," but that there's "you" and there's "the business" as two separate entities/identities. The things you do to show that you're separate entities are the "special requirements" mentioned earlier.

Here's a little side note about lawyer-speak: in that example above with "you" and "the judge," what the judge did is called "piercing the corporate veil," first mentioned in Chapter One. It really means letting someone attack you personally in court, despite the existence of a liability shield. The issues aren't with the act of "piercing the corporate veil," but with the name. "Piercing the corporate veil" is a cutesy name that makes people feel smart, like "QED" or "ipso facto." Most times "pierce the corporate veil" is used by someone who doesn't know what they're talking about and is generally making a threat. So, if you hear someone say "pierce the corporate veil," unless they're explaining the process to you, you can immediately assume one of a couple of things: (a) they don't know what they're talking about, or (b) you should be really, really concerned. And they're only eligible for (b) if the person saying pierce the corporate veil is a lawyer and you did something wrong.

John Says: "That's why just filing for an LLC or corporation is not enough. You have to do all the other things that companies do to be deserving of that protection."

The liability shield between you and your business is made up of all the rules, practices, policies, and paperwork you have regarding how to run your business. So, think about whoever is suing you as a raging berserker like the Tazmanian Devil (the cartoon, not the marsupial). The more layers of protection between you and them the better. The first and most powerful, in the view of a court, is notice. Does the berserker know that it is attacking a business, or does it think you're a person?

For example, given two names (1) John Smith Landscaping or (2) Green Lawn Landscaping, Inc., which one sounds like it's just a person getting paid for landscaping work and which one sounds like it's a separate business/company?

Different example. How about (3) Bill's Restaurant LLC or (4) Visionary Holdings? If forced to make a choice, these would rank in the following way (from strongest to weakest notice):

- Green Lawn Landscaping, Inc.
- Bill's Restaurant LLC
- Visionary Holdings
- John Smith Landscaping

The idea is that a member of the general public "gets" that it is a business, not just an individual. If they understand that it is a business, they are "on notice" that your liability may be limited.

Let's take a step back. In order to have an "Inc." or an "LLC," you have to file, with the state, to become a registered entity—another way of putting the public "on notice" that your liability is limited.

Generally speaking, the following are different layers of protection (additional strength for your liability shield) in order of their importance/strength:

1. Register with the state. Become a registered entity like an LLC or an Inc.
2. Your name should reflect your limited liability. Generally, the states require that your name include "LLC" if you're an LLC and "Inc." if you're a corporation. Also, choose your name carefully (think about the examples above). There may be good reasons to include your name (for example: Michael Jordan Nissan).
3. Don't let your business money and your personal money "mingle" in the same bank account.
4. Make sure the company is well capitalized. Does the business have enough money to do what it says it's supposed to do?
5. Defining document. You need to have a "rulebook" for how the business is run (notice I said, "how the business is run" and not "how you run the business" (remember, separate entities). For LLCs, the defining document is an Operating Agreement. For corporations, it is the corporation's bylaws.
6. Follow your document. This is (apparently) tougher than it would seem. If the Operating Agreement (or bylaws) says that the company will have quarterly owners' meetings, then have quarterly owners' meetings. It's not a rulebook if

the rules in the book aren't followed or enforced.

7. Have policies and procedures. Define, ahead of time, policies for important topics like payroll, sick leave, and vacation time, billing and collections, customer service, etc., so that you can show that you adhered to what the business says the rules are, rather than your own whims.

8. Be consistent. If the company's documents (Operating Agreement, bylaws, policies or procedures) say something should be done a certain way, do it that way. The documents are the company's way to give people (even you as an owner) instructions. As an owner if you want something done differently, change the document. Until the document is changed, do it the way the document says.

9. Number 1 and 2 have already been discussed.

"What do you mean, 'don't comingle funds?'" Well, for number 3, it means that you need to be able to show that you and the business are different and separate from each other. For example, if the business account pays your car payments, pays your lunch and your clothes, it starts to sound less and less like a company—everything you earn goes right into your personal bank account. In contrast, if the business pays you, say $500, then you deposit that in your account and then use it to pay your bills, now it looks much cleaner. Keeping the money separate (between what belongs to you and what belongs to the business) goes a long way in showing that you are two separate entities.

John Says: "Finances are a major source of errors that cause people to lose their limited liability protection."

Make sure that your business is well capitalized. Number 4, again, looks at the money. If your company is underfunded, you may be using it only as shield without really intending it to be a business. To show that the business is separate from you individually, it needs to be able to support itself—at least at some level.

For example, let's say you're in the business of buying and selling exotic collectors' cars. If you buy and sell Ferraris and Lamborghinis, but you only keep $2000 in your bank account and have no office, staff, equipment, showroom, or warehouse, how likely is that you're really intent on the business being successful in buying and selling the cars? Not very. A few thousand dollars to support what could or should be a multi-million dollar import/export/buy/resell business does not seem very realistic.

Or another example, let's say you are a freelance writer. Maybe all you need is a computer and a desk and you can work out of your home. In that case, maybe $2000 is a gracious plenty to show that the business is well funded. It's going to depend on your business and the particular situation.

For breweries, it generally needs to be a large number. Specifically, a brewery is a capital intensive business. Between equipment, facilities, aging inventory, and raw material investment, a lot of money is required to fund the business and the ongoing operations. On the good side, generally speaking, the equipment and physical assets are part of the capitalization, which feeds into that "number" to show how well capitalized the business is. But that number is tempered with how indebted the business is and whether there are any liens on the equipment.

Numbers 5 and 6—documents, policies, and procedures—are much more intricate. These set the tone and mode for the rest of the business (maybe for a very long time). Do NOT just use a "template" Operating Agreement or bylaws that you found on the Internet. Sometimes these are okay to use, but generally they are a little like "one size fits all" underwear. No matter what size you are, it's probably going to be uncomfortable. Talk to an attorney to get help in putting together your defining document (Operating Agreement, bylaws, or whatever). An attorney will make sure that you're not doing too much or too little and that the document is a good fit for the business.

This is especially important depending on your business plan. Specifically, as your brewery grows, the Operating Agreement or bylaws are what is going to govern the relationships between the owners and between the owners and the company. For example, these corporate-level documents are going to establish the ground rules around issues like:

- Who has what voting power or management authority in the company?
- Who is entitled to what percentage of the profits?
- What, in fact, are the "profits" of the company?
- What happens when there is a dispute between the owners or the owners and the company?
- What happens when one or more owners want to sell their interest in the company?

Number 7—policies, procedure—should be a collaborative effort between you and your attorney. There are certain things you should and should not do. An attorney can help guide you through what the important decisions to be made are and how the business can manage inherent risk. But, at the end, the policies and procedures of the business are the responsibility (and privilege) of the owners—they should be your decisions and your rules.

Documents, the last layer of protection, a terribly important one actually, is all up to you as the business owner, employee, manager, etc. If the document (whatever it is) isn't followed, it doesn't help protect you. Not following your own document is a little like buying really good tires for your car, then leaving them in the garage while you drive around on bald, slick tires in the rain. Sure, you've got good tires, but they're not helping you. If the document doesn't work, change it. But until you change it, follow what it says to do.

BUSINESS STRUCTURE CHOICE

Let us go back for a moment and talk about the actual structure of your business. This section discusses Sole Proprietorships, corporations, and Limited Liability Companies (LLCs) and often leads to the question, "Well, which business structure should I choose?" The short answer is (and you'll hear this a lot in this book)… it depends.

In terms of your business structure, you have to balance the following:

1. Your business-system "sophistication". How willing/able

are you to follow-up on specific requirements for the business and the owners year after year with consistency and accuracy?
2. Your risk tolerance. How willing are you to risk your investment or parts of the company or your personal assets?
3. Your funding strategy. How many owners or equity investors are you planning to have? And how are you going to "sell" that equity to those investors?
4. Your tax strategy. What's the best way to minimize your tax burden relative to your funding and available cash?

John Says: "But don't rush into it. Make sure you know why you're choosing which form or structure."

Strictly from a liability standpoint, either a corporation or an LLC is generally the way to go. Most lawyers (your author included) recommend forming an LLC as a "default setting." If you don't have a specific reason for doing something else, an LLC generally provides you the most flexibility with regard to addressing the above priorities while still keeping your personal liability limited.

Specifically, except in very rare cases, a corporation and an LLC will both offer the same liability protection for your personal assets.

PROACTIVELY LIMITING YOUR LIABILITY

Beyond the choice of business structure and building up your "liability shield," you should think about other ways to reduce your liability. What does that mean? Well, where does liability come from? Liability comes from you (or your business) doing something wrong (or, in some cases, doing something right) that results in injury to someone else, so that injured party deserves to be corrected or compensated for.

Some examples for your business might be:

- Glass shards in a bottle of finished product (that someone drinks and later has to go to the hospital)
- An employee or visitor being hurt by a tank falling on them at your brewery (actually happened)
- Being cited for a bartender serving alcohol to an underage person (remember, alcohol regulations can carry criminal or civil liability)
- A patron leaving the taproom trips in the parking lot and gets hurt (are they suing you? The landlord?)

What can you do to limit your liability (or maybe eliminate it) in situations like these? Well, it's difficult to say specifics and whether certain tools/techniques are even applicable or make sense, but there are some general guidelines:

- Have good signage that indicates known hazards (things like Hi-Viz tape on steps up or down that are easy to miss or signs that indicate processing hazards like "Danger! Hot Caustic in Use!")
- Have good, documented training for your employees about the various hazards and their responsibility to look out for each other, visitors, and patrons
- Reduce or eliminate known hazards when feasible (be sure there are handrails on stairs, etc.)
- Escort non-employees if they are in the brew space (tours should

be led. No one should be "wandering around" in the brewery.)
- Be sure to document observations when they happen (especially things like refusal to serve someone who is visibly intoxicated, calling a cab for a patron, refusal of an employee or patron to follow instructions)
- Keep good records, such as for purchases, tax payments, inventory, and product orders
- Develop procedures (or even checklists) for critical or hazardous tasks to ensure the task is done the same way every time (great for safety concerns, but also good for tax payments, bookkeeping, and managing day-to-day tasks)
- Act on information when it comes to your attention (for example, if you find out there's spilled beer on the floor in the taproom, don't ignore it—get it cleaned up or put some signage up ASAP. The same is true for non-safety issues.)
- Have clear policies for how routine issues are addressed (examples include policies for "drinking on the job," discrimination, or unsafe behavior.)

"John Says: Don't get complacent; you need to act on information in a timely manner."

The above are just some of the things you should keep in mind to make sure you are not creating unnecessary liability as you go about running the business. Specific actions to limit your liability need to be tailored to meet specific situations. Other tools include:

- Liability release or waiver (good for volunteers helping at the brewery)

- Non-disclosure agreements
- Non-compete agreements
- Limited liability clauses in contracts
- Insurance
- Dispute resolution procedures for administrative (internal to the company) or external problems

INSURANCE

The vast majority of this section is about the ways to limit liability, and that's important. Another major tool in managing your overall liability is insurance. You can get insurance for almost anything and for almost any reason. Jayne Mansfield had her breasts insured. The question isn't whether you need insurance. The question is what insurance do you need and how much?

John Says: "On the other hand, don't rely entirely on insurance to save you."

As with any business, insurance is a key component to the overall health of the business and the mitigation of risk to the operation. While most individuals understand the need for basic liability insurance to protect the business (or personal) assets from unforeseen circumstances, there are nuances that are likely apparent to a trained attorney which are not so apparent to a new business owner.

Keep in mind, there's also such a thing as "insurance poor" —you can't make any money because your insurance premiums take all your profits! So, it's important to manage your liability and your insurance based on risk.

Insurance and risk management is one area where the craft beer culture can be its own worst enemy. Craft beer appeals to the "rugged individualist," the "risk taking entrepreneur," and the iconoclast. Craft beer, as an industry, is filled with strong personalities that have overcome significant adversity to bring their vision to fruition. Craft beer as an industry is characterized by nimbleness and adaptive thinking. However, this also leads to a tendency to act before considering the possible repercussions. Often clients commit to, or take, actions without informing their insurance carrier. This leads to a dangerous situation where the insurance company could deny coverage in the event of a serious incident because the business owner exceeded their insurance coverage parameters.

Consider the brewery that holds an inaugural anniversary festival in their parking lot. A patron imbibes a little too much and stumbles over a curb (or slips on spilled beer or melting ice from a keg) and fractures their skull. The brewery then has to make an uncomfortable phone call to their insurance company to put them on notice and hope that the incident is covered.

UNDERSTANDING RISK

It can be helpful to think of the following matrix:

	Impact/Severity	
	High	Low
Very Likely (Likelihood)	A	B
Very Unlikely	B	C

If your issue is in quadrant A (very likely and high impact/severity) then you need to take active steps to manage the risk, and you probably want to make sure you have insurance to cover all (or substantially all), of the potential impact of the "thing" actually occurring. Hopefully you don't have too many "A" risks—if you have A risks, you're doing something wrong or you have a skewed definition of what can be "high impact."

Most of your risks as a brewery will fall into the B categories. "B" issues are those that are either high impact/severity but unlikely OR low impact/severity but likely to occur.

Examples of B issues might include:

- Someone sustaining a injury on your premises
- TTB or ABC action against you
- Loss of product due to contamination (before distributing to customers)
- Key employee quitting or leaving the company
- Power outages
- Broken glass
- Leaving a valve open when it should have been closed (or vice versa)

Whether you have insurance to cover the issue or are taking particular steps to mitigate the risk depends largely on the specific situation. You should get assistance from a lawyer and your insurance specialist (both should have experience with breweries) for guidance on your specific circumstances.

The items in the C category are really not a huge concern and probably should not be the subject of an insurance policy. Items in category C might include:

- Bartender "calling out" (i.e. not showing up for work)
- Keg never gets returned from customer
- Flat tire on the delivery van

These things could happen, and do happen, in the ordinary course of business. They are probably not worth discussing with your insurance carrier or having insurance on.

INSURANCE POLICIES

Like malt, breweries come in many different varieties and are often more complex than they first seem. And, there may be areas of liability that aren't intuitive that you may still want to cover with insurance (for example, intellectual property or cyber liability).

People often think that, as a brewer, all you need is general liability insurance coverage. Few things could be further from the truth—and this is where it is critical to get an insurance agent who understands your industry. There are several areas of insurance that, while not unique to breweries, often get overlooked. Some insurance policies or risk coverage you may want to consider include (most are not covered by a standard general liability insurance policy):

- Raw materials (damage to materials in transit, or from weather, insects, etc.)
- Contamination
- Process and processing hazards

- Packaging
- Storage and product transportation
- Events and festivals (even if they're on your own property)
- Intellectual property (for things like labels and marketing)
- Cyber liability (for things like storing or using credit card or personal information)
- Dram shop and liquor liability
- Workers compensation
- Product recall
- Business interruption

For almost any business owner, figuring out what insurance and how much you need (and what to budget for the costs) is a daunting if not impossible task. Get an insurance agent with experience with breweries. They can often help you work through the intricacies of your business to identify the right ways to manage your risk with insurance. Also, don't be afraid to shop around. Policies, carriers, and even costs vary from agent to agent.

CHAPTER THREE: FUNDRAISING

Very few people are sufficiently capitalized (i.e. "flush with money") to fund their own business venture. As a result, fundraising is a serious issue and priority for any small business. So, what's different about beer and alcohol businesses? For starters, the federal government says that certain kinds of people/businesses aren't allowed to own (or own part of) other kinds of businesses.

If you are "engaged in business as a distiller, brewer, rectifier, blender, or other producer, or as an importer or wholesaler, of distilled spirits, wine, or malt beverages, or as a bottler, or warehouseman and bottler of distiller spirits, directly or indirectly, or

John Says: "Whether you think it's right or not, the government (federal and all states) consider alcohol a highly regulated substance."

through an affiliate," you cannot have exclusive outlet agreements or have a "tied house;" you can't commit commercial bribery, or contract for consignment sales. The Code of Federal Regulations, Title 27, Section 6, also cited as 27 CFR 6, spells this out. That's all well and good, but the regulations also say:

> "...it is unlawful for any industry member [hint: that's you] to induce, directly or indirectly, any retailer to purchase any products from the industry member to the exclusion, in whole or in part, of such products sold or offered for sale by other persons in interstate or foreign commerce by any of the following means:
>
> (a) By acquiring or holding [...] any interest in any license with respect to the premises of the retailer;
>
> (b) By acquiring any interest in the real or personal property owned, occupied, or used by the retailer in the conduct of his business;
>
> (c) By furnishing, giving, renting, lending, or selling to the retailer any equipment, fixtures, signs, supplies, money, services or other thing of value, subject to the exceptions contained in subpart D;
>
> (d) By paying or crediting the retailer for any advertising, display, or distribution service;
>
> (e) By guaranteeing any loan or the repayment of any financial obligation of the retailer;
>
> (f) By extending to the retailer credit for a period in excess of the credit period usual and customary to the industry for the particular class of transactions as prescribed in §6.65; or

(g) By requiring the retailer to take and dispose of a certain quota of any such products."

27 CFR 6.21 *(emphasis added)*

Basically a bar owner (i.e. a "retailer") can't own part of a brewery (i.e. an "industry member"). The regulations also limit how much one segment can support another (such as through guaranteeing a loan, or "furnishing" items of value). Understanding this law is crucial so you won't have an issue in terms of who can own a piece of your company or who you can accept loans or gifts from.

That's the first (and biggest) distinction for raising funds to support your business. In practice, that means that, at the TTB, any owner of 10% or more must complete the owner application process and declare their other ownership interests, including their sources of income and their bank. Your local ABC may have a different threshold for percentage of ownership for reporting purposes.

But, even with that understood (and it's not always clear), there are some critical terms and concepts to appreciate as you go about maximizing your fundraising efforts.

John Says: "*The TTB treats LLCs like partnerships, so everyone has to apply because every partner is important. Meanwhile some states treat LLCs like partnerships and some treat LLCs like corporations.*"

SECURITIES

A serious issue for raising capital is the concept of securities. We've all heard of the U.S. Securities and Exchange Commission (the SEC). They're a regulatory body. But what exactly do they regulate? The SEC website at www.sec.gov says:

> *The mission of the U.S. Securities and Exchange Commission is to protect investors, maintain fair, orderly, and efficient markets, and facilitate capital formation.*
>
> *As more and more first-time investors turn to the markets to help secure their futures, pay for homes, and send children to college, our investor protection mission is more compelling than ever....*
>
> *The world of investing is fascinating and complex, and it can be very fruitful. But unlike the banking world, where deposits are guaranteed by the federal government, stocks, bonds and other securities can lose value...*
>
> *The SEC oversees the key participants in the securities world, including securities exchanges, securities brokers and dealers, investment advisors, and mutual funds. Here the SEC is concerned primarily with promoting the disclosure of important market-related information, maintaining fair dealing, and protecting against fraud.*

Uh, okay. Sounds great. But what does that *mean*? Let's start with what is a "security." The Securities Act of 1933 says that a security is "any note, stock, ...bond, evidence of indebtedness, certificate of interest or participation in a profit sharing agreement, ... [etc.]" So, for our purposes, the important bits in that are "stock," "bond," and "evidence of indebtedness." All of these are terms of ownership or debt, answering the question "at some time in the future, who owes who money?"

The SEC regulates securities (stocks, debts, etc.) and the selling of those securities. Why do we care?

One major way of raising funds for a business is to sell stock or shares (i.e. ownership) in the business. As we can see from understanding how the SEC operates, they'd better be involved.

John Says: "*Unfortunately, it's things like SEC regulations that really mean to say 'get a lawyer.'*"

However, there is an exception/exemption for certain types of equity sales (stocks, shares, etc.). The most important exemptions include:

- Private placements
    - Transactions by an issuer not involving a public offering
    - This generally means that it is
        - Offered to fewer than twenty-five people ("offerees")
        - The offerees have a "privileged" relationship (like relatives, certain employees, friends, etc.)
        - The offer is not advertised
        - Any restrictions on the rights of the offeree to sell or transfer the stock must be disclosed to the offeree
        - The offeree must be "qualified" (meaning that they're sophisticated enough to "fend for themselves" with respect to financial issues; they have the ability to assume the investment risk (i.e. wealth), and must have access to the type of information that would be included in the registration statement

- Accredited Investor Exemption
    - Transactions where the total offering is less than $5,000,000 are exempt if they're offered to Accredited Investors (known as Rule 501 of Regulation D)
    - Accredited Investors are
        - Certain institutional investors (Rule 215 and Rule 501)
        - Directors, executive officers, or general partners of the issuer
        - Individuals with a net worth of greater than $1,000,000
        - Individuals with an annual income of more than $200,000 each of the two most recent years (or joint income with spouse of greater than $300,000)
    - But, the notice of sale must be filed with the SEC
- Intrastate Offering Exemption
    - Transactions where the issuer and ALL offerees are persons residing within a single state
    - But
        - All securities must "come to rest" in the hands of investors who are residents of the state
        - Be sure to read up on Rule 147 (which clarifies some of these requirements)
        - The state may have separate regulations you have to follow

This book isn't designed to make you an expert on securities (it would take a lot more time, effort, and money to do that). The aim of this book is to at least introduce you to the topics so you can look into them with more background and be able to talk intelligently with co-owners, investors, lawyers, and insurance representatives about the issues.

Most small businesses want to avoid entanglements with the SEC and securities as a whole. Following one of the above basic exemptions should keep you on that path.

John Says: "Duh! This book isn't made to make you an 'expert' in anything!"

If, however, you want to make a big splash and register your securities so you can sell to the general public and/or advertise the investment opportunity, be aware that you should immediately seek out an attorney with securities experience. There are a myriad of laws and regulations that you need to be aware of and many of which take effect before you actually offer anyone anything. Finally, if you go this route, be prepared to spend a significant amount of money up front. Forming the registration packaging can cost many thousands of dollars.

We'll spend the rest of this chapter talking about means for fundraising which either fall into one of the exemptions or are outside the purview of serious SEC oversight.

GETTING FUNDS

With very few exceptions, there is no "free" money to be had out there. There are opportunities to avoid expenses or to get value for less than it's worth to you, but for the most part, "there's no free lunch." You're going to have to pay "something" to get cash/financing.

Generally speaking, there are two big categories of financing or getting money: equity and debt.

EQUITY

"Equity" is a way of saying "ownership." Specifically you can give away or sell equity in the company in exchange for cash now. It's what we're all really familiar with. When you hear about someone "buying into" a business or purchasing shares or some kind of ownership interest in a company, they're receiving equity (ownership) in the business for cash now.

Equity, or ownership, isn't an all or nothing thing. There are different kinds of equity and ownership. And, very rarely is there a single owner for most businesses, especially large or growing ones. Ownership can be shared and is often restricted.

> *For example, in an LLC, there can be Manager-Members and non-Manager-Members. Managers in an LLC are generally charged with running the business day to day and "managing" it. Managers, in this sense, aren't the same as "managers" when we talk about a manager of shipping or a manager of human resources. These are Managers with a capital "M." In this case, a member can be a non-Manager and have an ownership interest, but no real say in the day-to-day operations of the business.*

Also generally speaking, equity comes in several flavors. If the equity is in a company (like an LLC or a corporation), then the equity takes the form of membership or shares of the corporation. If the equity is in a partnership, then the equity must necessarily be as a partner.

How the equity is divided up or what rights of ownership go with it is up to the company, generally. A corporation or an LLC is typically much more flexible about how equity is used than most other forms of business.

In almost all cases, equity investors are looking to ensure that they can lose no more than they've already invested—i.e. they're looking for limited liability. As a result corporations and LLCs are highly favored.

When surrendering equity in exchange for cash, be sure you understand what control, rights, or privileges are tagging along with it.

John Says: "Many people say that 'equity is the most expensive money you'll ever get.' Once someone owns part of your company, they own it forever unless you buy it back. And they'll always be entitled to a portion of the value of the company. There are ways around this, but you have to be very careful and very specific about it in the beginning."

DEBT

The other major form of financing is debt, i.e. a loan. Both small and large companies (don't believe for a second that they don't carry debt) carry some amount of debt that's been used to finance the growth of the company.

Loans are a major way that companies raise money, especially capital, to fund operations. Most people have a good idea of how debt works—car loans, home loans, student loans; they're all about the same in that respect.

For small or new companies, banks or other lenders often want a personal guarantee from one or more of the owners. What does that guarantee mean? Well, it's like if you co-signed

John Says: "*Debt can be an advantageous thing. Remember that servicing a debt is a business expense. And that comes before awarding profits to owners.*"

for a loan for someone who has no credit. Essentially, as a guarantor, you're on the hook for the full amount. In most cases, even if there is more than one guarantor, each guarantor is liable for the full amount. When there is more than one guarantor, after the lender gets paid, the paying guarantor can go after the other guarantors for a contribution, but each guarantor is liable for the full amount.

Additionally, most lenders require a substantial amount of history, preparation, and a strong and detailed business case to support any loan to a new or small company.

VENTURE CAPITAL

Venture Capital and Venture Capitalists (VCs), often referred to as "private equity," are much less in the news than they used to be. In the late 1990s and early 2000s, VCs were all the talk. Many businesses benefitted from, and even depended, on them. Generally, VCs provide cash up front in often highly speculative or high-risk business ventures in exchange for a portion of equity or a significant share of the profits later.

In most cases, VCs manage pooled funds of others looking to invest. Institutional investors, funds, or asset collections rely on VCs to manage the funds for growth and investment income. These funds are mostly portfolios of investments which look too small or new to businesses with large opportunities to provide high return on investment, but often riskier, investments.

There are far fewer VCs with money to spend in the last five to ten years as the global economy, and the U.S. in particular, has suffered setbacks and a recession. Those that are around and active tend to have moved to more conservative investment strategies given the recent economic downturn. There are, however, VC markets available online which try to match businesses to investors. Additionally, there are capital brokers out there that try to play matchmaker with businesses and VCs, for a fee of course.

John Says: "Most of the VC stuff we see is for fairly 'large' breweries looking for money to grow, not generally start-ups."

ANGEL INVESTORS

Angel investors, or angels, are a special form of private equity and venture capital. Specifically, angels are generally a single investor investing their own private funds. In most cases the angel looks for a significant return on investment, or interest rate, for loans. When seeking equity positions, angels often take a large fraction of available ownership, even if it's not enough to control the company. Angels are often seen to fill the funding gap between friends and family and being able to take out significant business loans or other private equity funding.

CROWDFUNDING

Crowdfunding is probably the most exciting and is certainly the newest topic in business finance in recent years. Specifically, crowdfunding leverages small investments from many individuals

John Says: "These folks often fall into one of the Three Fs: Friends, Family, and Fools."

to aggregate into significant and usable amounts of capital.

However, a major issue in crowdfunding is the issue of "what" exactly investors are getting for their investment. Ideally, investors (and many companies) would like to be able to invest in exchange for a small piece of equity. As we discussed above, the SEC regulates securities offered for sale to the general public. Even if they're little securities, they're still securities and SEC has to try and figure out how to protect investors who are, likely, not qualified, or accredited, or sophisticated. In 2012, President Obama signed the Jumpstart Our Business Startups (JOBS) Act. The JOBS act incorporates a mandate to allow crowdfunding for equity and for the SEC to develop rules to manage that process. The SEC promulgated some guidelines, and the industry is in the very early stages of understanding how they work. Check with the SEC website and industry specialists for clear guidance.

Generally, the rules include provisions which would open the crowdfunding concept to the public (for equity positions), while still offering investor protection through the creation of new entities called funding portals. Some of the elements of the proposed rule(s) as of the time of this writing include:

- Capping the amount a company raises through crowdfunding to less than $1,000,000 every twelve months
- Investors with a net income of less than $100,000 can invest a maximum of 5% of their net income or $2000 (whichever

is greater) every twelve months
- Investors with a net income of more than $100,000 can invest a maximum of 10% of their net income every twelve months
- Securities bought through a portal would have to be held at least a year before being sold

Even though some states have crafted exceptions or statutes to allow crowdfunding for equity (if the investors and the business are within the state), until the rules are promulgated, it is critical for small businesses that utilize crowdfunding, and wish to avoid SEC issues, to make sure that they are not offering equity in the company in exchange for a crowdfunded investment.

Crowdfunding best practices generally include:

- Setting a reasonable/achievable target for your crowdfunding campaign based on your personal network
- Avoiding the perception (and certainly the action) of offering equity in exchange for the investment/donation/contribution;
- Building a social media presence prior to your crowdfunding launch
- Leveraging your existing contacts and relationships when the campaign begins (you can't do that if you haven't done the step before it!)
- Including video marketing and explanations in your campaign and in your social media outlets/website
- Ensuring that you're giving contributors high quality and "special" rewards (something they might only ever be able to get if they contribute now); and

- During the campaign, never stop promoting your campaign on social media, the Internet, and other outlets for your target audience.

Until rules and the processes are well defined, companies should look at crowdfunding as a donation—and should make that explicit in the crowdfunding "ask" for money. It is perfectly acceptable to offer tokens of appreciation, celebrations, accolades, or other nominal rewards in exchange for a crowdfunding investment, but any mention of equity or ownership position should be very carefully worded.

John Says: "There's a lot of movement around this type of funding regulation, both at the federal and state level. Make sure you research thoroughly before you pull the trigger on crowdfunding, especially when it involves equity."

For example, many crowdfunded breweries offer membership in a "mug club," special celebration or brewery tour experiences, pint glasses, T-shirts or other merchandise or incentives for different donation levels. This often works out very well for both the brewery and the investor as they see themselves as part of making the business "happen," while the brewery avoids the issues of equity.

Crowdfunding is still in its infancy and, though it seems a strong viable alternative to traditional financing or fundraising, we have not yet seen a final incarnation of a mature crowdfunding market that is free of challenges or ambiguity. Additionally, as crowdfunding matures and some of the law becomes more settled around the issues, crowdfunding appears to be a very strong contender to provide a robust distributor ownership network for Co-Ops or other share-based ownership programs/schemes.

GRANTS

Grants are the closest thing to "free" money that is available to small businesses. However, the major sources for grants are nonprofit organizations as well as state and federal government. In recent years funding and budgets for both government and nonprofits have seen a downward slide. As a result, competition for grants can be fierce, even for "small" amounts.

Grants can range in value from a few hundred dollars to hundreds of thousands of dollars or more. But, in most cases, the grantor is looking for a significant public or community benefit. Often grant awards are tied to job creation, training, or local capital investment. This quid pro quo in grants often makes it very difficult for small businesses, especially breweries, to compete for significant grant dollars. Coupled with in some areas strong political or patron pressure to avoid encouraging the alcohol industry (i.e. "the Bible Belt"), in many cases, makes this a non-starter for many breweries.

However, many nonprofits and, certainly, many state or local government agencies are in the business of economic development, job creation, and community revitalization—so don't rule grants out.

John Says: *"Grant money is a lot harder to get than you think. Especially if you're a for-profit company."*

That being said, smart counsel would not depend on grants as a major source of funding for a new or startup brewery.

SUBSIDIES

Subsidies are a special form of support, typically from a government agency or municipality. Subsidies often take the form of "cost avoidance," such as a city or town contributing to an infrastructure improvement as a way to entice a new business into the area. Examples of these kinds of subsidies include utilities improvements, roadwork, parking or other public access routes, or "partnering" with the local government to promote the business. Additional examples of subsidies might include reduced costs for utilities or other services for a specific period of time or construction or improvements to nearby public land or facilities to improve the attractiveness of your location.

These subsidies, while not putting cash in your piggy bank, can and do add up to substantial and tangible benefits to your business.

For example, a downtown district might be willing to upgrade the street lighting, install bike racks, benches, or other pedestrian accessories, as well as improve the sidewalks or available parking—all just to encourage you and your small business to move into a particular location. These improvements, while perhaps not strictly necessary, certainly add value to your business and, perhaps, might have been needed in the future as your business grows and brings in additional crowds.

Subsidies might also be available from some suppliers in the form of special rates for small businesses—though that seems to be rarer. Subsidies from whatever source can be a boon to small businesses and should be investigated, even if they do not contribute to the bottom line in terms of raising funds.

TAX BREAKS

Tax breaks are a major way that local and state governments incentivize businesses to invest in particular locations or to set up shop in their particular area. Tax breaks can be significant for lowering the barrier to entry for opening up a business, at least in terms of planning for your profitability, since you'll be more profitable if you minimize your tax burden.

However, understand that tax breaks are a very real cost to the local government (even at the state level). In many cases any tax break offered has to be approved by the city or county commissioners or even by the state legislature since these are tangible reductions in expected income (i.e. budgets) for coming years. The town, city, county, or state is of course banking on the hope that if you move to their area—in the long run—you'll generate more tax revenue than they're giving up in the short term. But even though it isn't always a slam dunk to get a tax break, even locally, you should always investigate the possibility when starting your business.

PAYING BACK FUNDS

No one really wants to talk about paying back funds, especially when you're still looking for money to start or run the business, but it is something to be fully aware of. Whether you're paying back a loan or you're distributing money to equity owners, keep in mind that whatever agreement you began with is likely going to control the outcome—unless the lender/owner agrees to modify the agreement.

So, when you're originally looking at the funding, whether debt or equity, note with special attention the conditions of when you have to start paying the funds back and at what rate.

> *For example, many Operating Agreements (remember, this is the controlling document for an LLC defining how the business is run between the owners) include a provision that the owners do not receive any return until the company is profitable overall including salaries (some of which may be going to other owners). However, this is usually included as a "default" provision. You have to look for it, ask for it, and make sure it's written in. On the other hand, there's no prohibition on the owners receiving funds before the company is profitable, though it is somewhat frowned on from an accounting perspective because it makes you look shady.*

In loan documents, look for the conditions for the payback of the loan. Is there a balloon payment? Is the interest rate adjustable? Also keep in mind that you can, in many cases, create your own conditions too. Think about including provisions where you don't pay anything back until you hit certain milestones (like construction, permitting, or profitability). If you insist on including some of these ideas, your interest rate will likely increase (because it's becoming a more risky investment for the lender) and the lender will scrutinize your business more to ensure that you're diligent in working to meet those milestones.

In LLCs, the Operating Agreement as hinted at above, can

be used to tailor the payback of certain investors or owners in preference of others, yet because it's in the Operating Agreement, all owners have to agree to that stipulation.

Likewise, in a corporation, different classes of stock may receive preferential treatment, which is referred to as Preferred Stock.

> *For example, Class A stock may receive $1.00 for every $0.50 that Class B stock receives. Or Class A stock gets paid a guaranteed return, even if there's little or no profitability. Specifically, many companies employ preferred stock where there's only a $500,000 surplus. Class A stock receives all of that and Class B stock doesn't get anything unless there's more than a $500,000 profit, and then only the surplus above $500,000 is divided among the Class B stock. You can see how what class of stock you own becomes extremely important—particularly when the returns are lean.*

Keep in mind that S-Corps can have only one class of stock so that everyone is treated equally. Now you can begin to see why there are certain advantages to being a C-Corp, even with the double taxation issue.

In any case, be sure to study the payback terms while you're raising funds—you don't want to be caught looking stupid. Also, many brewers believe that there's only one kind of financing or that the payback terms are set across the board. Lenders and investors do have more negotiating power in that sense, but you won't know if opportunities exist until you investigate them and ask the right questions.

CHAPTER FOUR: CONTRACTS AND AGREEMENTS

This section is one of the longest in the book. That is because agreements (i.e. contracts) form the basis of all our interactions in a business setting. There are so many things to think about and understand, it is surprising how many intricacies impact what could happen, might happen, and won't happen. So, let's start with the basics.

A contract is a binding agreement between two or more people to do (or not do) something. With a definition that broad, it's not surprising that contracts are everywhere around us—so much so that we often don't even realize that we're engaged in a contractual agreement.

For example, when you go into a restaurant and order something to eat, you're creating a contract—a promise that if they give you the food, you will pay for the food.

Most people see contracts as a written document signed by both sides, but that's not necessarily the case. If we break it down into the required parts, a contract is an agreement between two parties that creates an obligation to perform (or not perform) a particular duty or action. To have an enforceable contract, at its barest level, only needs

- An offer
- An acceptance
- A consideration (the value exchanged)

John Says: "Don't underestimate the importance of 'boilerplate'. AND don't just cut and paste 'boilerplate' from one doc to another. That stuff is there for a reason and you should make sure it's the right reason for you!"

There are, obviously, so many other issues to be worried about, but this is the general paradigm that we'll use to look at and understand contracts.

Just as in any negotiated agreement, there are standard issues that one must consider when drafting the document—often to protect both sides. The normal issues of disputes resolution, merger, choice of law, and other "boilerplate" type clauses won't be discussed here. Instead, we'll focus on the items that are different for the different types of agreements that are unique to the craft beverage industry or have unique aspects specific to the craft beverage industry.

FREEDOM TO CONTRACT

The ability to contract freely and without significant hindrance from the government is a basic tenant of most economies and, in particular, the United States. Generally speaking, people have the right and freedom to contract to do almost anything for almost anything. If people can agree, they're pretty much free to execute on it—and able to enforce the contract if the other person doesn't live up to their end of the bargain.

"No, they can't!" I hear you say. Well, it is true that in some cases there are prohibitions on contracts. For example, you cannot have an enforceable contract to do something illegal. You can't sue your (illegal) drug dealer for shorting you a gram, because it's (generally) illegal to sell illegal drugs. So you can't contract to do something illegal (hitmen don't often go to court to sue the person who hired them because they didn't get paid their full fee!).

John Says: "There are also laws that rewrite contracts, no matter what the parties actually agreed to. Take a look at the Franchise section."

And there are some laws which govern what goes into a contract and how that contract can be enforced—such as franchise laws, the Uniform Commercial Code (UCC), anti-trust laws, and of course some laws regulating alcohol production and sales, and the like. We'll discuss some of the most important of these as we move through this section.

But, you have to admit, you can contract (agree) for way more than you can't. Just think about all the agreements you form, execute, and complete every day: gas stations (promise to pay money in exchange for gasoline), coffee shops and diners (money in exchange for food), your utilities in your home (money in exchange for services), your employer or employees (money and benefits in exchange for work performed), or simply returning a favor ("Hey, I owe you one!"), maybe even your children! ("We can go to the mall after you clean your room.")

Contracts, and to a lesser extent equity, are central pillars of not only our economy, but also—to some extent—the very lens through which we see the world.

WHAT GOVERNS CONTRACT LAW?

Like many of the laws or regulations that we have discussed (and will discuss), there are multiple sources for laws that govern contracts and how we enforce them. The major groups of contracts that we'll discuss include:

- Services
- Goods
- Construction
- Employment
- Leases
- Franchises

Each of these has nuances and facets specific to the alcohol industry. And the sources of law that you need to worry about with respect to these types of contracts include:

- Federal statutes
- State statutes
- Administrative regulations (carrying the weight of laws)
- Common law

We'll address the specific sources of law within each contract-type discussion. But, be aware that there are often multiple levels of "law" impacting any one contract, and some may be harder to ferret out than others. And, often too, there may not be a single place to go to make sure that you're doing everything you're supposed to and not doing the things you're not supposed to. It's one of the big reasons for making sure that you have a good relationship with a lawyer licensed to practice law in your jurisdiction. When dealing with contracts, especially when significant effort or money is involved, it's definitely NOT better to beg for forgiveness later than to ask for permission to begin with.

REMEDIES

Before we get into the specific contract types and what to look for, we need to talk a little about remedies. Along with the concept of contracts, comes the idea that we should be able to enforce the agreement. If one person performs as required in a contract and the other refuses to pay or perform, we inherently see that as an injustice. So what do we do? We try to enforce the contract. There are two ways to look at enforcement: legal and equitable. If you do what you're supposed to under the contract, and the contract is breached, you've been "injured" under the law. You've suffered harm; you've been injured to the extent you didn't receive what was due you. If you've been injured, you need a "remedy." A remedy is the way a court redresses (or tries to correct) an injury. So, you'll often hear it phrased that there are two sets of remedies: remedies at law and remedies at equity.

Remedies at law are essentially damages awarded by the court. Damages, in this case as money owed, not damages as in "it's broken." Think of it this way—you're looking to "remedy" your "injury" under the contract. The measure of how "injured" you are is "damages"—how "damaged" were you as a result of the breach? A court of law can only give or award remedies at law, i.e. money. A court at law cannot order someone to do something, only to pay money.

John Says: "We get a lot of calls that say 'but it says in the contract that they have to do it! Why do I have to sue them to make them do it?' The issue is, only a court can force someone to do something. If they breach the agreement, in order to force them to do anything, you have to go to court."

Only a court of equity can order someone to do something, also known as a remedy at equity (or an equitable remedy). A court of equity can, for example, order that the other person perform under the contract (often called "specific performance") to cure your injury from the breach. Other forms of equitable remedy include injunctions ("stop doing that!"), rescission (the agreement never existed), and restitution (restoring to the way it was).

Now to make it even more confusing, both remedies at law and remedies at equity are often referred to as "legal remedies"—meaning that a court hears the case and awards a remedy. And, in the United States, most states have a combined court system, meaning that a single judge can judge cases in both law and equity—so, even though they are *technically* different (equitable vs. law), a single judge in a single court has the power to order either type of remedy.

Eyes glazed over yet? Not to worry. The important things to remember are:

John Says: "If you aren't at least a little confused and you didn't go to law school, then you don't understand the situation."

- Injury (how you were "hurt" by a breach of contract)
- Damages (money)
- Equity (fairness)
- Specific Performance (a court order to force someone to do what they agreed to do)

SERVICE CONTRACTS

A service is an intangible economic commodity. It has value, but you can't hold it, number it, or put it on a shelf.

For example, a bellhop's service isn't a tangible asset. Or, seen a different way, a pile of bricks and mortar is worth much less than an assembled brick wall. The mason's service changes one into another, but the service by itself isn't an asset.

Contracts for services are generally governed by state specific laws or the common law. Both of these can be highly complex and vary from state to state. But there are some general principles that we need to discuss and that you need to be aware of.

First, service contracts generally require an acceptance that is a "mirror image" of the offer. This isn't too much of an issue if the contract is written down, but imagine a verbal agreement:

Teenager: Hey, mister, I'll mow your lawn for $10. (offer)
Homeowner: Okay, I'll pay you $10 to mow my lawn. (acceptance)

Great! Offer = Acceptance. But what if…

Teenager: Hey, mister, I'll mow your lawn for $10. (offer)
Homeowner: Well, how about $5? (counter-offer, not an acceptance)
Teenager: I'll do it today for $5, if I can do it next week and you'll pay $10. (another counter-offer, not an acceptance)
Homeowner: Okay.

Now we have a verbal contract. But, what if…

Teenager: Hey, mister, I'll mow your lawn for $10. (offer)
Homeowner hands the teenager $5
Teenager goes and mows the lawn.

How much is the teenager owed?

It's a simple example, but you can see how quickly something can get out of control, especially if you're talking about, say, hauling off waste grain. Especially when you add in email and perhaps one side sends a check in the mail after a phone conversation, etc.

John Says: "The moral of the story is: if it's worth more than $5, write it down!"

So, in verbal service contracts, make sure that you are clear (and the other person is clear) on the critical parts of the contract. Be sure to specify:

- The service to be performed, including the scope of activity
- Any quality requirement(s) for the service
- When the service is to be performed
- The compensation and when it will be paid

But, let's get off of verbal service contracts for a bit. Assuming that you're going to get a written contract—which is strongly recommended—what should you look for? Well, for starters, you should include at least what you would have included in a verbal contract. In addition, make sure that the written agreement includes all of the terms and specifics, no "Oh, and this other thing, but we won't put it in the contract right now, we'll just take care of it on the side."

Also, what if there's confusion about what the terms mean? What if you think "on site" means at your brewery and they think "on site" means at their fabrication shop? Well, common law generally requires that the terms will mean (in descending order of preference):

- Plain meaning: if there's an obvious meaning from the context or the words themselves, we'll use that.
- Course of dealing: what has the term meant in the past when these same two parties have done business?
- Trade practices: what would the term mean to an ordinary professional in this trade?
- Trade usage: what would the term mean to anyone in the

John Says: "Practicing law would be really fun if it wasn't for clients. They always need things!"

general industry? Or how would it be interpreted outside the business between these two parties?

Believe it or not, lawyers *really* try to make a contract easy to understand and that the terms are plain... it just doesn't always work out that way.

So what's a breach of a service contract under common law? Well, there are a few different layers to that analysis. Is the breach *material*? Meaning, is the breach important to the main goal of the contract?

> *For example, if you hire someone to wire up your brewery and the contract says he has to park his van in the back of the building, but instead he parked on the street. Is that a material breach? Probably not. Not unless there was a significant reason for that specification. If you specified that he park behind the building because otherwise he would block the crane delivering your fermentation tanks, well, maybe that's a material breach. But, if you specified that he had to park in back just because you thought his van was ugly, that's probably not a material breach.*

Next, was the breach *fundamental*? Meaning, was the breach so bad that you just want to cancel the contract entirely AND that the other person hasn't done any work sufficient to entitle them to ANY compensation.

For example, you hire a rigging crew to install your 30 BBL fermenters. But the rigging crew never shows up. That's a fundamental breach. And, they never did any work that would entitle them to any compensation. But, if the rigging crew does show up, but they do a bad job—that's probably not a fundamental breach. Maybe they didn't understand the directions, or they placed the tank in the wrong spot, they did the job wrong—but they did work that entitles them to some compensation.

Or, was there *substantial performance* by at least one side?

For example, let's take the other side of the above example; you're in charge of the rigging crew. Your folks installed all the tanks exactly where the brewer told you to put them, except they installed one of tanks three inches to the left of where they were supposed to and they bent a handrail while they were doing it. Your guys worked really hard and did almost exactly everything that was asked. You substantially performed your part of the contract; the other side should have to live up to theirs.

The type and severity of breach will determine the best remedy in your situation. For some services, there's only one person or company that can do the service—when service contracts like this are breached, specific performance (i.e. forcing them to actually perform the service) is maybe the best option. On the other hand, if you've had to go to court to enforce the contract, do you really want this service provider in your brewery doing work they don't want to do? In that case, maybe money damages (and paying someone else to do or redo the work) is the best option. The severity of the breach, whether it's fundamental or the degree to which one or the other side performed under the contract, will influence how much you can recover in money damages or how much the breaching side is owed for the work they did do.

The common law analysis of breach in service contracts is also generally applicable for real estate contracts and intangibles (such as intellectual property, goodwill, or accounts).

There are other "boilerplate" provisions that we'll talk about later that should be included in nearly every contract.

GOODS AND CONTRACTS

John Says: If you're having trouble getting to sleep, may I suggest the UCC Article 2? Works every time for me."

Contracts for things (i.e. "goods") are a little different than contracts for services. In all fifty U.S. states, the Article 2 has been adopted in one form or another. Article 2 of the UCC involves sales and how those sales (and their contracts) are enforced.

Article 2 is a very comprehensive set of laws and regulations dealing with everything from what's considered an "offer" to how to resolve a dispute about the quality of the goods. We'll cover the main points to remember here, but the code is the ultimate source and (probably) covers the precise circumstances that you're interested in. Additionally, Article 2 is also at times counter-intuitive to what you think the "right" answer or process is.

CONTRACT BREWING AGREEMENTS

Each state is going to vary on its specific laws about contract brewing. This is especially concerning when the contract brewer (the one doing the brewing) and the principal (the one hiring the contract brewer) are in different states. The issue in that case is about making very clear who owns the beer when, and what the responsibilities are of each party. In general terms, issues to watch out for in contract brewing arrangements include:

- Definitive statements as to who owns the beer when. When (if ever) does the customer beer company take possession of the beer?
- Clearly defined responsibilities during the brewing process. Federal and state laws prohibit someone who is not licensed from producing alcohol. So, what part of the process is "brewing?" It's not entirely clear. The general rule is that the client company's representative should not add the hops (a major differentiation between malt extract production and making wort for beer) and should not pitch the yeast (a major distinction between wort production and making beer).
- Quality requirements for acceptance of the product. Too often brewers will design a product and contract with someone to make the product without ever deciding on the characteristics of an "acceptable product."

John Says: "Some states even regulate WHO is eligible to do contract brewing or who can enter into a contract brewing agreement."

- Clearly defined regulatory and licensing responsibilities. Who is responsible for the COLA (Certificate of Label Approval)? Who pays the taxes? Will the taxes be reimbursed by the client company, or will they be subsumed in the price of the finished goods?
- Specifics on who will provide what raw materials or ingredients. If the company wants a specialty ingredient, will they provide it? What about special bottles or labels different from the standard ones the contract brewer uses?
- Agreed-on payment terms. The excise tax is due when the product is "removed" from the brewery. Even for professional distribution companies, it is often thirty-sixty days before they're paid for the beer that's been sold. When does the client company need to pay the contract brewer?

ALTERNATING PROPRIETORSHIPS

Alternating proprietorships are unique beasts. If you're not familiar with the concept, it's sort of like renting someone else's equipment to make your beer, but they're not brewing your beer, so they're not a contract brewer. Alternating Proprietorships (APs) are a very good solution to a very narrow market need. For the TTB, as well as many ABCs, the issue of ownership of the brewery is an important distinction. First, if you do not own the equipment that the beer is made in, you can't be called a "brewery" or a "brewing company." Hence, the producers of Sam Adams® are Boston Beer Company, rather than Boston Brewery—they started out as having all of their beer contract brewed. APs were an attempt to reduce the capital equipment cost of opening a brewery while still owning a brewery.

The idea behind APs is the brewery (i.e., the equipment making the beer inside the building) actually changes ownership (it "alternates") on a periodic basis (typically every day or two). So, you end up with a negotiated agreement where Brewery A owns the equipment Monday, Tuesday, and Thursday, while Brewery B owns the equipment Wednesday, Friday, Saturday, and Sunday. This allows two companies to own and share the same equipment, but still be two different breweries according to the TTB and the ABC. Again, this is important for licensing issues.

It's clear that there are economic advantages to this arrangement. One example is that the "brewhouse" (where the wort is made) can normally make two to three batches of wort in a day, but it takes fermentation (where the wort is made into beer by the yeast) at least several days to make something like a final product. So, once all your fermentation tanks are filled, your brewhouse sits idle until fermentation space opens up. That means there's unused capacity in the brewhouse. An AP is one way to try to utilize that unused capacity.

Issues to think about when drafting an AP agreement include:

- Setting the schedule. While it may be tempting to set a definitive schedule for the equipment forever and ever, production concerns do not always work out to support that. There must be a system for determining who "owns" the brewery at any one time. It must also be flexible enough to allow the parties to make amendments from time to time (keep in mind, the TTB may need to be informed) as capacities and growth demands.

- Clear responsibilities as to who owns what when. In an AP, there may be two different breweries' beers fermenting in adjacent tanks at the same time. What happens when there's an issue with Brewery B's beer while Brewery A is in possession of the brewery?
- Reporting. Again, because of the shared equipment (including, in many instances, packaging equipment), how are the tank and product volumes accounted for across the breweries to ensure that reporting (for tax purposes) is clear and consistent? The last thing Brewery A wants is to have Brewery B cause tax problems for them.
- Maintenance. The equipment is shared, so who is responsible for the maintenance, calibration, and—in some cases—upgrading/improvement of the equipment?
- Termination and amendments. It is almost certain that one brewery will grow at a different pace than the other. As one brewery decides it needs more capacity, can it kick the other off the system? Or what if Brewery A decides to build its own brewery, what are Brewery B's options when faced with increased overhead by not sharing the equipment?
- Facility issues. Who is responsible for the building/space? Likely, the breweries did not simultaneously execute the lease or purchase the property together. Who is ultimately responsible to the landlord? What are the other parties' responsibilities for facility upkeep and preservation?
- Taproom use or existence. Nearly every brewery has a taproom or tasting room. The margins versus wholesale are just too good not to. Though the TTB and ABC allow for alternation of brewery equipment, there is no

such provision for the alternation of the taproom. The general rule is that a single address can only have a single retail license (at least in North Carolina). So, who gets the taproom? Who has to move their retail beer sales offsite? Or sell it at the other brewery's taproom (back to wholesale margins)? Or do neither get to have a taproom?

"John Says: "AP and Contract Brewing Agreements can make or break you as a brewery. Please be sure to get some legal help on this. Don't rely on a handshake."

AGREEMENTS WITH SUPPLIERS

The main subject for contracted supplies is hops. Following the "hop shortage/crisis" of 2008, breweries are now routinely committing to hop purchases two to four years in advance. Previously, very few breweries had any contracts for hop purchases beyond the current year's brewing. One of the principle issues causing this shift in practice is that for many years leading up to 2008, hop plantings were decreasing year after year, while hop demand was increasing year after year (principally due to the rise of craft beer). Prior to 2008, hop prices were at an unsustainable low. To make hop farming economically feasible, the market had to make an "adjustment." Spot market purchase prices for hops went through the roof. In some cases, only those breweries with contracts were able to get certain varieties or volumes. This economic shift coupled with the fact that hop plants take two to three years to have commercially viable yields (and the public seems to be demanding ever new and different hop varieties), hop contracts have to be in place to secure reasonable costs, available quantities, and a sustainable marketplace.

That said, there are, of course, agreements with other types of suppliers, particularly glass, cardboard (packaging), aluminum cans, yeast, specialty ingredients, and malted grain. There are specialists in the market that deal in only one of these areas, but there are also one-stop shops that can provide multiple types of supplies for the burgeoning brewer or distiller.

Many times, the supplier/customer relationship, especially in smaller breweries and distilleries, is governed by a simple purchase order and invoice system. But, when evaluating or developing a supplier contract, issues to consider include:

- Shelf life. The majority of the ingredients for brewing and distilling are not shelf stable. Hops, malted grain, yeast, and specialty ingredients all degrade with age. They degrade with age whether or not they're at the brewery or in a warehouse at the supplier. So consider the dating/freshness even before receipt by the end-consumer.
- Quantities. Be sure that the client is clear on the volume of the item they're ordering. Certainly there are advantages to ordering more at a time (bulk discounts), but it is also a serious issue if the brewery orders a year's worth of packaging material and then has nowhere to store it or has to deal with losses (due to moisture, weather, heat, accidental destruction, etc.) as they spend a year working through their packaging material—assuming that their forecasts were right and the beer is still selling well in eight months! The other issue, more likely to affect smaller companies, is the material handling. I know of a client that ordered a "super-sack" of malted grain. When the

malt showed up, there was no way to unload it; the shipping company assumed the brewery had a forklift, while the brewery assumed that the truck would have one on board.

- Duration and termination. The market for craft beer and craft beverages in general seems to be only going up. There is double-digit growth year after year, even after the Great Recession. But, even growth can be chaotic and difficult to plan. Make sure that there are terms that allow the termination of the contract if the market or demand changes (even if it goes up). I've seen brewers outgrow suppliers only to be stuck in the contract, so they end up with two small-ish orders from different suppliers (because the initial supplier can't meet demand) and lose some of their purchasing power.

John Says: "Far too often people just don't think to include important terms in their agreements. If it's not written down, it's hard to prove later that it was important."

LICENSING AGREEMENTS

Licensing agreements for breweries and distilleries are largely similar to other licensing agreements. However, there are a couple of nuances to consider:

- Franchise laws. Licensing agreements, depending on their terms, can implicate franchise laws and distributor-type relationships. Care should be taken to avoid this overlap. More on franchise laws later.
- Prohibited practices. With alcohol, there are also prohibited

practices in marketing and selling alcohol. If the license agreement involves a novice company, (on either side) make sure that all parties (and the contract) are clear on the do's and don'ts of alcohol marketing.

John Says: "Unless you have experience with franchise laws and distribution agreements, be careful here. But, that said, license agreements can be a powerful tool in managing your intellectual property."

- Duration and termination. Too often, license agreements are left as "perpetual" in duration—particularly if the agreement is used as a tool to settle a trademark dispute. Be sure to have terms where the license is either mutually renewed, renegotiated, or terminated on a periodic basis.

- Dispute resolution. In most license agreements, the parties are in different states. For some small businesses, this makes legal action to enforce or fight the agreement cost prohibitive. This can be a serious issue for one side or the other or both depending on how strongly they've relied on the license (for an entire brand, in some cases). Be sure that alternate dispute resolution or non-legal avenues for resolution are available. → mediation

EQUIPMENT LEASES

Most of these types of agreements are very similar to non-alcohol circumstances and do not warrant in-depth discussion. However, there are a few critical points that are often overlooked even by seasoned transactional attorneys. Some points to consider include:

Most brewery and distillery equipment is purchased outright or bought on installments, rather than leased. One major exception to this is beer kegs. Beer kegs are, for the most part, stainless steel. There are stories that the purchase of kegs can account for nearly half of the required capital for startup. As a result, there are several services which allow breweries to lease kegs.

- For beer kegs, be sure that the lease discusses or somehow addresses:
    - Lost kegs. It's surprising how often this happens.
    - Found kegs. What if a keg that was leased to Brewery A ends up being returned to the keg leasing company? Or to Brewery B? It's surprising how often this happens.
    - Damaged kegs. Are they repaired? Returned? Who's responsible for the damage? Does it depend on the age of the kegs?
    - Responsibility for keg maintenance. In the last several years, there have been at least three separate instances where a keg has ruptured and caused the death of a brewery employee.
    - Transportation. Who is responsible for shipping kegs to/from the lessor?
    - Flexibility. As a brewery installs a bottling line (typically a second-tier purchase in most brewery's growth plans), they may need fewer kegs. Or more kegs if they're growing quickly. Make sure that there is some way to expand or contract the brewery's keg inventory.

For other equipment leases, many of the same principles apply. However, be aware that there may be some security (collateral) or finance piece (including a personal guarantee) on equipment leases that can impact your credit and credit rating.

COMMERCIAL/RETAIL SPACE LEASES

Despite the statements of myriad landlords and brokers, there is no such thing as a "standard lease." The landlord (or broker, in some cases) has a strategic advantage in—typically—drafting the lease and presenting it to you the tenant. If you're not 100% comfortable with every single solitary piece of the lease's wording, make sure to have it reviewed by a lawyer. Several times clients have said, "It's okay, I've had my brother-in-law look it over and he's a [insert tangentially related occupation]." Too often, clients have relied on non-lawyers for legal advice when it comes to a lease. If you're committing to two, five, ten, or more years at (potentially) thousands of dollars a month in rent, isn't it worth the couple hundred dollars it would cost for a professional review?

John Says: "Even though there isn't a 'standard lease,' real estate is one of those areas where—depending on your local laws—the statutes can rewrite your agreement, no matter what you agreed to."

For retail space, such as a taproom or a bottleshop, leases will be very similar to any other retail business. Most issues that come up with respect to retail space have to do with the immediate surroundings or neighboring businesses/homes. For example:

- Places that serve alcohol are typically open later than many other businesses. Is that an issue for the landlord? Or neighboring homes?
- Taprooms or tasting rooms often feature live entertainment. Is that an issue?
- Because alcohol is involved (and there may be intoxicated people on the premises), how does that affect the landlord's expectation of insurance or liability protection?
- If you're putting a retail space in an industrial or commercial environment (such as when a brewery moves into a warehouse-type district, and has a taproom), does that affect the premises, ingress and egress? What about the parking and access to neighboring businesses?
- Many taprooms are open only certain days of the week or certain hours. If you're in a retail space with other retailers, does the landlord have an expectation of certain hours?
- Also, if you're changing the use of the building (from, say, an industrial assembly facility to a retail taproom), make sure that you are informed about the parking rights, privileges, or availability.
- Think about any retrofit for Americans with Disabilities Act (ADA) compliance or retrofitting of existing spaces, particularly historic spaces.
- Especially for a long-lease term, consider incorporating a clause that gives you, as tenant, first right of refusal if the landlord looks to sell the building, etc.

In addition, your local municipality (or state, in some cases) may have special requirements for retail alcohol establishments.

And, it may be important that the lease specifically states the purpose of the business with respect to the sale of alcohol.

Production and distribution space leases are more intricate. In particular, if you're not regularly in the business of these businesses and their lease requirements, you (or the landlord) may overlook some of these. Most nuances are relatively obscure, but can become critical:

- Noise/odor. Be sure that the landlord is aware that the business is a production brewery/distillery and alcohol is, essentially, an agricultural product. Malted grain has to be milled before it can be used—this causes noise and dust. Wet grain tends to get very smelly after a couple days. This can be a serious issue if the brewery is located in a strip mall and the wet grain stored out back is causing complaints from the upscale jewelry store next door.
- Infrastructure. Even in commercial and industrial zones, the building infrastructure is often insufficient for brewery needs. For example, full fermenters can weigh thousands and thousands of pounds—is the floor up to the task of supporting that kind of weight? If not, who retrofits it, and how is it retrofitted? Or, many breweries use 3-phase electricity. Does the building have access to 3-phase? If so, can it support the electrical load from the brewery? If not, who retrofits it and how is that retrofitted? Roof penetrations for vents or equipment installation, roof reinforcement for chillers, adding trench drains, reinforcing walls, enlarging doors and adding unloading docks—the list goes on and on. Be careful, too, when changes are extensive enough to

trigger other retrofitting (like ADA compliance, sidewalks, or upgraded restrooms).

- Access. Particularly in retail zones, make sure that the landlord is aware that a large semi may be parked in front (or around back) for hours at a time multiple times a week delivering raw materials, equipment, or picking up product.
- Common areas and outdoor areas. Particularly in light industrial or industrial areas (but also in retail spaces), be sure that the landlord understands that the brewery or distillery may be using the outdoor or common areas in ways different from the other tenants. It's not often that a machine shop hosts a festival at their business, but it's fairly common for a brewery.

Leases will almost always include a requirement for a personal guarantee for one or more of the owners. The issue here is that, especially if the company is new, the company has no credit history and so it is very difficult for banks or the landlord to determine how likely it is that the business will pay its debts. As a result, landlords require a personal guarantee that the owners, individually, will promise to pay if the business cannot or will not. Some breweries have had some success in negotiating a termination of the personal guarantee depending on a certain period of time (usually years) of on-time, in-full rent payments. This termination of a personal guarantee can be a great way to, over time, reduce your personal liability on company debts.

DISTRIBUTION AGREEMENTS AND FRANCHISE LAW

Distribution agreements and franchise law (and its reform) are hot topics right now in the craft beverage industry. To understand alcohol distribution and franchise laws, you need to understand the genesis of the three-tier system. The three-tier system applies equally to beer, wine, and distilled spirits. For the purposes of this discussion, we'll focus on beer. But be aware that the principles are the same, though the actors (like the state in the case of the distribution and retail sales of distilled spirits) may be different, and vary state to state. This book will talk more specifically about distribution and franchise laws later, but be aware that distribution rights are generally governed by two things:

1. A distribution agreement AND
2. The state laws governing distribution of alcohol in your state

John Says: "Distribution and Franchise Law get their own sections later on. They're that important."

The same basic contract law applies to distribution agreements, BUT the agreement is "overwritten" by the statutes in most cases—that is, even if you can AGREE to certain things, the LAW may make the contract different than what you agreed on.

INTERNATIONAL AND OUT OF STATE AGREEMENTS

It's surprising, but at a very fundamental level, out-of-state agreements and international agreements are treated very similarly by courts. For just a peek at that distinction, check out your state's Secretary of State website and look for "foreign corporation registration." ("Foreign corporations" are any companies that were not originally formed in the state.)

In the United States, however, contract law is broadly similar from state to state, so it is less of a risk for the small business to contract with companies in another state. Nonetheless, it is important for the parties contracting to know and understand the "choice of law" specified in an agreement. Specifically, any contract between companies in different states should have an express clause which specifies what laws apply to the contract.

Keep in mind that, if you're dealing with a party in another country, you may run into a situation where what you agree to is overwritten by the country's laws or by an international treaty. For example, take a look at 1980 United Nations Convention on Contracts for the International Sale of Goods (CISG).

John Says: "The biggest issue to watch out for here is if something goes wrong, where can you sue AND get relief? If you're here and the contract says here, but the company is located in China can a state court order them to do something AND have it be enforceable?"

"BOILERPLATE"

This is a popular, but horrible, term. The term "boilerplate" makes the issue seem like it's not important. To say that these issues are unimportant would be to seriously understate the importance of how these terms can make or break your business—especially in the event of a dispute. When "boilerplate" is mentioned, it's more because the contracts are broadly similar and, especially when used by a lawyer, refers to template language that can be used again and again in agreements. When discussing "boilerplate," it should be that many of these pieces are seen over and over, but each one should be clear and included in (nearly) every agreement you sign on to. Important pieces to address include:

John Says: "I hate the term 'boilerplate'. It devalues the importance of those sections and how hard lawyers work to make sure that the agreement is fair to their client. Maybe if we called the section 'boilermaker' it'd get more respect."

- Choice of law—what laws apply to the agreement?
- Notice—how (and where) will each party learn (from the other) about important issues with the agreement?
- Jurisdiction—this seems pedantic, but it is critical to determine what courts have the authority to enforce the agreement.
- Venue—where will lawsuits or other "official" proceedings about the agreement take place?
- Termination—how will the agreement be terminated or concluded?
- Term—how long will the agreement be in force? This sounds

like the same as the one above, but they're different to the extent that the one above is about how to get out of the agreement. This one is about when the agreement may expire—with or without your action.
- Severability—what if part of the agreement is determined to be illegal or unenforceable? Do they throw out the entire agreement? Or just that part?
- Merger—is this the entire agreement between the parties? Or are there side agreements going on?
- Dispute resolution—if there's a dispute, how will the parties resolve the dispute? Without a specific procedure, the only way to get to a resolution without mutual agreement is with a lawsuit (arguably the most expensive way to get someone to say what the contract means).
- Confidentiality—is it important that the other side not reveal important stuff about the agreement?
- Attorneys' fees and costs of enforcement/collection—if someone has to sue to enforce the agreement, does the losing party have to pay the winner's attorneys' fees?

CONSTRUCTION CONTRACTS – GENERAL

Construction contracts are difficult in that they include goods, services, unknowns, and contingencies. Because construction naturally involves substantial transformation of an existing asset (typically a piece of property), it can be very difficult for the end product to be pinned down with real specificity. Additionally, when construction takes more than a few weeks, there are typically intermediate payments before the final approval—this can make things more complicated as you can easily pay for something that you haven't yet approved or isn't specified in the agreement. Essentially, and especially for construction agreements, the agreement detail should be proportional to the investment in the construction. For example, a $500k construction agreement should probably not be controlled by a two-page agreement. Conversely, an agreement for a $5,000 bar in your taproom should not require a 28-page document. The idea is that the detail, attention, and specifications for your construction agreement should track with the amount of money at risk.

CONSTRUCTION CONTRACTS – HISTORIC SPACES

Breweries are famous (notorious?) for revitalizing historic and older facilities. There are special concerns for these unique spaces. Some of the intricacies that could (or should) concern you are often not as intuitive as you might think. Without significant research, using a historic space can be a real risk from a financial and a legal perspective.

There was a client who was looking to locate a nanobrewery in a really nice, historic, just-off-the-beaten-path town. In fact they were looking to remodel the 1950s-era gas station that had been abandoned for twenty-plus years and turn it into a brewery in the garage area with the taproom inside (pretty neat idea, huh?). Well, the town told them, "No way, we don't want a brewery in our town. Breweries are like bars and we don't want a bar in the [historic] downtown." The client tried to explain,

"Hey, we'll refurbish that vacant eyesore over there and bring you foot traffic, festivals..." The town just flat shut them down. The nano moved down the road to a different (more friendly) downtown area. Town's loss.

Point is, whether it's zoning issues, political issues, or whatever, make sure that you've identified the issues you're going to face and know what you're up against. In the case above, even if money were no object, the town was going to throw up every barrier it could to make it harder for the brewery because that wasn't the vision the town had for itself. Make sure your vision is shared by the municipality.

When it comes to infrastructure, in the South even the old/historic construction is fairly new. Heck, most of Florida wasn't built until after the invention of central air conditioning. But, whether it's recently-old or old-old, be wary of the infrastructure that you might have to deal with.

Most brewers can immediately spot electrical issues (requiring rewiring), substandard/inadequate electrical service (doesn't have 220 or the panel isn't big enough), or even roofing or structural issues. But, what about what you can't see? Are the drains sufficient? How long have they been building up sediment? Do you even know where the drains/plumbing lead to? (This is especially an issue in buildings built in the early 1900s and before.) You might have a great space in this really nice building, but do you know where the hole in floor drains to?

What about the incoming water? I talked to a client a while back who was looking to start a nanobrewery on a farm he had just acquired. "Great idea," I said. "Where are you getting your water?" "Oh, from the well." Uh... maybe not a great idea.

If you're using a well, do you know if the well can meet your water demand (remember, even SUPER conservation-minded breweries are still using upwards of three plus gallons of water for each gallon of beer produced). If the well can meet your demand, do you know what's in the well? In many rural areas, you may have groundwater contaminated by heavy metals, pesticides, or other chemicals that may be below threshold values for residential purposes, but maybe not when you're pulling a lot of water out of the ground.

Same thought process goes for streams or surface water sources. Oh, and make sure that when you start pulling your water, you don't adversely affect your neighbor's wells, streams, etc.

Lastly, on the subject of infrastructure, here's something not so easy to gauge from a simple visual inspection—can the floor stand the weight? Remember, you're going to be putting several tons of grain, liquid, and equipment on that floor. And, just because it's concrete, doesn't mean it can stand the strain. You really don't want to explain to the landlord that your fermenter just broke the foundation.

One serious, often too costly, approach involves retrofitting historic or older spaces for use as a brewery/taproom. Consider, however, that some municipalities may be able to waive certain requirements, often as part of a program to revitalize or profitably use the space. Without appropriate waivers, remember that when you're retrofitting, you generally have to bring the building up to standard code regardless of what your requirements are. That can be seriously costly. One client had to add a handicap access ramp from the parking lot to the front door (four feet above the ground) before they could serve at their taproom. That new handicap ramp required an almost twenty-five foot run to get up a not-too-steep slope. That was a lot of concrete they weren't expecting to have to pay for. In fact, they were moving into an old factory (really pretty space), but because they were adding a taproom to serve the public (changing the use of the facility), they couldn't shelter behind a "grandfathered in" sort of rule.

On the other hand, many towns, counties, and even states have various programs to encourage rehabilitation of older buildings or revitalization of certain areas. Some clients have received a grant of money from the state as part of the economic development of the area. And, while everyone would like the incentives to come in the form of a check, they can also be very useful as tax breaks or joint cost sharing.

What is "joint cost sharing?" Well, for example, another client was looking to move into a historic building with inadequate electrical service. The town offered to pay for the service upgrade to get the power to the building, if the brewery would pay for the inside rewiring. This was a significant cost avoidance for the brewery. Other issues could include sidewalk upgrades, city bike racks, or redoing some of the city/town parking to support your business. All I'm saying is that you need to think out of the box. Brewers are pretty good at doing that anyway.

EMPLOYMENT AGREEMENTS

Employment agreements are a special beast. In rare cases it takes a specialist in employment law to sort out precisely where you stand with respect to your own employees. However, there are some general provisions and concepts for you to keep in mind

John Says: *"Also check out the section on Human Resources and Employment Law for different details on this."*

or be sure to address. But first, do you even need an employment contract? Well, that depends…

Employment agreements are important tools in specifying the relationship between the company and the employee. It is even more advisable in some states over others. For example, North Carolina is a "right to work" state where either party can terminate the employer/employee relationship for almost any reason and at almost any time. So, why would that not be a good reason? Well, it leads to a definite incentive for disloyalty in a field where there can be a fairly brisk movement of people between companies. Additionally, if there are specific aspects of the relationship that you want to make absolutely clear—like, say how the employee can earn an equity position in the company—you definitely want to put that in writing.

Many of the general basics of contract law apply to employment agreements, but there are some tweaks that you should be especially aware of. These include:

- Deliverables and goals—how does the employee understand what their specific requirements are with respect to the business? This is especially important for key employees, like brewers or marketing/sales reps.
- Authority boundaries—does the employee know the limits of their authority when acting for the company? This is critical for employees like the taproom manager, marketing manager, and head brewer where they have the potential to "speak for

the company" and commit money or time/effort.

- Inventions and creativity—if the employee creates something, who does it belong to? This is particularly important for the brewer position where they may be creating specific ideas, inventions, or creativity that becomes part of your brand.
- Term and termination—does the employee know how/when they can get out of the agreement or the penalties of breach? This can be critical if you're providing certain paid benefits (such as help with education) or equity in the company. *pay after the fact, not up front...*
- Confidentiality—what can the employee share after they leave the company? There may be parts of your process, sales strategy, or overall business that you do not want former employees sharing.
- Exclusivity—can the employee work somewhere else while working for you? Generally you can't prohibit someone from working more than one job, unless it's part of an employee agreement. Brewers are especially notorious for collaborating on other projects that may involve teaching or writing often to better their own brand—is that okay?

Consider whether you need an employment agreement for one or more key employees of the business. If so, be sure to get some help from professionals in designing this agreement to meet your specific business needs and concerns.

CHAPTER FIVE: INTELLECTUAL PROPERTY

Intellectual property can be thought of in four main categories: trademarks, copyrights, patents, and trade secrets. In whatever form, intellectual property represents an intangible asset that is incredibly valuable to your business and to your brand, so it is important that you understand the basic issues.

We will talk about each in some length, but you can generally think of the following breakdown:

- Trademark—protects the brand and the reputation of the supplier or source of goods or services
- Copyright—protects "works;" original works of art, literature, or performance—items which can be reproduced, and the specific arrangement of that reproduction is critical (i.e. "works")

- Patents—protect "things;" objects, processes, or tangible items which are new, novel, or unique, or a special way of producing something (i.e. "things")
- Trade Secrets—protect ideas, things, processes, or details that are critical to the business but not intuitive—they may constitute a competitive advantage

PATENTS

Patents protect "things" or the making of "things." So, what's a "thing?" Generally, a "thing," at least in this sense, is an object or something that has been assembled, manufactured, created, or grown. A thing, for the purposes of patent protection, is not the text in this book. It's not the music recorded on a CD or streamed to your device. It's not a brand name or descriptor. A thing is an idea that can be reduced to physical form. Examples of things might be a network router, a USB hub, a stapler (can you tell I'm looking around my desk?), or a computer monitor.

John Says: "*I learned early, I don't wanna do patents.*"

At one point or another, each of those things may have been eligible for patent protection.

TYPES OF PATENTS

Consider that there are three types of things that are eligible for patent protection. These are:

- Useful articles (protected by utility patents)
- Ornamental articles (protected by design patents)
- Plants (protected by plant patents)

Utility patents are the protections that we think of most often when someone mentions "patents." Utility patents protect an inventor's rights in a new invention so long as the invention is new, non-obvious, and useful. These patents carry a twenty-year protection life from the time the invention is recognized by the United States Patent and Trademark Office (USPTO).

Ornamental patents protect the "ornamental" features of a product or packaging. An ornamental design is eligible for protection only to the extent that it is purely decorative, without any function on its own. Ornamental patents protect the design for fourteen years from the date of issuance.

Plants (aka flora) are also eligible for patent protection if they are capable of being asexually reproduced and are not "tubers" (non-tuberous plants). Plant patents also carry a fourteen-year protection life.

Most of the time, breweries and other craft beverage manufacturers do not have a lot of opportunities to develop something that is patent-able under a utility patent, but it does happen.

When people think of "patents," in general they think about utility patents. The formula for utility patentability is a new, novel invention that is not obvious to someone ordinarily skilled in the art. This means that the item or way of doing something is not only new, but it is NOT something that someone who is "ordinarily skilled in the art" would be able to come up with—it must be a leap forward in technology or understanding. For example, if you came up with a new kind of fluid pump to be patentable, it cannot merely be an incremental improvement on an existing pump design or idea. It must be so different from technology that someone "ordinarily skilled in the art"—say, a professional pump designer—would not see it as an obvious improvement or change.

On the other hand, a brewery may be interested in looking to protect a design or packaging with an ornamental patent. This may include things like the shape of the brewery's bottle (if it's unique). For example, Coca-Cola's bottle shape (the distinct curvy one) is protected under both an ornamental patent and as a trade dress trademark.

Unless the brewery, winery, or distillery is into creating new and novel plants, a plant patent is not really in the picture for a brewery's intellectual property portfolio.

USPTO

The United States Patent and Trademark Office (USPTO) is the governing entity for the Patent Registration process in the U.S. Patents can be expensive and that's not just the USPTO fees. Patent attorneys are regularly one of the highest paid legal specialists. The work is very detailed, and the required knowledge and training is not something even most lawyers collect in their education. In fact, to even be allowed to practice as an attorney before the Patent Board, you have to have a law degree AND a degree in science, math, or engineering. The USPTO fees start around $500 and can range in to the tens of thousands for filing fees, search fees, examiners' fees, etc., and that does not include hiring an attorney to represent you. For a simple patent application/issue, the rule of thumb that we use for clients is that they should look to spend somewhere between $10,000 and $40,000, assuming that the patent isn't challenged.

Recall that, because it's the *United States Patent and Trademark Office*, the protection of the patent only extends to the borders of the U.S. There may be treaties with other countries that extend some protection to U.S. patents or that allow patentees preferential treatment in that country's patent system, but there are no guarantees. Check out the Patent Cooperation Treaty (PCT) if international patent protection is something that is a concern for the business/product.

John Says: "It's always interested me why patents and trademarks were lumped together in the same agency. The focus of each is very different from the other and the examining skill set (that is, how the agency personnel characterize and analyze the applications) is almost mutually exclusive. It would almost be like a company that specializes in car stereos and baby food. Yes, they both have to be 'manufactured,' but how it's done is very different."

COPYRIGHT

Copyright is protection the author or creator is given in the reproduction of a "work." The phrase is often heard, "copyrights protect works." So, what's a "work?" A work is a collection of content that has been created and the control of the reproduction of that content belongs to the author/creator of the content. Examples of works include: this book, a music recording, a painting or other artwork. In some cases even an artistic performance is eligible for copyright protection. The issue here is who gets to decide who can reproduce (exactly or substantially exactly) the work created by someone? For example, let's say that the estate of J.R.R. Tolkien owns the copyright to *The Hobbit*. Can anyone start printing copies of *The Hobbit* and sell them at their local bookstore? No. *The Hobbit* is subject to copyright protection and cannot be reproduced without the permission of the copyright holder.

Copyright owners get a host of protections and rights that they can enforce. These include:

- Right to reproduce the work or a portion of the work
- Right to prepare derivative works
- Right to distribution of the work
- Right to control any public performance of the work
- Right to public display of the work

There are a few cases where breweries, wineries, or distilleries need to be concerned about copyrights, but not many. For example, the company's website is subject to copyright. Do you want someone else to be able to exactly duplicate your website on their own server? No. You should be able to control the content and reproduction of that created content. The website should contain reference to copyrights and dates to put the world on notice that you claim those copyrights and that they cannot simply reproduce the website in part or in whole on their own. Check out http://www.copyright.gov/circs/circ66.pdf for details on registering websites at the U.S. Copyright Office.

John Says: *"Make sure you own the rights to your own artwork."*

Additionally, if you hire a graphic designer, artist, or anyone to prepare content for you, make sure you inherit or retain the copyright for that work. The last thing you want is to have a logo you want to use, but the artist who created it has the copyright on that logo!

TO COPYRIGHT OR NOT TO COPYRIGHT

There are also questions, in terms of copyright, as to whether or not it is worth the effort to try and protect your intellectual property. This comes down to two questions: (1) how likely is it that someone will try and pilfer your work? And (2) do you care?

> *For example, if the business is a brewpub, there will be a menu that someone has written. Technically, that menu is eligible for copyright protection. So (1), how likely is it that someone will try to pilfer the content of the work? Not very. Not a lot of call for "black market" or "bootleg" menus. And, (2), do you care if they do? Not really. How "bad" will it be if someone copies your menu? There is not going to be a lot of damage to your business if someone uses a copy of your menu at their restaurant or home. So, it may not be worth your effort to secure copyright protection for your menus. Each piece of copyright-eligible material should have at least a cursory evaluation as to whether or not it is worth securing copyright protection.*

However, registration at the Copyright Office does provide some additional rights for the registrant and is nearly a requirement for anyone that wants (or expects) to have to engage in litigation for copyright infringement. But, just like patents through the USPTO, the registration of copyrights and their protections with the U.S. Copyright Office (USCO) only extend to the U.S. borders.

SECURING AND DEFENDING COPYRIGHTS

The U.S. Copyright Office is the keeper of the registration of copyrights in the U.S. The process to register a copyright is simple, almost mind-numbingly so. Our office regularly advises clients not to hire an attorney to help you with registering your copyrights. The USCO has several "walk-through" guides to help you do this for yourself with reasonable fees. Check out http://www.copyright.gov/ for details.

Defending your copyrights is another matter. You should engage an attorney to help you identify your rights and find out the appropriate means and methods to stop any copyright infringement.

TRADE SECRETS

Other than trademarks, trade secrets are probably the most important intellectual property topic for craft beverage makers. Adopted in most states, the Uniform Trade Secret Act (UTSA) governs most legal issues with trade secrets. The UTSA defines a trade secret as:

"information, including a
- formula
- pattern
- compilation

- program
- device
- method
- technique
- process that:
  - derives independent economic value, actual or potential, from not being generally known to, and not being readily ascertainable by proper means by, other persons who can obtain economic value from its disclosure or use, AND
  - is the subject of efforts that are reasonable under the circumstance to maintain its secrecy."

"Say, what?" I hear you mumble. Here's the crux: if it's a special thing or process that you use that no one else knows and it makes a difference to your product, and you take steps to keep it a secret, it's a trade secret.

So, examples of trade secrets might be recipes (like Stone Brewing's infamous refusal to disclose the recipe for Arrogant Bastard, even though they make their other beer recipes known), Sierra Nevada's Torpedo device for extracting hop flavor/aroma (if they hadn't told everyone about it), or Dogfish Head's continual hopping for their 60-, 90-, and 120-minute IPAs (if they hadn't told us about it). If everyone knows about it, it is not a good trade secret. So, naturally, there aren't a lot of public examples to list here.

John Says: "Sometimes you have to make a decision. Is it better to keep it a secret or create a buzz by talking it up?"

RECIPES

Recipes are a big one for a lot of breweries. As an attorney in the industry, I sometimes get asked about how to protect recipes. This is a two-edged sword and, I believe, a non-issue in most cases. How do you protect recipes? By keeping them trade secrets. Don't disclose the recipes, and be sure that the recipes, logbooks, and brewers' notes are secured and not easily found or discovered. Seems simple. There are two things that argue against treating your recipes as trade secrets:

1. The exact same recipe produced on two different brewing systems will make two different beers. Even large breweries like AnheuserBusch-InBev have to adjust recipes from facility to facility to get consistent flavors across the different breweries for Bud Light. Even if Stone Brewing publicly released the recipe for Arrogant Bastard, no one could make Arrogant Bastard without adjusting the recipe because no one else has Stone's exact combination of brewing system, water, yeast, etc. If the flavor profile and taste of Arrogant Bastard is what someone wants to create, they can almost always do so by reverse engineering a sample of the beer. Where do they get a sample of the beer? From the brewery selling the beer!
2. Someone wants to make the exact same beer you make. Why?
    a. If they're a homebrewer and want to make a clone of your beer at home, okay. That's probably not going to stop them from buying your beer. The homebrewer

may want to make a clone of your beer because they can't get your beer in their hometown. But if they can, they're probably still going to buy your beer—ask most homebrewers, it's not a "cheaper way to get the same beer." Even if making your beer causes someone not to buy your beer, even if every homebrewer stopped buying your beer because they can make it at home—that's still less than 0.5% of the U.S. population. If your business depends exclusively on homebrewers buying your beer, you may need to revise your business model anyway.

b. If it's a commercial brewery that wants to make your exact same beer, based on your recipe, why? Commercial breweries, and the industry in general, thrives on differentiating their product from everybody else's. Commercial breweries are highly unlikely to advertise, "Hey, we make the same exact same beer as [insert your name], come buy it here instead!" It is just not a winning business strategy. They're more likely to say that "we make beer better than [whoever]" and "better" has to mean "different" and "different" means "not your recipe."

So, while there are reasons to protect your recipes, and it is not hard to do, make sure that you have a firm understanding of why you are protecting your recipes.

On the other hand, if you have a "mystery" ingredient or a unique process to making your beer, that is definitely something that you want to think about protecting as a trade secret.

PROTECTING TRADE SECRETS

We know what a trade secret is. How, exactly, do you protect trade secrets? Companies should take steps (and document those steps) to protect the information of the trade secrets. Examples might include:

- Make it known—Tell those who know the trade secret that it is a trade secret, and that you want it to be treated as a secret and as confidential information. "Those who know" might include employees, business partners, vendors, owners, etc.—anyone who has a reason to know the information you want kept confidential.
- Confidentiality Agreements—Document the agreement to keep the trade secret information confidential. Confidentiality Agreements can be used between companies and vendors, owners, and employees. Confidentiality clauses should be included in your standard employment agreements and in the business's organizational documents.
- Securing the information—If the trade secret is stored electronically, make sure that it's stored in a password-protected file. If the information is stored on paper, be sure that paper records are locked and secured by physical means. If the information is some special piece of equipment, make sure that the equipment is not generally visible (such as on tours of the facility). Whether it is stored electronically, written on paper, or hidden behind a curtain in the brewery—controlling access to the information is key to establishing the security of the information itself and to showing that this information should be treated as a trade secret.

CONFIDENTIALITY, NON-DISCLOSURE, AND NON-COMPETE

These topics play into how you control your intellectual property, which can be a serious and valuable asset to your business.

CONFIDENTIALITY AGREEMENTS: GENERALLY

With respect to confidentiality agreements, there are some things to consider if you're going to implement one. Identify those who need to keep information confidential. These can include business owners, vendors, employees, and even some customers. Confidentiality agreements need not be a separate document. Agreements can contain confidentiality provisions even if the focus of the document is something else. For example, consider including confidentiality requirements in

- Contract Brewing/Production Agreements
- Employment Agreements
- Business Organization Documents (like Operating Agreements or Shareholder Agreements)
- Equipment Purchase Agreements
- Leases (depending on what you are leasing)
- Consulting or Professional Services Agreements

CONFIDENTIALITY AGREEMENTS WITH EMPLOYEES

In many states, a confidentiality agreement between an employer and an employee cannot be forced onto an employee after they are employed. In those cases, there is often a requirement that there is some additional "consideration" provided to the employee beyond the continuation of their employment. An example might be illustrative:

Miguel is the Assistant Brewer at Third Street Brewing. He's been working at Third Street for three years now without any written employment agreement. In Year Three, the President of Third Street comes to Miguel and says, "Hey, I need you to sign this confidentiality agreement. It says that you agree to keep certain information confidential, even after you leave the company."

John Says: "*Confidentiality and non-disclosure are not necessarily the same thing. And neither means non-competition. Understand the differences and what's important to you.*"

> *If Miguel has never had an employment agreement (and assuming he's an employee in the legal sense), he's been doing his job and has not been required to keep information confidential up to now. So now, he has a new job requirement because of this confidentiality agreement? This agreement might not be enforceable because it is one-sided: the company gets confidentiality, Miguel gets nothing in exchange. That's not a contract. That's a demand.*

Miguel's boss says, "No, in exchange for the confidentiality, Miguel gets to keep his job going forward." This might not be enforceable because it is now (almost) extortion. At best, it looks like Miguel is being forced to sign something by having his job threatened. Not a fair bargain.

Miguel's boss says, "Hey, Miguel, we're going to promote you to Packaging Manager and you're going to have some people reporting to you now. The pay is the same, but we're looking to move you to Head Brewer after some time as Packaging Manager. But, as part of this new job, we need you to also agree to this confidentiality agreement." Okay. Now Miguel is receiving "value" (even if it is not money) in exchange for confidentiality. He's receiving value in the form of a new job or opportunity. This is probably enforceable.

So, it is smart to identify those individuals who need to maintain confidentiality early (probably at hiring) and have them sign on to a confidentiality agreement at that time.

NON-DISCLOSURE AGREEMENTS

Non-disclosure agreements are sisters of confidentiality agreements. The idea is that one party is going to share some confidential information with the other side. Sometimes, both parties will share confidential information with each other—typically referred to as mutual non-disclosure agreements. But, in any case, the issue is that confidential information is going to be shared with respect to some particular transaction.

> For example, if a brewery is looking to expand and wants to get several bids on construction from several contractors—none of which are guaranteed the job—the brewery may ask for a non-disclosure agreement with the contractor in exchange for the opportunity to bid on the job. The brewery would share confidential information (such as batch size, equipment layout, timeline for expansion, etc.) that the contractor may need to effectively bid on the job, but the brewery wants to make sure that the contractor doesn't disclose that information to anyone who absolutely doesn't need to know.

> Or, another example might be when a brewery is in talks about purchasing another brewery. A brewery may want to start talks with another brewery about buying them out, but does not want that brewery to disclose the fact that talks are ongoing. The same is true about sharing information about the business to a prospective buyer—if the deal falls through, the party that shared the information wants to make sure that the prospective buyer does not disclose business information to other parties.

The differences between a non-disclosure agreement and a confidentiality agreement may not be immediately obvious. Here is an example of how that may work out:

> Imagine talks with a brewhouse equipment company about designing equipment for a new brewhouse.

> Brewery says to designer, "Hey, we want to talk about the

details of this brewing system. We've got some special things that we want to do that are going to make a major difference, and it's a proprietary design. We haven't decided who will put the system together. We'd like to talk to you about it; would you sign a non-disclosure agreement?"

Designer signs the non-disclosure agreement and the brewery starts passing the designer information about the new "proprietary" system.

At some point, the brewery decides to hire the designer to build the system.

Brewery now says to designer, "Okay, now that we know we're going to hire you, we need to give you a lot more information about the details of the installation, the way we'll use the system, the process, etc. To get the job, you need to agree to a confidentiality agreement."

In practice, what this means is that a non-disclosure agreement says that:

> "I'm going to give you some confidential information. When I give you information, I'll tell you when it's something to keep confidential and not disclose. I'll probably even label it 'confidential information.' You promise not to disclose any confidential information that I give you to any third party."

A confidentiality agreement may be more along the lines of:

"We're in business together or my business relies on you and information you have. Some of that information I may have given to you is information we may have discovered in the course of our relationship. Here are the types of information that are really important and should be kept confidential: X, Y, Z, etc. You promise to keep that information confidential, even after our relationship has ended."

NON-COMPETE AGREEMENTS

Non-competition agreements are something of a fluid topic. The law of non-competition agreements is not only in flux in many ways (thanks in part to global changes in technology and working remotely from the employer), it also varies pretty substantially from state to state.

Some states, such as California, simply refuse to enforce any non-competition agreement. Some states are 180 degrees away from that and will enforce non-competition agreements so long as the parties agree to it and the terms are "reasonable."

John Says: "Even with more than 7000 breweries in the U.S., it's still a fairly small market. People talk, especially at the local level. Be careful with non-competition agreements and don't burn bridges."

This book will talk a lot about "reasonable," a term that does not have the normal, every-day meaning that you may think of. What is meant by "reasonable," in the legal sense is whether it is objectively reasonable: that is, is it just, fair, rational, appropriate, usual, or standard in those circumstances? It is sometimes used in terms of a "reasonable person"—meaning with reference to the standard of care that a reasonably prudent person would observe or the opinion of that person under a given set of circumstances.

The general rule for non-competition agreements is that, to be enforceable, they must be reasonable in terms of:

- Scope (pertaining to what jobs or businesses are "off-limits")
- Duration (the time in which someone cannot engage in the prohibited activity)
- Geography (the area in which someone cannot engage in the prohibited activity)

Scope

The scope of a non-competition agreement speaks to how broadly it restricts a person's activities. For example, it is unreasonable, in a non-competition agreement, for a brewer to say that his former brewer may not work in any beer or alcohol-related business. A restriction like that would essentially deprive a person of their livelihood. It would be like telling a professional engineer that they cannot "do engineering" anymore. That is an unreasonable restraint on a person for the purposes of non-competition. For breweries and craft beverage producers, a typical limited scope would be the exact same or similar position in another company. For example, if the brewer leaves the company and is subject to an enforceable non-competition agreement, it may prevent that person from working as a brewer, assistant brewer, head brewer, operations manager, or similar positions.

But it might allow them to work in a related job, like quality assurance, sales, or perhaps working for a distributor or supplier.

The same is true as to the scope. Can a brewer leave the company and become a distiller without violating the non-compete? Maybe, maybe not. Can a cellerman leave a brewery and become a general manager at a bottle shop? Probably. The issue comes down to how closely the employee is associated with the brand and the company. There are individuals who, as consumers, will follow the brewer to a new brewery—something the company wants to avoid. Does a cellerman have the same relationship as to reputation and creativity? Generally not, but in certain circumstances (such as a well-known sour beer brewery with a strong barrel program, where the barrel master is well known), you may have an issue. The same is true of distillers versus barrel masters when aging spirits.

Duration

Duration addresses how long the non-competition restriction is in place. For example, what if the non-competition agreement for the brewer above said that they could never brew beer professionally again? That would essentially deprive that person of their livelihood and main profession. Preventing a person from ever working in a similar capacity to work they did in the past is unreasonable. How long is too long? In most instances, a year or two is a typical duration for non-competition agreements. However, if it is related to a highly specialized skill or an extreme set of circumstances, a longer duration may be "reasonable." Conversely, if it involves a very common set of skills or a lower paying job, a year or two years may be too long. For example, it may be unreasonably long to prevent a grocery store cashier from working at another grocery store for a year.

Geographic Extent

With respect to geographic extent, enforceability again depends on the specific skill set and industry. For example, for a hairdresser it is probably unreasonable to say that they cannot work as hairdresser anywhere in the same county. How far is someone going to drive to go to a hairdresser? Conversely, if it is a highly specialized skill or a very mobile industry, it may be very reasonable to prevent someone from working in a particular profession anywhere in the country. For example, there are only a relatively few biological pharmaceutical companies in the U.S. If an engineer with very specialized experience in biological pharmaceuticals leaves a company, it is reasonable that one of the direct competitors of his former employer may be on the other side of the country. For breweries and craft beverage manufacturers, a regional prohibition (like the state or a group of states) is typical, but in rare cases, a nationwide limitation may be enforceable.

And, as the craft beverage industry grows, this seems ordinary and simple to police. However, despite the now over 7000 breweries in the U.S., the industry is still comparatively small. The vast majority of those 7000 breweries are small two-to-ten employee operations. And, one finds that the movement within the industry is largely local or semi-local. So, for example, there may be a comparatively small number of jobs with breweries in any one state (just ask someone looking for a job in a brewery!). Compound that with brewer reputations that are largely only locally recognized, and you've got a real question as to what is a reasonable geographic scope. Certainly there are brewer rock stars who are known nationwide/worldwide, but most are personalities known in their home county or state or region. So, where can we prohibit these craft brew folks from working should they decide to leave the company? The advice I generally give to clients is that you can likely enforce a non-compete within the state, but trying to enforce it let alone nationwide, regionally, may be very difficult.

RECIPES

In terms of non-disclosure, the single biggest question that surfaces is how to protect beer "recipes." This question comes up from nearly everyone who hasn't worked in a brewery. The issue of recipe guarding is only critical where the recipe secrecy itself is important to a brand. For example, Stone Brewing closely guards their recipe for Arrogant Bastard Ale. For many of their other beers, they regularly share recipe, ingredient, and process information. The secrecy of the recipe for Arrogant Bastard Ale is part of their branding and marketing strategy. Mitch Steele, Head Brewer at Stone, has said on numerous occasions that Stone's owners have told him that Arrogant Bastard is the one recipe he can't disclose.

One of the primary reasons that recipe secrecy isn't a high priority for many breweries is that, while the ingredients and their proportions are important, the final product is very closely tied to the process and the equipment used in the production. Brewers all over the world generally agree that the same recipe made on a different system by a different brewer will give you a different product. The artistry and the combination of ingredient, equipment, and process is the purview of the brewer. So, even if the recipe were given precisely to another brewery, if it were produced on a different system without adjustment, you'd get a different beer—defeating the goal of getting the recipe to begin with. Said differently, a highly trained and technical brewer can likely reproduce a competing beer (or nearly so) on their system, but the resulting recipe would likely be quite different that the competing beer's recipe on its home system. The same analysis applies for distillers. The equipment shape, geometry, and parameters lead to an almost unique product based on the way the equipment is used—not just on the initial mash recipe or the specific aging time or barrel. In fact, there have been stories about distillers taking extraordinary measures to replicate equipment precisely (down to replicating the same dent in the same spot on a new still!) when installing new equipment or expanding capacity.

John Says: "I really think people put too much emphasis on protecting recipes. Even if they could reproduce it, who wants to advertise 'Hey! I make the same beer as that guy over there!'? The whole point is to differentiate your product."

However, of much stronger concern for craft beverage businesses is the sharing of proprietary technology or process information. Among brewers and distillers, especially smaller operations or highly innovative companies, there are often either equipment or processes that have been developed in-house to solve specific issues or to get specific effects in the final product. For example, see Sierra Nevada's "Hop Torpedo." Additionally, issues like account lists, equations for equipment utilization, logistics, calculations, or other information developed in-house are likely items to be closely guarded.

So, the key in non-disclosure agreements is to specify the type of information that you're looking to protect.

CHAPTER SIX: TRADEMARK

Intellectual property, overall, is a hot topic in the alcohol industry. But right now trademark reigns as king because trademark and brand awareness are continuing to grow with social media. And the marketplace is becoming crowded with breweries with similar ideas, beers, and brands. This is all complicated more by the specific restrictions placed on alcohol manufacturers, distributors, and retailers with regard to advertising and marketing.

WHAT IS A TRADEMARK?

Not often does a legal definition make sense to a non-lawyer, but this one works:

Trademark, n—A word, phrase, logo, or other graphic symbol used by a manufacturer or seller to distinguish its product[s] from those of others. The main purpose of a trademark is to designate the source of goods or services. In effect, the trademark is the commercial substitute for one's signature. (*Black's Law Dictionary.* Third Edition. Garner, Bryan A., Editor. West Publishing, 2006.)

Or you can use a more succinct description, "the commercial substitute for one's signature." That really puts things in perspective and gives additional insight as to why trademarks can be such a personal/emotional issue. A trademark is your identity.

A trademark (or mark) is set of characters (text) or design (logo) that is used to market goods or services by the seller of those goods or services and is used to identify the source of those goods or services as to the quality of the product. The easiest way to describe a trademark is by example. Think about marks like Nike®, Coca-Cola®, or Apple®. These are some of the world-class examples of trademarks, and not just trademarks but also companies that are serious about managing their trademark rights against infringement and protecting the reputation of the company. These companies are some of the folks that lawyers look at for examples of ways to enforce and police marks, and develop their mark portfolios.

But what's not in that definition? Registration, exclusivity, ownership rights, infringement, etc. When individuals think of trademark issues, they often read in a lot of stuff that is not there, at least not necessarily there. The key thing to remember is that a lot of the terms discussed in a casual way are actually terms of art that don't have their regular everyday meaning. Think of it this way, the physical boundary between two pieces of property can be a lot different than the legal boundary between those pieces. For example:

> "Yep, I reckon the property goes down thar a fur piece and runs between da big oak tree that Billy done ran into with da tractor and da field where Bubba's barn used to be—you know where that two-headed mule was borned?"

versus

> "The property boundary is a line extending from an iron stake located near the NW corner of Thurmond St and Johnston Ave heading 76°32'21" NNE for 245.8 feet and terminating in the middle of the creek bed."

You get the idea. So, when words like "likelihood of confusion" are tossed around in conversation regarding trademarks, throw out your common sense and remember that these are legal conclusions, not intuitive descriptions.

John Says: "Think you are pretty comfortable with trademark law? Ask a trademark attorney about 'related goods' or 'likelihood of confusion.' Then wait for your head to explode."

YOUR BRAND

One of the most important issues with developing a brand is choosing a name that (1) is easily identified by your target consumer, (2) encapsulates or represents the core ideals of the brand, and (3) can be protected from intrusion by others.

When choosing a name for a brand, the business should avoid:

- Offensive names (because they cannot be approved by a labeling authority and/or they cannot be protected by trademark registration)
- Geographic or purely descriptive names (like North Carolina Brewing or Ted's Brewery, see http://carolinabrewery.com/ v http://www.carolinabrew.com/)
- Common industry terms or ideas (like "hops" or "IPA" http://www.mutineermagazine.com/blog/2012/01/cease-and-desist-letters-can-be-fun-freetail-brewing-co-and-hopasaurus-rex/)
- Names on/with common variations (like 3rd Street Brewing vs. Third St Brewery)

When choosing a name for a brand, the business should:

- DO A GOOGLE SEARCH!!!! You'd be amazed how often this isn't done.
- Attempt to make the name personal or as specific as possible. There are a lot of generic/abstract names out there like "Iconoclast Brewery." Is that too close to "Heretic Brewing?" http://hereticbrewing.com?

- Understand your core demographic. The industry as a whole has achieved a state of growth where the target audience for a new brewery cannot simply be "all beer drinkers" or "everyone in North Carolina who drinks craft beer."
- Invest early in help with research for trademark protection before investing time and money into building a brand you can't protect, or worse, one that someone else already owns!

John Says: "Start by doing a Google search. But, just because you don't find anything, that doesn't mean it's okay. And, just because you find something doesn't mean it's not okay. Either way, you need to know what's out there."

USPTO AND MARK STRENGTH

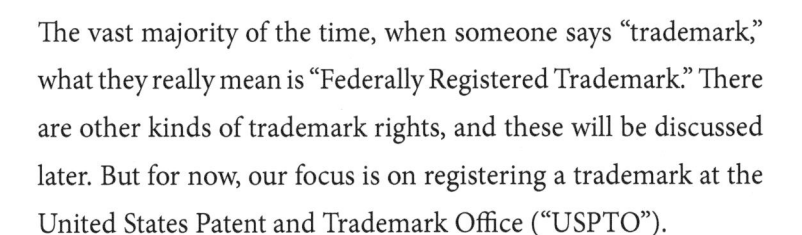

The vast majority of the time, when someone says "trademark," what they really mean is "Federally Registered Trademark." There are other kinds of trademark rights, and these will be discussed later. But for now, our focus is on registering a trademark at the United States Patent and Trademark Office ("USPTO").

The gold standard for brand or trademark protection is USPTO registration (http://www.uspto.gov/) and the spectrum of weak marks to strong marks is used by the USPTO and others to analyze and characterize marks and their "protectability." A great way of thinking about this is:

Protection	Mark Type	Example
None	Generic	Bike (bicycles)
↑	Descriptive	Tasty (bread)
↕	Suggestive	Greyhound® (bus lines)
↓	Arbitrary	Apple® (computers)
Strong	Fanciful	Kodak® (photography)

Generic marks are generally not eligible for protection through the USPTO or otherwise. Generic terms are terms that the purchasing public sees as a common class name or descriptor for the entire spectrum of similar goods or services. Examples of generic terms might be "shoes," "cookware," or—more pertinent here—terms like "beer," "brewing," and "ale."

Descriptive marks are those that describe an ingredient, quality, characteristic, function, feature, purpose, or use of the goods or services. For example, a mark that is merely descriptive might be something like "The Good Beer Company," or "Hoppy Beer Brewery," or "Dark Ales Brewing." A good example, that actually set some of the law on the subject, was when someone tried to register the mark, "Bed and Breakfast Registry." The court said that the term, "Bed and Breakfast Registry," when used in conjunction to market an actual bed and breakfast registry/database, is merely descriptive of the product and did not deserve trademark registration.

John Says: "But some marks which are merely descriptive may become eligible for registration if the mark is used for a significant amount of time. A mark has acquired sufficient 'acquire distinctiveness' that would allow it to meet the protection threshold."

Suggestive marks are those that, if applied to the goods or services, require imagination, thought, or perception to reach a conclusion as to the nature of the goods/services. A classic example, which again set some law in the area, was that of "Speedi Bake" frozen dough. "Speedi Bake" on its own does not directly describe the product, but is related or suggests an aspect to the product that "only vaguely suggests a desirable characteristic." Examples for the brewing industry may be marks like "Mashhouse

Brewing," "High Gravity Brewery," or "Session" for beers.

Arbitrary marks are words that are in common linguistic use, but when used to identify a particular good or service, do NOT suggest or describe an ingredient, quality, or characteristic. Examples of arbitrary marks might be "Galaxy" for automobiles, "Canon" for cameras, or "Mystery" for beer or brewing. Arbitrary marks often make good trademarks for breweries because they ARE words that people recognize but are not closely tied to the product itself. These often give the mark holder the opportunity to connect to values, ideas, or culture of the brewer in terms of the product and brand they tout.

Fanciful marks are marks that have been invented for the sole purpose of functioning as a trademark. These are either made-up words (like "Pepsi" or "Sony") or are words no longer commonly used (like "Donnybrook" or "Quince"). Fanciful marks are the strongest marks because they have the least attachment—in the mind of the consumer—to the goods or services being offered.

John Says: "What about brands that were distinctive or even fanciful before becoming generic? Like 'Kleenex,' or 'Xerox,' or 'Scotch Tape'?"

USPTO PROCESS

The overall process for registration is as follows:

1. Determine if your mark is eligible for registration.
   The following, for example, are not eligible for registration:
   a. Geographic names
   b. Generic terms

c. Goods or services which are not "in commerce"
2. Do full a mark search, looking at all combinations, permutations, similar connotations to your mark on the USPTO database, Google, and—really—anywhere you can look up companies or brands.
3. Determine whether you have priority rights in the mark. Priority rights are established as
   a. Sufficiently different from other marks
   b. First use of the mark "in commerce"
   c. Current use "in commerce"
   d. Exclusive use for a period of time
4. Submit an application for registration.
5. [wait three months]
6. A USPTO examiner will do a preliminary assessment of the mark
   a. If there are no issues, go to step 13
   b. If there is an Office Action, go to step 7
7. There is an Office Action.
   a. An Office Action is, essentially, a problem report with an application. It's a letter from the examiner outlining the reasons that your mark should not be registered.
   b. About two-thirds of all USPTO trademark applications are rejected initially (i.e. they receive an Office Action).
   c. Of that two-thirds, approximately half will be able to overcome that initial rejection and still register.
8. You have six months to respond to an Office Action.
   a. After six months, the application is abandoned.
9. You can provide arguments, amendments, or fixes to the application to try to address the Examiner's requirements.

10. The Examiner will re-evaluate the application and your response to the Office Action.
    a. If the Examiner agrees with your response, go to step 13.
    b. If the Examiner disagrees with your response, go to step 11.
11. If the Examiner disagrees with your arguments to allow your registration, you will receive a Final Office Action.
    a. A Final Office Action is the USPTO's determination that your mark does not meet the necessary requirements for registration.
12. The only way to overcome a Final Office Action is to file a petition at the Trademark Trial and Appeal Board (TTAB).
    a. This is where things get expensive and you definitely need an attorney.
    b. This is, essentially, a trial for your mark rights—suing the USPTO in their own court. Does that sound like it will go well for you?
    c. Depending on your business, at this point, we often recommend our clients to save their money and pick a different mark name if they really want to register their mark.
13. Once the USPTO Examiner finds no issues with your mark or application, they will place it in queue for publication.
14. [wait ~ thirty days]
15. The mark will be scheduled for publication with a Notice of Publication.
16. [wait ~ thirty days]
17. The mark is published in the *Weekly Gazette*, a government publication showing all the applied for marks that are

currently in process and "published."

18. The mark must be published in the *Weekly Gazette* for thirty days to give anyone the opportunity to oppose the registration.
19. After the thirty days of publication, wait ~ thirty more days to give anyone the chance to file the Opposition with the USPTO.
20. If no Opposition is filed, the mark is slated for registration.
21. [wait ~ thirty days]
22. The mark is registered, and you'll get a pretty little certificate in the mail.
23. Congratulations! You've got a registered trademark which must be renewed every ten years to stay current.

So, some notes on that process:

John Says: "Can you do all that without a lawyer. Sure. How many folks have I met that did that successfully for them-selves and weren't already a lawyer? Not many."

- Notice how there are several things capitalized or in quotes, and you're not sure why? They are technical terms of art and have special legal meanings. They do not mean what you think they mean.
- You will also notice that, if everything goes perfectly and no one misses a step, the process will still likely take more than nine months from start to finish. If there are issues or TTAB proceedings, it can go on for years.
- A common rejection for many brewery trademark applications is that the applied-for mark is "confusingly similar" to an existing mark. That typically means that there is a

registered mark that is too close to the applied-for mark. It means that the examiner has determined that the applied-for mark meets the requirements for the Likelihood of Confusion standard (based on the DuPont factors, call or look it up if you want a crash course on these). This is essentially saying that your mark is too similar to another mark that has priority. These rejections, though highly subjective in some cases, are notoriously difficult to overcome.

John Says: "If you really want to know about the DuPont factors and you don't do trademark stuff for a living...you are a sick individual."

INTENT TO USE VS. IN USE USPTO APPLICATION

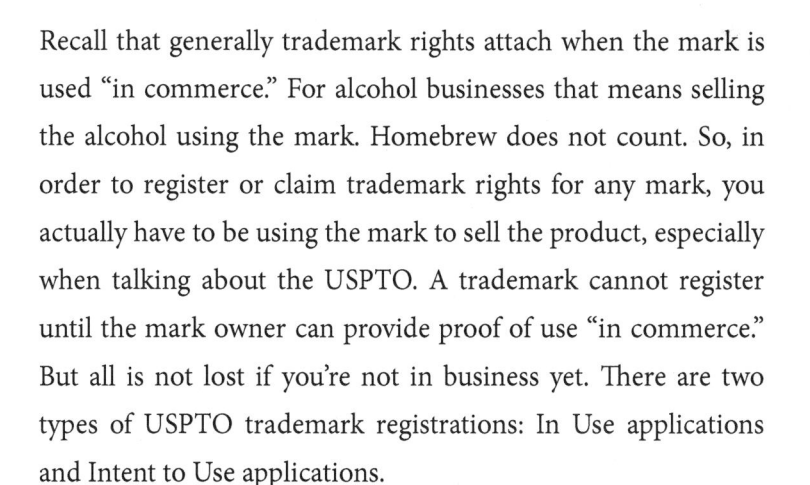

Recall that generally trademark rights attach when the mark is used "in commerce." For alcohol businesses that means selling the alcohol using the mark. Homebrew does not count. So, in order to register or claim trademark rights for any mark, you actually have to be using the mark to sell the product, especially when talking about the USPTO. A trademark cannot register until the mark owner can provide proof of use "in commerce." But all is not lost if you're not in business yet. There are two types of USPTO trademark registrations: In Use applications and Intent to Use applications.

In Use applications are those where the mark is currently being used in commerce and the mark owner can demonstrate that use. These are the "typical" mark registration applications that people

John Says: "Let me say that again...a trademark cannot register at the USPTO until it is used 'in commerce.' And, the words 'in commerce,' don't mean what you think they mean."

think of when they talk about trademark registration.

Intent to Use applications (ITUs) are an opportunity for a mark owner to "put a stake in the ground," and to put the world on notice that they intend to use that mark, but they are just not ready to do so yet.

For an ITU, a mark owner submits an application and the mark is analyzed, examined, and generally goes through the exact same process as an In Use mark, but if everything goes well in the application process instead of becoming "registered," it becomes "allowed." Being "allowed" is the equivalent of the USPTO saying, "Okay, we think this mark should register, and we'll register it just as soon as you provide us proof of use in commerce."

For an allowed ITU mark application, from the time the mark is allowed, the mark owner has six months to show use of the mark in commerce. Bad news: the mark owner has six months to show use in commerce. Good news: the mark owner can ask for an extension of time for an additional six months, and keep getting six-month extensions up to a total of three years. After three years...well, USPTO seems and believes that if you cannot make it happen within three years, you probably do not deserve a mark registration anyway.

TRADE DRESS

In addition to the "text" mark or a "design" mark, a certain "overall impressions" may also be eligible for protection as a trademark. This type of protection is called trade dress. Trade dress is basically a product's "total image and overall appearance [...] as defined by its overall composition and design, including size, shape, color, texture, and graphics." An example is something like the iconic Coca-Cola® curvy, ribbed bottle and label placement. But, in order to be eligible for trade dress protection, it has to have developed an "acquired distinctiveness" through use, typically five or more years.

DO I NEED AN ATTORNEY?

You do not NEED an attorney to help you through trademark work, but you SHOULD have one. Trademark registration is very technical and counterintuitive. There are literally dozens of exceptions, serious nuances, different answers depending on language and connotation, and hundreds of rules, etc. For example, the TMEP (Trademark Manual for Examination and Prosecution), the manual that the examiners use, is hundreds and hundreds of pages long! So long, in fact that no one really uses the paper version any more—the electronic hyperlink version is the one to use: https://tmep.uspto.gov/RDMS/TMEP/current. An attorney can help keep you from wasting time and money.

In the day-to-day exercise and practice of USPTO work, common mistakes or mis-steps include:

- Forgetting to search in adjacent classes
    - For purposes of USPTO practice,

John Says: "By the way, attorneys LOVE it when you call and say, 'Yeah, I did my own search and application. I don't need an attorney, that's a waste of money.'"

the general rule is that beer (class 032) is a related class of wine and distilled spirits (class 033). A registered mark in one will prevent the USPTO from allowing a new mark registration in the other.
- Not checking alternate spellings, different languages, and associated ideas
    - "Iconoclast" vs. "heretic"
    - "Dust" vs. "dirt" vs. "earth"
    - 3rd St = Third Street = Th3rd St = Dritte Strasse (German equivalent)
    - Colorful = Colourful = Kolorfull
- Proposing marks close to marks owned by large breweries
    - See Natty Greene example: http://www.bna.com/anheuserbusch-opposition-natty-b17179891562/
- Failing to show use "in commerce" by selling the actual product using the mark
    - That means that registering the company name with the Secretary of State when forming the company, selling T-shirts with the mark on it, or homebrewing DO NOT qualify as use "in commerce."
    - Not even TTB and ABC label approval show use "in commerce": approval for sale is not the same thing as selling or marketing to sell.
- Failing to think ahead about how to show use "in commerce"
    - Nightmarish example: one brewery looked to register their brewery name as their mark. Typically, a keg ring (label for the final packaging of a keg to ship to a retailer) would suffice. But the brewery used keg rings where they handwrote the brewery name under the brewery's logo.

This is not sufficient, since anybody could write anything on a keg ring. Normally a tap handle would also work, except the brewery used their very distinct logo as the only reference to the brewery on the tap handle. Sometimes the kegs themselves are branded with the name of the brewery—but not this time. Their pint glass is a great example of their name next to their logo, but pint glasses and T-shirts are marketing tools, and don't show the use of the mark "in commerce" for the class of goods. How about an invoice to a wholesaler or retailer? Nope, they must show they sell the product using the mark.

WHY REGISTER?

What does registration get you? Well, if you need to sue someone over a trademark (say, infringement for example), you would need to prove in court that:

1. You are the rightful owner of the mark
2. The mark is used in commerce
3. The mark is used in a particular geographic area
4. The mark has come to be associated with you and your business/product
5. The other party is using the same or (too) similar mark
6. The other party, by using the mark, has caused injury to your business

But, if it is a federally registered mark, numbers 1, 2, 3, and 4 are already taken care of for you. You only need to show that your mark is registered, someone else is using it, and that someone else has hurt your business by using the mark—that's much simpler than proving all six items.

Also, keep in mind that you do not necessarily need to be able to register a mark to be able to use the mark. For example, there's a Raleigh Brewing Company in Raleigh, North Carolina. They cannot register the name because it's a geographic name, but they can still use the mark without fear of someone telling them to stop. On the other end of the spectrum, however, you can get into trouble in some cases. For example, Carolina Brewery and Carolina Brewing Company are two different breweries located quite close to one another and are often confused one for the other by folks not-in-the-know.

There are downsides to registration as well. You will never receive a notice from the USPTO that someone is violating your trademark. That's not how the system works. It is incumbent on the mark owner to police their own mark through the country (and the world, if that's important). As the mark owner, you must be diligent in looking for people violating your mark rights. It is up to you to enforce those mark rights.

John Says: "Don't bother to register if you're not going to do anything to protect, defend, or police your mark."

In some cases, if you do not enforce your mark rights, you lose the ability to enforce them. For example, if you've known about a competitor using a very similar mark to your registered mark, and you know they've been doing it for ten years, you've missed your chance to say something (typically three years from the time you learned of the issue). Now a court will not allow you to try and enforce those rights. It's called *laches* and it means if you're too lazy to bother about it at the time, it must not be that important to you, so you can't come back later and make a stink.

Before we talk about trademark disputes, there are two other classes of trademark protection to understand.

STATE REGISTRATION

Not much time will be spent on this as its importance has decreased rapidly since the advent of the Internet. Essentially, each state's Secretary of State (or other designated department) maintains a state-level registration for goods and services similar to the federal registration. This was especially important when shipping products—or more likely advertising—out of state was more difficult or expensive, so most products or services were never sold "far from home." In that case, it was very useful to have a state-level registration for your products or services that would be recognized at your local state courts (as opposed to federal court) so issues could be resolved relatively easily.

Now that the Internet is such a substantial driver in consumerism and purchasing, and because it is nearly free to advertise nationally, or even internationally, federal and international trademark registration or protection is becoming more critical than state registration. Registration at the USPTO has become the workhorse for trademark rights throughout the U.S.

While on the subject of state registration, be aware that forming your company and reregistering your company name with the state Secretary of State DOES NOT qualify you for any trademark protection and has nothing to do with "use in commerce" for trademark purposes.

INTERNATIONAL REGISTRATION

International registration is worth discussion as well. The USPTO is the world-class standard for trademark protection. Most of the rest of the world, other than the UK and the EU, treat trademarks very differently. Some have reciprocal treaties with the U.S. and USPTO, but many do not. And, countries that have reciprocal arrangements do not enforce those trademark rights in the same way we do. Other countries are notorious for lack of trademark rights/enforcement. Depending on the product, international trademark registration may be a concern. However, the U.S. exports relatively little craft beer to other countries, and the vast majority of breweries have no intent to do so, so your risk is low. If you're concerned about international trademark rights, you should definitely contact an attorney for help.

COMMON LAW TRADEMARK RIGHTS

This subject is sometimes tough for folks to understand. So let's try this example:

> *Ed opens Ed's Dry Cleaners on Main Street. Ed runs Ed's Dry Cleaners for twenty years without a problem. In Year Twenty One, someone else opens Ed's Laundromat right next door to Ed's Dry Cleaners. Something is clearly wrong, yes? Well, Ed's Laundromat is very close in name and idea/connotation to Ed's Dry Cleaners. And, everyone knows that Ed's been there for a long time. Wouldn't it be confusing to someone walking up to the two storefronts? "Oh, Ed has opened a Laundromat*

to go with his dry cleaning business!" There is a likelihood of confusion in the mind of potential consumers.

Even if Ed never registered his trademark, he still has rights in his name. The basic formula for trademark rights is that one has rights in a trademark if the mark has been *used exclusively*, in a *certain geographic area*, and for a *certain period of time*.

How far the rights extend depends on the specifics of the "exclusive," the "geography," and the "time." For the example, Ed certainly wasn't the only "Ed's Dry Cleaners" in the whole world or even the whole country. But he was probably the only one in the city, county, or maybe even the state. Geography? Well, how far do people go to get their dry cleaning or laundry done? Most of the time, people will use these services relatively close to their homes; rarely will someone travel outside their county or state for simple convenience services like these, so the geography that Ed was effectively using is probably fairly small. With regard to time, Ed was there for a long time using the mark exclusively in his geography, and he probably has stronger rights than if he had opened Ed's Dry Cleaners only the year before.

The details of how this example may apply to your business depends on how unique the mark is, as well as the other components. The key here is that a mark does not have to be registered to have trademark rights. Unfortunately, while registration provides broad protection on certain items, common law trademark rights are very dependent on the specific situation and need hard data to back up ownership damages, etc. Trying to enforce common law trademark rights can be very costly as well.

POLICING YOUR MARK

Whether registered at the state level, the USPTO, or simply relying on Common Law trademark rights, you—as the mark owner—are responsible for policing your mark and enforcing your mark rights. No U.S. or state agency is going to send you a notice that they've found a mark that is too close to yours. That's your job. As a mark owner, it is incumbent on you that you're looking for infringing marks, marks that are too close to yours, or other issues that would impact your mark rights. It is highly recommended to sign up with a trademark monitoring service to help keep you informed of potential issues.

TRADEMARK DISPUTES

Another topic of discussion is the growing litigiousness of alcohol companies when it comes to trademark protection. Almost daily, we hear news about one or more breweries in a dispute about who owns a particular mark or who is infringing on whom. There is a great story (and beer) that highlights the best of the brewing industry:

> *Russian River Brewing (Sonoma, California, http://russianriverbrewing.com/) and Avery Brewing (Boulder, Colorado, http://averybrewing.com/) discovered in the early 2000s that they both had a beer called "Salvation." Neither had registered the mark with the USPTO, and there was some confusion as to first use and geographic spread/overlap. Both sides' attorneys advocated legal action to determine who had*

exclusive rights to the mark. The owners of the company (also the only/main brewers at the respective companies at the time) met over a beer at an industry event. They had been acquaintances and soon became friends. They and they and their families frequently vacation together now. They decided that there was plenty of room in beer for both beers which, incidentally, were nothing alike. In the mid-2000s (I think it was around 2004), they produced one of the industry's first "collaboration beers" and named it "Collaboration Not Litigation," blending the two dissimilar beers to create something new and different fromeither separately. Now, they brew the beer once a year and distribute the product as an Avery Brewing beer nationwide. (http://averybrewing.com/collaboration-not-litigation-ale/)

John Says: "I got into the industry because of stories like this. Unfortunately, with more and more breweries, some of this camaraderie is going away. It's not personal, it's just business. But, you don't need to be a jerk either."

Doesn't that warm your heart? What other industry could do something like that? Don't you love beer?

Unfortunately, at the time of this particular dispute, there were about 1500 odd breweries in the U.S. The industry was smaller and much more collegial. Today there are over 7000 open or in planning, and competition is intensifying (https://www.brewersassociation.org/statistics/number-of-breweries/). For business owners, it's getting more and more difficult to "take the high ground" while protecting your mark AND not looking like a colossal jerk on social media. The social media movement has led to the development of a shoot-from-the-hip, any-publicity-is-good-publicity approach to dealing with mark disputes. Breweries are vilified by a public that doesn't have all the facts and *certainly* doesn't understand the law at play in those facts. In the event of a mark dispute, it is critical for attorneys not only to provide sound legal advice, but also to help their clients intelligently manage their market reputation and interactions with other breweries and industry members.

Trademark litigation is a specialized field, and you definitely need an attorney when you're headed down that road. This book will not address the details of litigation, but will give some pointers on things to think about when you're faced with a potential dispute.

When evaluating a mark dispute, you'll need to:

- Work very hard to avoid litigation. In almost all cases, the parties are in different states and it may be prohibitively expensive for you to engage a much larger brewery in protracted litigation in federal, or worse yet, remote state litigation.
- Focus on interest-based negotiation. Neither party wants bad publicity and neither wants to give up their mark. But what do you really want? You may want not to throw away the $50k (which makes up the bulk of your advertising budget for the year) you just spent on merchandise and packaging. You may not want to be seen as giving in to the "big bully."
- There may be opportunities to work together, cross promote, do a collaboration beer, host an event for charity, etc., that triggers your idea of fairness, your favorite causes, or your sense of respect for the other guy (and hopefully his for you).

Almost every time I talk to a mark attorney for another brewery, the interaction goes like this:

- I introduce myself and my client
- I describe the issue we have
- The other attorney strongly disagrees with our position (sometimes telling us that we're infringing on them—that's always fun)
- I ask them to discuss it with their client
- I follow up with a letter
- I follow up by phone a short time later
- They reiterate that they strongly disagree with our position and that there is "no way" they will stop doing what they're doing or pay anything
- I try and discuss non-monetary options (you'd be amazed how often the issue is not about money)
- They reiterate that they're in the right and outline all the reasons that we would lose at court, but they'll ask their client how much they'd offer us
- I talk about how neither side wants adverse publicity and we should look for common solutions
- They say they'll talk to their clients and get back to me
- I have to follow up with them again
- They say that they think a "mutual coexistence" agreement is a good solution and "that's more than you'd get in court"
- I spend the next several weeks convincing them that
    - We're serious
    - We've got a strong case
    - We probably don't want any money
    - My client just wants to talk to their client and see if they can work it out

John Says: *"Not sure why, but trademark attorneys seem to be some of the biggest bullies I know. Many try to bluff and bluster you into submission rather than talk about the issue. If you're being bullied, get help from an attorney before you try and bully back."*

Again, every time (well, almost every), time I get the two clients talking to each other to work out a solution. It's only when the lawyers get involved that it seems to get acrimonious and litigious.

That said, the trend in the industry seems to say that litigation is the go-to tool for resolving these disputes. Since 2014, almost every week there is an article or website announcing a new trademark dispute. Some of the most interesting lately have been:

LAGUNITAS VS. SIERRA NEVADA

http://beerstreetjournal.com/lagunitas-files-legal-complaint-sierra-nevada/ (and the inevitable Internet backlash): http://www.chicagotribune.com/bluesky/technology/ct-lagunitas-sierra-nevada-backlash-20150114-story.html

BELLS BREWING VS. INNOVATION BREWING

http://detroit.eater.com/2015/3/11/8191539/bells-brewery-innovation-brewing-north-carolina-michigan-trademark-lawsuit-craft-beer

(and the fallout): https://www.facebook.com/BellsBreweryInc/posts/865382180167157

STEELHEAD BREWING VS. FREETAIL BREWING (NOT ACTUALLY A LAWSUIT, BUT AN INTERESTING DISPUTE)

http://brewerylaw.com/2013/03/freetail-brewing-for-the-win

http://goodbeerhunting.com/blog/2016/2/11/this-is-illegal-san-antonios-freetail-brewing-company

MAGIC HAT VS. WEST SIXTH

http://www.kentucky.com/news/local/crime/article44427750.html

AB-INBEV VS. NATTY GREENE'S

http://www.bna.com/anheuserbusch-opposition-natty-b17179891562/

The issue is that lawsuits, USPTO proceedings, and even minor mark disputes can have an enormous impact on the companies involved; they can be expensive in terms of fighting a legal battle, they can have an adverse impact on your company image in the craft beer industry, and they can be a major distraction from the focus of the business. And while the litigation may be meritorious, or even an absolute necessity, the dispute is going to have an effect on the business. That's not always for the best even if your business is right or the law is on your side.

MORE ON TRADEMARK DISPUTES

The author of this tome wrote a blog post about a dispute between Starbucks® (yes, that Starbucks®) and Exit 6 Brewing.

The blog highlighted the discrepancy between managing trademark rights and managing public reputation. The blog post is reprinted here in its entirety:

TRADEMARK SNARKINESS

Recently, I'm sure you probably saw it (it got a lot of coverage, even from NPR). Exit 6 Brewery got pretty snarky with Starbucks. And Starbucks defended itself (somewhat) here. I had several people ask me about this; what my thoughts were, what I would have done, etc. So, here we go…

Exit 6 is surprised?

Exit 6 Brewery (in Cottleville, Missouri) got a Cease & Desist letter from Starbucks Corporate HQ saying, in essence, "Hey, uh, the word 'Frappuccino®' is our registered trademark, please stop using it." Jeff Britton, the CEO, responding for Exit 6 to the Dec 9 Starbucks letter, decided to make a "statement." We'll get into what made it snarky later. Here's my question/concern. Exit 6 was marketing a beer called "Frappicino…" Wait, let's look at that again…

Frappuccino (Starbucks registered trademark)

Frappicino   (Exit 6 beer)

Was Exit 6 surprised that Starbucks would have an issue with this? Did they think changing TWO letters was enough to make their mark distinct and avoid legal "likelihood of confusion?" I'm betting they didn't ask their attorney. This is so close it could border on intentional infringement.

And, we're talking about Starbucks Coffee Co. here. We're not talking about a trademark owned by Bob's Dry Cleaners in Bethesda, Maryland. This is Starbucks, who work so hard on their brand that internationally, all the uniforms, restaurants, and products match even in the grocery store. These are not unsophisticated, "Hey, whoa! We never thought something like this would happen!" guys.

If Exit 6 Brewery really were surprised, they are way uneducated about the business and, in particular, the beer industry. If they weren't surprised, then they decided to flaunt the mark and see what happens. Seems like a jerk move to me.

Snarky, really?

Jeff's letter and the $6 check (the profit earned from the sale of the Frappicino beers to go toward legal fees) was pretty funny, right? Well, yes, and no. Sure, that was pretty cute he made Starbucks look like a big, bad dummy. But what did it really tell us?

Well, first see my previous blog about why some trademark attorneys can be jerks; I touch on why Cease and Desist Letters are written like that.

Then let's think about the two parties involved. No large business (like Starbucks) wants the negative publicity of "smacking down" the "little guy." My guess is that Starbucks probably would have negotiated some agreement along the lines of, "My bad, we won't do it again." Instead, they didn't get the chance to do that; a small brewery in middle America just made them look stupid EVEN though Exit 6 was in the wrong and maybe intentionally so. I'm betting that Starbucks never really wanted to "punish" or "squash" Exit 6, but in order to maintain their trademark rights, they HAVE to police the people/businesses that violate those rights. My guess, too, is that they never wanted this to be this public.

The whole situation made Exit 6 look, to the unenlightened, like a hip, quick-witted, small business showing the big guy "what's what." But, once you dig a little deeper, it really says that maybe the Exit 6 guys were just looking for publicity at the expense of someone else.

Caution

So here's the part that really concerns me: okay, fine, Exit 6 burned a bridge with Starbucks, no big whoop. But the craft beer industry is small, and brewers depend on each other to reflect well on the profession. What if this had been another small brewery? Would they have been as snarky (and *public*) about the response? If this is how Exit 6 treats a multi-billion dollar corporation, how would they treat someone—like another brewer—that might not be able to fight back as effectively?

Even though the industry, is still experiencing double-digit growth year after year, it is small enough that you'd better be really sure that it's a bridge you want to burn before you set it on fire. There just aren't that many bridges out there for the small brewer to use as kindling.

For example, look at last year's debacle between Magic Hat and West 6th. Both breweries came off looking like jerks. No one wins. I'd also bet that the argument between Magic Hat and West

6th probably forever foreclosed the possibility of a future collaboration or even them treating each other civilly in the event of a future dispute.

So my thoughts are these: (1) don't be so quick to jump on a publicity bandwagon with a snarky response; you might burn a bridge you'll need later, and (2) look at the facts before you support one side or the other.

MORE ON TRADEMARK ATTORNEYS

For a small industry (or relatively small), like brewing, it is wise not to burn bridges or unnecessarily anger potential collaborators. I wrote a popular blog post about this topic too, and the apparent tendency for trademark attorneys to bully the opposing team. My blog post is reprinted here in its entirety:

WHY ARE (SOME) TRADEMARK ATTORNEYS JERKS?

I do a fair bit of work in intellectual property and, especially, trademark issues. It always surprises me what bullies, blusterers, and even a$$holes trademark attorneys can be. The general jerky-ness of attorneys is well-publicized in social media and the vast number of lawyer jokes out there (for example: http://www.jokes.com/funny-lawyer-jokes). But, even among lawyers, trademark attorneys have a special reputation—almost as severe as personal injury attorneys (degradingly referred to as "ambulance chasers"). Even so, trademark attorneys seem to tip the scale of jerk-ocity like no one else.

I consider myself a trademark attorney. Am I a jerk? I don't think so. Well, at least not about legal stuff. Other stuff maybe.

Anyway, why is it that (some) trademark attorneys are the way they are? Let's look at the issues here:

Background

Trademark is as close to traditional "creative" pursuits as most lawyers get. Many business lawyers, criminal lawyers, and even patent lawyers (maybe especially patent lawyers) look at trademark lawyers like they practice some weird, soft, feel-good, squishy, ill-defined branch of law. Looking at the way marks "generate an image or feeling in the mind of the general public," or how certain words "connote a different emotion" in the way color is used, or how the line-art is shaded causes even some attorneys' eyes to glaze over.

So, like it or not, trademark attracts a certain breed of attorney/person. Layer on top of that the fact that trademarks often involve a business owner and owner's self-identity, and you get an emotional powder keg with (potentially) real money involved.

Like we talked about above, whether a mark is "too similar" depends on a lot of factors including phrasing, connotation, technical definition, and color tones, shades, etc., along with markets, classes of goods or services—the list goes on and on. Oh, and no one wants to pay either attorney to sort the matter out.

The Conflict

Let's take a step back and think about how trademark problems come up:

- Step 1: Someone (let's call them Allan's Ales) comes up with a word, phrase, or picture that they use in their business
- Step 2: Someone else (let's call these guys Bill's Beer) comes up with a word, phrase, or picture that they use or want to use to promote their business
- Step 3: Allan thinks that Bill's Beer is using Allan's Ales' mark. Bill disagrees. Allan yells at Bill. Bill makes rude comments about Allan's mother.
- Step 4: Allan and/or Bill call attorneys—sometimes at the same time

At this point, let's assume that we're the attorney for Allan. Allan tells us that

- He's been using the mark since the dawn of time
- He tried to be nice and work something out with Bill
- Bill is totally unreasonable
- Bill is clearly trying to destroy Allan's business
- Allan is mortally wounded at the mere assertion that the mark might not be protectable and wants us to (legally) beat Bill into submission and make him pay through his excretory orifice.

Okay, now that the situation is set up, let's see how this plays out...

Training

Lawyers are trained to be advocates for their clients whether their client is right or wrong. In fact, in most states, there is a legal requirement that an attorney be a *"zealous* advocate" for their clients. If you think that's not a big deal, think about how we view the term "zealot" in our larger culture. Do we think of zealots as rational, reasonable, willing-to-see-the-other-side folks? Generally not.

So what does the attorney do?

The attorney assumes that the other side isn't represented (or if they are, it doesn't really matter). The knee-jerk reaction is to claim, without reservation, that my client is right and you (or your client) is wrong, and if you can't see that, you're a bumbling idiot.

So the attorney puts together the most aggressive, decisive, one-sided letter he or she reasonably can, based on the facts their client has given them, hoping that, on receipt of this letter, you totally cave in and admit defeat. Essentially a warning shot.

Nearest I can tell is that it's far easier for an attorney to try and bluster his or her way through and intimidate whomever they can into caving in. It's fast and cheap and easier than explaining the law (to you or their client). And it makes them (or their client) feel like their attorney is doing a good job.

Let's face it: if you're paying me to defend your mark, you want me to stop the other person as quickly and effectively as possible. Maybe that can be done with a single, aggressively-enough worded letter. Then I've done my job well, right?

Really?

I call foul. Bullying and intimidation through legal threats and pompous, arrogant language are some of the reasons that lawyers have such bad reputations with the general public in the first place. The better attorney is always willing to explain the law and listen to the other side. Now, just because they're willing to listen doesn't mean that you're going to change their mind, but they are willing to be civil about it.

In fact, I've found that the better the attorney, and the more right they are, the less aggressive and bellicose they are. Often the loudest attorney has the weakest case. Don't take that as a rule. Loud attorneys can be right too, I'm just sayin'.

So, what do YOU do?

When you get an aggressive (or even nasty) communication from an attorney, here's the first thing to understand: they don't mean it personally. "Are you kidding me?" I hear you say, "They just said that I'm stealing and that I did it on purpose and…!" Yeah, well, that's just the game they play.

I'll be honest, I don't like the game much myself, but it seems to be pervasive. And, again, the attorney isn't meaning this as a personal attack (even though it sounds like one), they're just trying to make their strongest, most assertive point up front and "get your attention."

So, when you get a letter, *do not* respond to it right away. Most attorney letters give you some time to respond. Use the time. Cool off. Get some others' opinions about what's going on. Maybe even (gasp) talk to your own lawyer. Even if you handle the response and everything else yourself, it's good to make sure that you really understand the situation the way you think you do.

When you respond, make an offer. Generally, that's what the

attorney and the other side are really looking for to begin with. Think about responding with, "Okay, you asked me to do X. I can't do X because of A, B, and C reasons. But I want to resolve this too. I can do Y. Will you accept Y instead of X?"

This kind of response gets the dialogue open and moving. Generally, the attorney (and probably the other side) didn't think you were really going to go for X anyway (but if you did—hey, WIN). Now that they know you're paying attention, we can get down to business and get a resolution. Both sides are satisfied because, hopefully, we're moving toward a resolution, and it won't be too expensive. And the lawyers are happy (because they're probably billing by the hour) and back off the "in your face" tactics.

What if that doesn't work?

Unfortunately, some attorneys continue to push and bully and threaten. In that case, get a lawyer. Sometimes, for whatever reason, lawyers don't think the other side is serious until they're talking to another lawyer. I guess, at some level, it says that the other side takes it seriously enough to spend money to address the issue. It also says that, with an attorney involved, you're a lot harder to bluff and bully. I've had to have conversations with other lawyers twhere I was saying, "Hey, lay off my client. Talk to me. Neither I nor my client are as stupid as you seem to think we are." Usually, this has made things more civil and somewhat less aggressive.

Conclusion

So…

I got all the way through that discussion, and I still don't know if I answered the question of "Why are some trademark attorneys jerks?" But maybe I've given you some things to think about and some background as to the attorneys' thought process. Here are the takeaways if you receive a cease-and-desist letter.

- Don't take it personally
- Cool off
- Make an offer
- Negotiate a resolution

And, somewhere in there, talk to your own lawyer if you need to.

CHAPTER SEVEN: THE THREE-TIER SYSTEM

This section is pretty technical. The first time I wrote this section, my editor had a meltdown because I started with the sentences: "The underpinnings of the 'three-tier system' between alcohol manufacturers, wholesalers and retailers in the United States come from the history of beer and pre-Prohibition economics. Understanding the regulatory and legal issues of alcohol distribution means understanding the three-tier system." And that's why lawyers need editors. So, let's try this again:

We have the three-tier system because people were worried. Why were they worried? Because drinking, drunks, and drunkenness were causing major social issues in the early 1900s. That's how we got Prohibition. When we repealed Prohibition, we got the three-tier system as a form of protection for the public. To understand how we got to where we are, we need to understand where we've been. So, hang in there with me, here we go!

ONE MAN CAN TURN THE TIDE OF HISTORY!

It can be argued that the current system of "three-tier" regulation is the result of one person, though not in the way you might expect. Machinist and locksmith Andrew Muhl (1831-1892) was the first to devise and patent a commercially viable means of manufacturing ice. Ice gave beer a longer shelf life than the limited one derived by the Arrhenius equation, which gives you the speed of staling.

$$x = Ae^{\frac{-Ea}{RT}}$$

Where X is the speed of staling (i.e. how fast the beer goes stale), A, Ea, and R are constants, and E is the inverse of the natural logarithm and T is temperature. Before your eyes glaze over, the details are not important; what is important is that for every 10°F increase in temperature, the beer goes stale twice as fast. So, for example, if the beer goes stale in two weeks at 50°F, it will go stale in one week at 60°F, 3.5 days at 70°F, etc.

John Says: "They said that every formula will cut the book's appeal in half, but I can't help it, I'm an engineer at heart."

Prior to Muhl, there was not a great way to keep beer cold other than harvesting ice, shipping ice to the brewery, and packing ice in wagons or rail cars to be shipped. As a result, breweries could not distribute their beer far from their home base. In the pre-Civil War United States, most towns had their own brewery and that beer almost never left the town, certainly not the county.

Brewing was local, and limited in scale.

However, with the rise of non-ice-harvesting refrigeration, that began to change. The company that would become known as Anheuser-Busch was the first brewery in the U.S. to use pasteurization to keep beer fresh. They invested heavily in refrigeration and refrigerated railcars, so by 1877 Anheuser-Busch owned a fleet of forty refrigerated railcars.

THE RISE OF THE TIED HOUSE

Being able to distribute their beer from a central location hundreds of miles afield allowed breweries to take better advantage of economies of scale. In the 1890s, brewers could make larger and larger breweries to supply thirsty people farther and farther from the birthplace of their beer. This, in combination of an increasingly mobile citizenry, thanks to a national railroad system and the advent of air travel starting in the early 1900s, created the opportunity for regional and national beer brands.

With beer brands and breweries becoming larger and larger, breweries began to exert an almost unnatural power on the market for beer. Breweries figured out that if they were supplying beer, they could also supply the rest of the "experience" for patrons. Soon, "tied-houses" sprang up with increasing frequency. Although they were ostensibly run by an "independent retailer," that retailer had little control over his destiny. A tied house was a bar that was required to buy some or all of its beer from a particular manufacturer. In exchange for this tied house arrangement, the brewery would often help the retailer get started in business, provide equipment, materials, and other financial help, needed to effectively sell beer. Tied houses still exist, though in a slightly different flavor. In the United Kingdom, bars (or "Public Houses") can be either a free house or a tied house.

Consider this: as you drive down the street in your hometown, you see a CVS drugstore across the street from a Walgreens drugstore, or a Burger King a block away from a McDonald's. In pre-Prohibition America, you might have seen an Anheuser-Busch pub across the street from a Michelob pub which was just around the corner from a Falstaff pub. You want a Falstaff, but your friend wants a Miller? Well, you'll just have to see that person some other time because you'd be headed to different bars.

These were pubs operated by independent owners but were required (in most cases) to sell only one manufacturer's product.

LET'S DIGRESS FOR A MOMENT...

A bar that sells just one brewery's beer? Really? Well, that's crazy unless it's a craft brewery or specialty store. But you mean that any old "average Joe's Bar" would have to be something like "average Joe's Michelob Bar?" It sounds unthinkable today, but we still have that sort of situation in every town in the United States! Have your doubts? How about:

- Where can you buy a McDonald's hamburger? At a McDonald's, probably owned by a local owner but required to sell only McDonald's products.
- Where can you buy a Ford truck? At a Ford dealership, owned

by a local owner, but required to sell only Ford products.
- Where can you buy Shell gasoline? At a Shell gas station, owned by a local owner, but required to sell only Shell gas.

What do these all have in common? They are franchises. A "franchise" is a business model where a producer of some commodity (the "franchisor") grants exclusive rights to market and sell its products to a local representative (the "franchisee"). That franchisee is guaranteed to be the only supplier of that franchisor's product for some territory. You want to open a McDonald's? Or a Taco Bell? Or a Subway? Buy a franchise.

But the franchise comes with responsibilities on both ends. As the franchisee, you get exclusive rights to sell the product, but it's also the only product you can sell. If you're a Ford dealership, you can't just up and change to a Chevy dealership overnight. No, you're tied to that franchisor with its sometimes strict rules.

To make matters more complicated, as a result of post-Prohibition regulation, alcohol franchise laws are very different from most franchise arrangements. If you open a McDonald's franchise, you are governed by a franchise agreement between you (the franchisee) and McDonald's (the franchisor). And, generally, those agreements are going to dictate the terms of the relationship of the franchisor and the franchisee. *Not so with alcohol franchise laws.* For alcohol, every state has a set of laws that *overwrite* whatever agreement

John Says: "We'll talk more about it, but suffice it to say that alcohol is regulated in some very strange and strict ways."

exists between the distributor and the manufacturer. It's as if the legislatures were saying, "Yes, we know that you know your business. But we know what's best for you, and *this* is the way your relationship is going to work. Your contract? That's cute. Nope, you need to use these terms *here*. Run along now, and good luck with your little business!"

Only a very few areas of franchises are treated this way. The other major examples, in addition to alcohol, are automobile retailers and gas/oil retailers.

We'll discuss alcohol franchise laws in more detail later on.

MORE ON TIED HOUSES

So, with these tied houses under the thumbs of breweries that were growing larger, things got more competitive. To quote the Associated Beer Distributors of Illinois: "Pressure was exerted on retailers to maximize sales without regard to the well-being of customers or the general public."(http://forgottenchicago.com/features/tied-houses/). As a result, sales tactics became seriously cutthroat.

In a time when labor unions were not as strong as today, laborers were paid pennies an hour and, in some urbanized and lower economic areas, food was scarce. Tied houses began offering "a free lunch." Sometimes the offer was with the purchase of a beer or two. Sometimes the offer was just "a free lunch" of some salty stew or cheese with dry bread. When patrons needed to slake their thirst, the manufacturer's beer was the only liquid at hand. Convenient, eh? Dollar signs hung in the air above the tied house. One description goes like this:

"A typical free lunch started with rye bread, followed by an over-seasoned bologna, blood sausage in a German bar, or summer sausage in others. Most also provided a heavily salted, dried herring. Baked beans were another regular fixture, along with thin slices of yellow cheese sitting next to a bowl of hot and spicy brown mustard. Garnishes included green onions and radishes when available, set out next to the ever present dill pickles. No tavern owner was totally altruistic and generous, they knew they'd make back threefold in beer sales what it cost to provide 'free' lunches and other giveaways." (http://www.beerhistory.com/library/holdings/taverngold.shtml)

In urban and industrial towns and cities, tied houses began to play host to growing labor union movements, often with the union treasury picking up the tab in order to get people to attend the meetings or rallies. In addition, the immigrant influx to the U.S. from the late 1800s well into the Great Depression fed the tied house machine by becoming a gathering place for people from "the old country" to talk, socialize, and learn about their new homeland.

With the brewing industry becoming more industrialized and the rise of the Beer Barons (Schlitz, Pabst, Busch, and others), the goal tended to be to maximize profits. The political cartoons and commentaries of the late 1910s were rife with references to the negative effects of alcohol on the family unit, marriage, spiritual salvation, and—

John Says: "Would we have had Prohibition at all without this confluence of events?"

yes—even, the very future of the United States as the country prepared for the Great War.

In addition to the effect of tied houses on the masses and "widespread drunkenness," tied houses also competed against each other. There are stories of breweries subsidizing the local tied house to enable below-cost sales of beer to drive other saloons out of business. Both legal (at the time) and illegal actions were employed in a "spy vs. spy"-esque game of competition between tied houses. So the tied-house trade affected not only direct consumers but also the entire commercial system.

The social, economic, and political tides came to a confluence that left the U.S. with the Eighteenth Amendment to the United States Constitution. Welcome to Prohibition. This book won't deal further with the "dry years," except to say that when the Eighteenth Amendment, aka the Volstead Act, was repealed by the Twenty-First Amendment, the United States wanted to put into place a sound system of regulations which would ensure that the excesses and near vertical integration of breweries to retailers of the pre-Prohibition era would not soon be revisited. And, from this impetus, we get…

THE THREE-TIER SYSTEM

The basis for our current regulatory system stems from the 1935 enactment of the Federal Alcohol Administration Act (FAA Act, Title 27 of the United States Code, Chapter 8). From the Tax and Trade Bureau (TTB) website, I quote:

FEDERAL ALCOHOL ADMINISTRATION ACT

The FAA Act provides for regulation of those engaged in the alcohol beverage industry, and for protection of consumers.

To ensure the integrity of the industry, the FAA Act includes provisions to:

- Require a permit for those who engage in the business as a producer, importer, or wholesaler of alcohol beverages
- Issue, suspend, and revoke permits
- Ensure the integrity of the industry by preventing persons who are not likely to operate in accordance with the law from entering the trade
- Protect the revenue and consumers by ensuring the integrity of the industry members

To protect consumers, FAA Act includes provisions to:

- Ensure that labeling and advertising of alcohol beverages provide adequate information to the consumer concerning the identity and quality of the product
- Require that alcohol beverages bottlers and importers must have an approved Certificate of Label Approval (COLA) or an exemption certificate before the product may be sold in the U.S.
- Prevent misleading labeling or advertising that may result in consumer deception regarding the product

The FAA Act includes provisions to preclude unfair trade practice. These provisions:

- Regulate the marketing and promotional practices concerning the sale of alcohol beverages
- Regulate practices such as exclusive outlets, tied house arrangements, commercial bribery, and consignment sales (https://www.ttb.gov/trade_practices/federal_admin_act.shtml, Aug 5, 2016.)

The FAA Act established the Federal Alcohol Administration which, for the purposes of this text, continues in the Tax and Trade Bureau.

This regulatory framework also sets up the now familiar "three-tier" model of alcohol production, distribution, and sales.

The general rule for the three-tier system is in two parts:

1. There are three types of alcohol industry members: manufacturers, wholesalers, and retailers.
2. No company or person may own or control more than one tier of a product's chain from manufacturing to retail sales.

John Says: "Repeat after me: 'There are always exceptions. Except when there are no exceptions, but that is the exception.'"

There are, as one might expect, exceptions to this general rule. But the main focus of the rule is to protect businesses from undue influence by manufacturers and to protect consumers from unscrupulous business practices of retailers.

In today's craft beer market, where many breweries are small, one-or-two employee operations, it is hard to imagine "undue influence" by manufacturers of beer. But at the time of the enactment of the FAA Act, breweries were large and powerful players in the market, able to pressure and leverage their influence over local distributors and small bars or restaurants.

Though the FAA Act lays out the main points in broad strokes like most other federal legislation, the government and industry heavily rely on the Code of Federal Regulations to figure out how the law will be implemented. For our purposes, the sections that are of interest are:

- 27 CFR 6 – Tied house
- 27 CFR 7 – Labeling and advertising of malt beverages
- 27 CFR 8 – Exclusive outlets
- 27 CFR 10 – Commercial bribery
- 27 CFR 11 – Consignment sales
- 27 CFR 13 – Labeling proceedings
- 27 CFR 16 – Alcoholic beverage health warning statement
- 27 CFR 25 – Beer

Additionally, in the Internal Revenue Code (IRC) at Title 26 of the USC, Chapter 51 lays down the rules on taxation of alcohol.

Through this enabling legislation, the federal government takes on the role of licensing manufacturers and wholesalers, collecting revenue, and ensuring that only licensed manufacturers are producing alcohol. These functions are now housed in the TTB (for licensing and revenue collection) and the Bureau of Alcohol, Tobacco, Firearms, and Explosives (for the enforcement).

Yet the FAA leaves the regulation of selling and distributing alcohol to the individual states. As a result, there are nearly fifty different schemes for regulating alcohol sales, and no uniform set of laws applies to all fifty states (other than the federal framework).

THE THREE-TIER SYSTEM: MANUFACTURERS

As brewers, you are automatically part of the manufacturer tier of the three-tier system. So, what does that mean to you? It means that you need to grasp a few things.

First, what is "beer?" Well, beer is an alcoholic beverage. And, according to the federal government, an alcoholic beverage is "any beverage in liquid form which contains not less than one-half percent of alcohol by volume and is intended for human consumption" (27 USC 214(1)). The states have similar or analogous definitions for regulatory purposes as well. Federal regulations further divide alcoholic beverages into beer (malt beverages), wine (including mead and cider), and distilled spirits (anything which achieves its alcoholic content by means in addition to, or other than through, natural fermentation). Beer, or a malt beverage, is defined as "a beverage made by the alcoholic fermentation of [...] potable brewing water, [...] malted barley with hops, [...] with or without other malted cereals, [...] with or without carbon dioxide, and with or without other wholesome products suitable for human food consumption." (27 USC 211(a)(7)). And that's just the "important" parts. The idea is that, essentially, anything fermented with any malted barley and any other carbohydrates is considered a "malted beverage" for federal regulatory purposes, i.e. beer.

So, as a manufacturer, if you make any beverage that is fermented and contains malted beverage, you're a beer brewer as far as the government is concerned. This becomes a more and more challenging proposition as brewers become more and more creative about ingredients and processes: the industry begins to outpace the regulations. This situation is further complicated by the way the state laws and regulations do, or in many cases do not, align with federal regulations. The brewer is strongly cautioned to distrust their intuition about how laws should (logically) work since intuition often fails when it comes to alcohol regulations.

John Says: "By the way, if you're a brewery and serving to the public, you're going to be subject to the regulations of both manufacturers and retailers."

One such example would be how labeling requirements are applied to manufacturers. By way of illustration, malt beverages may not use the word "strong" or allusions to "high strength," "full strength," or such descriptions in their labeling (27 CFR 7.29(f)). Not so with cider. With the recent uptick in cider production and its increasing market availability, cider is stocked right next to beer in the refrigerator section of your local grocery store. But cider is a wine for federal labeling purposes, and wine has no such prohibitions against the word "strong" on a label (27 CFR 4.39). Does cider have an unfair advantage in being able to use the word "strong" on their product competing with malted beverages? Maybe. Maybe not. But the point is that though you stand in the refrigerated section staring at apparently similar products, they may be regulated very differently.

John Says: "I tell my clients (often) that 'just because it makes sense to you, doesn't mean that it works that way.'"

So, what about products that include malted barley and grapes? Is it a wine? Is it a beer? What about mead, traditionally regulated as a wine by the federal government—what happens when it contains malted barley? When is it a beer with honey or a mead with grain? These are questions of degrees and can have a significant impact on whether or not you have the right license to produce the product and, if you do, how does it need to be labeled? This is the part where the brewer is strongly urged not to trust their intuition.

THREE-TIER SYSTEM: WHOLESALERS

The role of the wholesaler is to take the product from the manufacturer and sell it to retailers and promote the brand. Details on this relationship will be covered in more depth in the section on franchise law. But, it is important to understand the role in terms of the three-tier system, not only because of the franchise relationship, but also because an increasing number of states allow some manufacturers (breweries) to self-distribute or self-wholesale.

The ability to self-distribute is a state-level choice and has to be specifically enabled by legislation/statute.

Even if the state allows a brewery to self-distribute, that action of distribution is regulated differently than manufacturing. Many states require that, even when self-distributing, a manufacturer be licensed as a wholesaler as well. And because the manufacturer is now classified as a wholesaler, tax is due when the beer is removed from the premises for consumption—something that, technically, only wholesalers can do (i.e. take a malt beverage product from the brewery and deliver it to a retailer).

As a brewer who also operates a taproom at the brewery, you should think of your business as not just a brewery, but also a wholesaler/distributor (even if you're just distributing to yourself), and a retailer.

THE THREE-TIER SYSTEM: RETAILERS

The final link in the chain from raw material to beer to consumers is the retailer. The role of the retailer is to take the product from the wholesaler and sell it directly to the consuming public. The retailer is regulated almost exclusively by the state and local authorities. Even after Prohibition was repealed, counties, and some whole states, were "dry" until they decided to allow alcohol sales. Famously, Jack Daniel's whiskey is produced in a dry county (at Lynchburg in Moore County, Tennessee). So the company can produce the alcohol, but not sell it in its home county.

Situations like that of Jack Daniel's whiskey were widespread in the years after Prohibition. In the intervening seventy-odd years, these circumstances have largely been ameliorated as more and more states and counties have loosened their alcohol production, sales regulations and ordinances.

That said, the local government, including the state's ABC, the county government, and even the city, have a much larger role in keeping retailers "in line" as far as regulations go. And, the local laws about the sale of beer vary wildly from state to state and even within states as counties (and even cities) can, in some cases, set their own requirements or limits.

Lastly, in terms of the retail aspect of the beer-to-consumers chain, the risks, liability, and consumer protection issues are very different from those of either the wholesaler or the manufacturer. It's often the case that if operating a retail outlet for your brewed product, your retail establishment may be scrutinized much differently from the rest of your operation.

GENERAL GUIDANCE ON HOW TO VIEW THE THREE-TIER SYSTEM

	Manufacturers	Wholesalers	Retailers
Federal requirements and oversight	• Brewer's Notice (permission to produce) • Label Approval • Formulas (in some cases) and Health Statements	• Wholesaler Approval/ Registration • Importer Approval/ Registration	N/A
State requirements and oversight	• License • Label Approval • Product Registration	• Wholesaler Approval/ Registration	•License
Local requirements and oversight	• Business License • Privilege License (in some cases)	• Business License • Privilege License (in some cases)	• Business License • Privilege License (in some cases)

CHAPTER EIGHT: FEDERAL LICENSING

Not surprisingly, the federal government has a role to play in the production, distribution, and sale of alcohol. Throughout recorded history, alcohol has been a part—often a critical part—of human society. As a result, alcohol production and its sale have been one of the very first targets for taxation and government regulation. One of the earliest recipes for beer dates from the First Babylonian Dynasty during King Hammurabi's reign extoling the virtues of the goddess of beer, Ninkasi. Not surprisingly, the earliest regulation we have for beer comes from that same period in the seminal work of ancient law-giving, the Hammurabi Code, that set severe penalties for brewing "bad" beer.

Now fast forward to the post-Prohibition world in the United States, where the regulatory and taxation role is taken over by what used to be known as the ATF (Alcohol, Tobacco, and Firearms) division of the Department of Treasury. In 2002 the ATF's regulatory and taxation role was sequestered as the Tax and Trade Bureau (TTB), the main federal agency regulating the alcohol industry.

The role of the TTB is to license breweries (as well as distributors, distillers, wineries, firearm manufacturers, and fuel alcohol producers) and to collect the appropriate tax on their licensees. This section of the book will discuss the role of, issues for, and some guidance regarding the TTB.

WHAT IS IT?

As far as alcohol goes, the TTB regulates beer, wine, and distilled spirits. But what about the other…stuff? Generally speaking:

Product	Definition	Label/Formula Standards	Taxed as:	Permit Required
Malt Beverage	FAA	TTB - Beer	Beer	Brewer's Notice
Wine	FAA (>7%)	TTB – Wine	Wine	Bonded Winery
Cider / Perry (>7%)	IRC Ch 51	TTB – Wine, Agricultural Wine	Wine – Cider	Bonded Winery
Cider / Perry (<7%)	IRC Ch 51	FDA – Wine, "Still Wine"	Wine – "Hard Cider"	Bonded Winery
Sake	For production and tax, considered a Beer (IRC) For labeling and advertising considered a wine (FAA)	FDA – Wine, TTB Wine	Beer	Brewer's Notice
Mead	IRC §5388 (0.5-24%) FAA (>7%)	TTB – Wine	Wine	Bonded Winery
Flavored Malt Beverage	Treasury Decision 21 (TD-21)	TTB – Beer	Beer	Brewer's Notice
Gluten Free Beer	TTB Ruling 2012-2	FDA - Beer	Beer	Brewer's Notice

*IRC = Internal Revenue Code

THE TTB

- Regulates trade practices
- Issues rulings impacting industry members
- Collects excise taxes
- Approves formulas for non-traditional alcohol products
- Approves labels for products crossing state lines (Certificates of Label Approval, or COLAs)
- Issues federal permits necessary for the production, importation, or wholesale of alcohol

WHAT ABOUT THE FDA?

The Food and Drug Administration ("FDA") plays a role in the regulation of alcohol in the United States, but probably not the role you would think. FDA is mainly concerned with food safety, and because beer and other alcohol may be considered a "food," the FDA has some real interest in regulating, supervising, and inspecting alcohol production facilities instead of leaving this aspect of regulation exclusively to the TTB.

From time to time, every few years or so, there is a discussion (or rumor or threat) that the FDA might take a bigger role in alcohol regulation. In the mid-2000s, there was a concern that beer producers, by adding coffee to beer to make a coffee stout, were crossing the line into FDA territory. It took some months to resolve, but the TTB (and to a lesser extent, the FDA) agreed that merely adding coffee to beer did not make it "food" for FDA purposes. Thus far, though issues like this come up on occasion, the FDA has asserted significant regulatory authority on the alcohol industry only in certain very specific areas.

The FDA does have jurisdiction over alcohol production to the extent of:

- Food safety (ensuring that all food products sold to the public are safe and not adulterated and are not processed or stored under unsanitary conditions)
- Food Facility Registration (see below, next paragraph)
- Food additives and Generally Regarded as Safe (GRAS: additives or substances added to a food product)

John Says: "It's important to know what it is you are before you assume that you're doing everything right."

There is an issue that new producers must understand: Food Facility Registration. Following the 2002 passage of the Bioterrorism Act, alcohol producers are considered to make food for a limited purpose for the FDA. That is, to safeguard the U.S. food supply, the FDA has assembled a database registry of all the "food production facilities" in the United States. For this limited purpose, breweries and wineries are considered "food production facilities." This means that as an alcohol production facility owner you are required to register your facility with the FDA. This registration process is simple and straightforward—the FDA just wants to know that your business exists and where it is located. Registration on this list does not subject you to additional regulations, inspection, or other governmental authority. Additionally, the FDA has some jurisdiction when it comes to labels.

The FDA has rules for labeling which apply in two circumstances:

- Wines—Wines less than 7% Alchol By Volume (ABV) (i.e. wines that do not meet the Federal Alcohol Administration definition of "wine")
- Beers—Beers without hops and beers made with a barley substitute (i.e. corn, rice, or wheat)

These may seem like odd descriptions for classes of beverages that the FDA is concerned about, but consider that the FAA act only covers wines over 7% ABV. The FAA gives label supervision to the TTB. Additionally, the FAA act defines "malt beverage" (i.e. beer) to include malted barley and hops. A traditional cider (<7% ABV) would be neither a beer nor a wine under the FAA. Therefore lower alcohol "wines" or "beers" made without barley or hops (such as wine coolers, "malternatives" or "alcopops," sake, and cider) would have no labeling oversight without the FDA requirements.

FDA LABEL REQUIREMENTS

FDA labeling is different from TTB label requirements—which will be discussed shortly. The FDA does not do a "pre-market" clearance or approval on labels. In this sense, the FDA oversight is much more reactive than the proactive approval of TTB labeling. As such, there is no need to submit labels for FDA-covered products to the TTB or the FDA. However, the FDA (or the TTB for that matter) can take regulatory action after the product is "on the shelves" if they find that the products do not meet their requirements.

So, it is important to ensure that FDA-covered product labels are in compliance with FDA requirements before they hit the market. FDA label requirements are codified in 21 CFR Part 101 and are extensive. Read over all the requirements to be sure you understand the issues. These requirements can be found at:

FDA website: http://www.fda.gov/Food/GuidanceRegulation/default.htm

and

Electronic Code of Federal Regulations: http://www.ecfr.gov/

The biggest difference between FDA and TTB requirements is that the FDA requires the inclusion of the Nutrition Facts Panel and an ingredient statement (these elements are optional, but not required for TTB products). Some label claims are also regulated by the FDA, such as "Fat Free," "Light," "Low Calories," etc. The FDA also requires a statement that declares all major allergens such as egg, fish, and peanuts, etc.

However, an alcohol product can avoid some of the FDA requirements, especially the Nutrition Facts Panel, through the Small Business Nutrition Labeling Exemption. This exemption, essentially, only applies when fewer than 100,000 units of product are sold per year and the company employs fewer than 100 full-time employees.

Even though the FDA requirements are somewhat different from the TTB, they both require many of the same items, namely:

- Government warning statement
- ABV statement
- Country of origin
- Sulfite statement (for wines)

BACK TO THE TTB

Despite the above tangent regarding the FDA, as a brewery owner you will mostly be concerned with the TTB. It is the primary federal agency that most breweries will go to for:

1. Licensing (Brewer's Notice)
2. Label approval (COLA)
3. Formula approval (for non-traditional ingredients)
4. Excise tax payments

TTB LICENSING

The TTB licenses alcohol production facilities. This includes not only beer, wine, and distilled spirits, but also alcohol production for fuel use. In this discussion, the primary concern is, of course, brewery licensing. The TTB licensing process is lengthy and can be complex. The application is quite detailed and can be confusing for the layperson embarking on this adventure for the first time.

When getting your application approved by the TTB, the time from submission to approval can vary wildly. In June of 2015, the average processing time was varied from 70 to 90 days. As of June 2016, the time varied from 130 to 180 days. Though the timing varies in recent years, the general trend is that it is taking more and more time to approve applications due to a confluence of two issues:

1. For economic reasons, the federal government is under more and more pressure to cut costs and utilize online technologies to reduce overhead. Result: in 2016 the TTB has approximately the same number of staff it did in 1985.
2. The craft beverage industry is growing exponentially. Result: in 2015 the TTB had over a couple thousand applications submitted (or more than twenty times the number in 1985).

It turns out that you cannot double (or triple) the workload of the agency without extending the timeline to approve the applications. Therefore, the sooner you can apply to the TTB, the better. But expect to wait as long as four to six months for approval.

GETTING TO (TTB) "YES"

So, unless you can provide more staff to the TTB, your role as a brewery owner is to make it as easy as possible for the TTB to say "yes" to your application. That means having all the required information in your first submission and making sure that you answer the questions in a way they are expecting to see, rather than what makes sense to you.

For your TTB application, you will need an OOI(s) and the Permit Application. Both of these applications are submitted via PermitsOnline at https://www.ttbonline.gov/permitsonline/.

The OOI is the Owner Officer Information application and must be filled out for anyone who is:

- An officer of the organization
    - Such as President, Secretary, CEO, COO, Chief Brewing Officer, etc.
- An owner of the organization
    - If your organization is a corporation, each owner owning more than 10% of the outstanding stock must fill out an OOI application
    - If your organization is a limited liability company (LLC), each owner owning any membership interest must fill out an OOI application
    - The TTB treats LLCs like partnerships, so each owner is important. However, if there are many de minimus owners (for example, two major members holding 40% each and twenty members each holding 1% each), the TTB may waive these de minimus owner applications.

The OOI application includes:

- Personal identification information (such as name, height, weight, hair/eye color)
- Citizenship information
- Background information
    - Addresses for the previous ten years
    - Reference from a banker
    - Four references from personal/business associates
- Criminal history
- Federal permit history
- Employment history

The Brewer's Notice Application is more extensive and includes:

- Articles of Organization (LLC) or Articles of Incorporation (Corp.)
- Operating agreement (LLC) or bylaws (Corp)
- Federal Employer Identification Number (EIN)
- OOI applications
- List of all owners and officers identifying the percentage of voting ownership and amount of funds invested
- Source of funds invested (documentation)
- Diagram of premises
- Description of property (metes and bounds description, i.e. "legal description" from the deed)
- Description of the building (location of doors, windows, equipment, etc.)
- Environmental information
    - Number of employees
    - Amount of waste
    - Amount of energy used
    - Disposal of solid waste
    - Disposal of liquid waste
    - Disposal of waste to navigable waters
    - Brewer's Bond form
    - Or Consent of Surety if using a surety to post bond
- Lease agreement or deed for property
- Assumed name (trade name) registration, if applicable
- Security statement and information (how the premises are secured/protected)

John Says: "Buckle up, this is just the beginning."

- Main contact person
    - Copy of government-issued photo ID for the contact person
- Signing authority—granting authority to speak to the TTB on behalf of the company
- Power of attorney (if being filed by an attorney)
- Brewer's Bond payment
- Other documentation (for example, any variances requested, historic building designation)

John Says: "Starting January 2017, the TTB has eliminated the need for a Brewer's Bond if you anticipate that you will owe less than $50,000 in excise tax in the coming year. That's almost all startup breweries!"

Unfortunately, the TTB expects certain answers or types of answers to these questions. For example, there is a question which states: "Describe the fuel source and energy usage per year in BTUs." Questions like this can be extremely daunting to someone working on their first brewery and TTB application (and wanting to get it right the first time!). Recall this is the same application that MolsonCoors fills out to open one of their new million-barrel-a-year breweries. Now you, nano-brewery-in-your-garage, are trying to fill out the same sort of questions. For the question, "Describe the fuel source and energy usage per year in BTUs," the TTB is looking for one of two answers:

John Says: "Also, they can always ask for more information or additional details. The key is to provide enough information to make it easy for the TTB to say 'yes' but not too much information so as to open up more questions."

- The fuel source and the number of BTUs you plan to use to make beer that year OR
- "Natural Gas" or "Electricity" and "Sufficient to make less than 60,000 BBLs per year"

The trick here is to know that (as of 2016) 60,000 barrels of beer a year is the threshold for a "small brewery" for tax purposes. This tells the TTB three things: (1) you are a small brewery, (2) the tax rate/bracket for your brewery, and (3) you are not producing a lot of beer (globally speaking), so that changes their scrutiny of your fuel use, waste products, etc.

How would you know to use those "magic words"? Because you've done it before. Unfortunately, there is not a great resource or tool for the newcomer to identify the right way to answer questions for their certain set of circumstances. This is why it was said earlier that you can do most of this stuff yourself but you might not want to.

John Says: "Far too often, I get clients who have seriously messed up this stuff."

THE TTB APPLICATION PROCESS

After completing all of the OOIs and the Permit Application and uploading all the documents (and there are many) that you need to, you're finally ready to submit.

You must submit your OOI application(s) before your Permit Application. Once the OOI applications have been submitted, they will be reviewed by a TTB Specialist. The OOI review is pretty short and straightforward. By the way, once you submit your OOI application, be sure to write down the OOI number that is assigned to your application. Within a few days, the application status should go from "submitted" to "accepted." You can submit your OOI applications at any time, and you do not have to wait until you have completed your Permit Application.

Once your OOI applications are accepted (and you've filled out your Permit Application), you're ready submit your Permit Application. Once the Permit Application is submitted it will receive a cursory review (or triage) to make sure that, at least, all the pieces are present. The Triage Specialist does not review the individual answers; they just make sure that all the questions have been answered and all the appropriate documents are present. If there are any issues, the Triage Specialist will send you an information request.

If you receive an information request at the triage stage of review, you have ten days to respond. If you do not respond completely (that is, all the questions the triage specialist raised are answered to their satisfaction) within 10 days, the application will be *Abandoned*, and you'll have to start over. That means that, if you receive an information request from a Triage Specialist and you wait until Day 9 to answer the request, you may be out of time if the Triage Specialist needs additional documents besides what you submitted. Here's a worst case example:

> You submit an application and then go on vacation for a week. While you're gone, you receive a Triage Specialist request for

John Says: "Don't laugh, it happened."

a signed Operating Agreement (the one you submitted wasn't signed) and a copy of your driver's license (the one you sent isn't legible). You get back to town on Day 7. You get a signed copy of the Operating Agreement and send it to the Triage Specialist. On Day 9 you remember she also asked for a copy of your driver's license. You quickly scan a copy and send it to the Specialist. Also on Day 9, you get an email from the Specialist that your Operating Agreement's pages 3-8 didn't come through on the scan. So, also on Day 9 you rescan the Operating Agreement and email it to the Triage Specialist. Day 10, while you're in the brewery supervising some last minute construction, you receive an email saying your driver's license picture was still not legible, could you resend it with the picture more clearly? Unfortunately, you don't get that email until after 5 p.m. Eastern Time (close-of-business on the east coast) and Day 10 is past. The next morning you receive an automated email saying that your application is Abandoned.

The moral of the story here is, don't wait. Reply to the Triage Specialist (or any TTB Specialist) as soon as possible. Just like with the application, it may take more than one try to be able to adequately answer what the TTB believes to be a simple request. The TTB is most serious about their deadlines. There are no extensions and no "fudging" of when things were submitted, so be sure you know when the deadline actually is.

After the Triage Specialist is satisfied, you will move into a status similar to "Specialist Review." This is the all-encompassing "bucket" of statuses that includes everything from "waiting for specialist assignment," "waiting for specialist review," "specialist reviewing," "specialist thinking about what you submitted," "specialist deciding whether to ask you more questions," "specialist getting cup of coffee," "specialist quit*," etc. Specialist Review is the only system status that will be shown for the vast majority of the time the application is under review.

*Note: this actually happened. Just after the application was assigned to a specialist, that specialist left the TTB. Unfortunately, in the ensuing turmoil, there was no way to ensure that all of the applications got re-assigned to other specialists. This application went into limbo and this travesty wasn't discovered until nearly eighty days later. Credit to the TTB, once the issue was discovered, the TTB Specialists were very apologetic and bent over backwards to correct and expedite the review to get the application approved in a timely manner. It worked out well in the end, but the incident does provide some insight into the difficulties that face the TTB, even with their own electronic systems of checks and balances.

DIGRESSION: A PERSONAL WORD ON TTB SPECIALISTS AND TIMING

The TTB Specialists are generally super-nice people and are working very hard to meet the expectations of their supervisors and the industry. There have been many comments that the TTB is "lazy" and has "no sense of urgency." This has not been the experience of our office.

There have been comments such as "call the TTB every week to make sure that your application is 'on track.'" This is,

John Says: "I suggest that you not go out of your way to piss off the TTB staff."

in the experience of our office, a bad idea. The TTB Specialists are, generally, working on applications in the order they receive them. Constantly badgering them about your application does nothing but frustrate and annoy the Specialist, and it takes time away from the application they should be working on. If there is an issue, the TTB Specialist will reach out to you for clarifications or questions. Generally, no news is good news.

My recommendation is within the first couple weeks after assignment to the Specialist, send a short email indicating that you're available and would be happy to answer any questions they have. Then, wait. Approximately a week or so before the "average" processing time from when you submitted your application, call the TTB and let them know you haven't heard anything and wanted to know if there were any issues with your application. These two touch-points are more than enough to "check-up on" your application.

John Says: "Unfortunately, it takes as long as it takes."

If, however, you are approaching thirty or more days *after* the "average" processing time, then you should start calling more frequently until you understand what is holding up your application. Remember, the "average" processing time is just that, the average. Some applications will take less time, some will take longer.

There have been comments suggesting to "call your local legislature and see if they can call the TTB on your behalf." Again, based on our experience this is a bad idea. This is a little like telling a patron at the taproom, "If you're waiting too long for a beer, find the owner and get them to tell the bartender to serve you." It may get you a beer faster, but you have certainly gotten the bartender very upset with you. At that point, you had better hope that there is nothing wrong with your Permit Application and that you never need another one.

PERMIT APPLICATION APPROVAL

After you receive your approval, there are a few documents you need to download and keep at the brewery. These documents (issued by the TTB) are critical to show that you are licensed to do what you are doing. You should download

- A Brewer's Notice (often needed to apply for your state license as well)
- A Brewer's Bond (this is the original form you submitted, but countersigned and approved by a TTB official)
- Instructions on paying excise tax

After you have these, at least as far as the federal government is concerned, you are ready to brew beer.

[*Side note:* remember that the Brewer's Notice is a license to PRODUCE, not a license to SELL. You should not be producing any beer in/on the premises without first being permitted.]

CERTIFICATE OF LABEL APPROVAL

The TTB also approves labels for alcohol beverages that cross state lines. The requirements for beer are listed at https://www.ttb.gov/beer/beer-labeling.shtml. There is a helpful brochure at https://www.ttb.gov/pdf/brochures/p51903.pdf. Generally, the specific requirements can be found at:

§ 27 CFR 7.25 Name and Address

§ 27 CFR 7.71 Alcohol Content

§ 27 CFR 7.27 Net Contents

§ 27 CFR 7.29 (and TTB Ruling 2004-1) Caloric and Carbohydrate Representations

§ 27 CFR Part 16 Health Warning Statement

§ 27 CFR 7.23 Brand Name

§ 27 CFR 7.24 Class and Type

§ 27 CFR 7.24(d) & 7.71 Non-Alcoholic Malt Beverage

§ 27 CFR 7.11 Use of Ingredients Containing Alcohol

§ 27 CFR 7.22a Voluntary Disclosure of Major Food Allergens

Requirements are things you must do. There are also things you must not do. These prohibited activities are listed at:

27 CFR 7.29 and also at https://www.ttb.gov/beer/beer-labeling.shtml. As of 2016, the things you CANNOT do/have on a label are (and I am quoting the whole regulation here):

> *(a) Statements on labels. Containers of malt beverages, or any labels on such containers, or any carton, case, or individual covering of such containers, used for sale at retail, or any written, printed, graphic, or other material accompanying such containers to the consumer, must not contain:*
>
> *(1) Any statement that is false or untrue in any particular, or that, irrespective of falsity, directly, or by ambiguity, omission, or inference, or by the addition of irrelevant, scientific or technical matter, tends to create a misleading impression.*

(2) *Any statement that is disparaging of a competitor's products.*

(3) *Any statement, design, device, or representation which is obscene or indecent.*

(4) *Any statement, design, device, or representation of or relating to analyses, standards, or tests, irrespective of falsity, which the appropriate TTB officer finds to be likely to mislead the consumer.*

(5) *Any statement, design, device, or representation of or relating to any guarantee, irrespective of falsity, which the appropriate TTB officer finds to be likely to mislead the consumer. Money-back guarantees are not prohibited.*

(6) *A trade or brand name that is the name of any living individual of public prominence, or existing private or public organization, or is a name that is in simulation or is an abbreviation thereof, or any graphic, pictorial, or emblematic representation of any such individual or organization, if the use of such name or representation is likely falsely to lead the consumer to believe that the product has been endorsed, made, or used by, or produced for, or under the supervision of, or in accordance with the specifications of, such individual or organization: Provided, That this paragraph shall not apply to the use of the name of any person engaged in business as a producer, importer, bottler, packer, wholesaler, retailer, or warehouseman, of malt beverages, nor to the use by any person of a trade or brand name that*

is the name of any living individual of public prominence, or existing private or public organization, provided such trade or brand name was used by him or his predecessors in interest prior to August 29, 1935.

(7) *Any statement, design, device, or representation that tends to create a false or misleading impression that the malt beverage contains distilled spirits or is a distilled spirits product. This paragraph does not prohibit the following on malt beverage labels:*

(i) *A truthful and accurate statement of alcohol content, in conformity with §7.71;*

(ii) *The use of a brand name of a distilled spirits product as a malt beverage brand name, provided that the overall label does not present a misleading impression about the identity of the product; or*

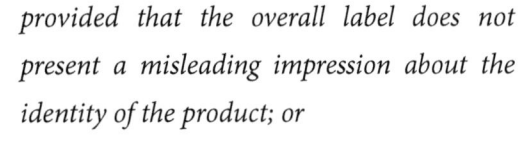

(iii) *The use of a cocktail name as a brand name or fanciful name of a malt beverage, provided that the overall label does not present a misleading impression about the identity of the product.*

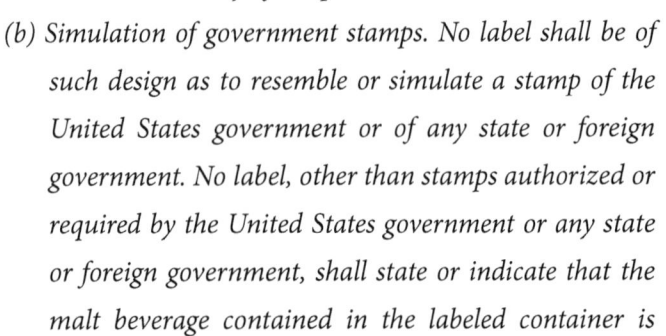

John Says: *"Believe it or not, all these indents make it easier to read!"*

(b) *Simulation of government stamps. No label shall be of such design as to resemble or simulate a stamp of the United States government or of any state or foreign government. No label, other than stamps authorized or required by the United States government or any state or foreign government, shall state or indicate that the malt beverage contained in the labeled container is brewed, made, bottled, packed, labeled, or sold under, or in accordance with, any municipal, state, federal, or foreign government authorization, law, or regulation, unless such statement is required or specifically authorized by federal, state, or municipal, law or regulation, or is required or specifically authorized by the laws or regulations of the foreign country in which such malt beverages were produced. If the municipal or state government permit number is stated upon a label, it shall not be accompanied by an additional statement relating thereto, unless required by state law.*

(c) Use of word "bonded," etc. The words "bonded," "bottled in bond," "aged in bond," "bonded age," "bottled under customs supervision," or phrases containing these or synonymous terms which imply governmental supervision over production, bottling, or packing, shall not be used on any label for malt beverages.

(d) Flags, seals, coats of arms, crests, and other insignia. Labels shall not contain, in the brand name or otherwise, any statement, design, device, or pictorial representation which the appropriate TTB officer finds relates to, or is capable of being construed as relating to, the armed forces of the United States, or the American flag, or any emblem, seal, insignia, or decoration associated with such flag or armed forces; nor shall any label contain any statement, design, device, or pictorial representation of or concerning any flag, seal, coat of arms, crest or other insignia, likely to mislead the consumer to believe that the product has been endorsed,

made, or used by, or produced for, or under the supervision of, or in accordance with the specifications of the government, organization, family, or individual with whom such flag, seal, coat of arms, crest, or insignia is associated.

(e) Health-related statements:

(1) Definitions. When used in this paragraph (e), terms are defined as follows:

(i) Health-related statement means any statement related to health (other than the warning statement required by §16.21 of this chapter) and includes statements of a curative or therapeutic nature that, expressly or by implication, suggest a relationship between the consumption of alcohol, malt beverages, or any substance found within the malt beverage, and health benefits or effects on health. The term includes both specific health claims and general references to alleged health benefits or effects on health associated with the consumption of alcohol, malt beverages, or any substance found within the malt beverage, as well as health-related directional statements. The term also includes statements and claims that imply that a physical or psychological sensation results from consuming the malt beverage, as well as statements and claims of nutritional value (e.g., statements of vitamin content). Statements concerning caloric, carbohydrate, protein, and fat content do not constitute nutritional claims about the product.

(ii) *Specific health claim* is a type of health-related statement that, expressly or by implication, characterizes the relationship of the malt beverage, alcohol, or any substance found within the malt beverage, to a disease or health-related condition. Implied specific health claims include statements, symbols, vignettes, or other forms of communication that suggest, within the context in which they are presented, that a relationship exists between malt beverages, alcohol, or any substance found within the malt beverage, and a disease or health-related condition.

(iii) *Health-related directional statement* is a type of health-related statement that directs or refers consumers to a third party or other source for information regarding the effects on health of malt beverage or alcohol consumption.

(2) *Rules for labeling:*

(i) *Health-related statements.* In general, labels may not contain any health-related statement that is untrue in any particular or tends to create a misleading impression as to the effects on health of alcohol consumption. TTB will evaluate such statements on a case-by-case basis and may require as part of the health-related statement a disclaimer or some other qualifying statement to dispel any misleading impression conveyed by the health-related statement.

(ii) Specific health claims.

(A) TTB will consult with the Food and Drug Administration (FDA), as needed, on the use of a specific health claim on a malt beverage label. If FDA determines that the use of such a labeling claim is a drug claim that is not in compliance with the requirements of the Federal Food, Drug, and Cosmetic Act, TTB will not approve the use of that specific health claim on a malt beverage label.

(B) TTB will approve the use of a specific health claim on a malt beverage label only if the claim is truthful and adequately substantiated by scientific or medical evidence; sufficiently detailed and qualified with respect to the categories of individuals to whom the claim applies; adequately discloses the health risks associated with both moderate and heavier levels of alcohol consumption; and outlines the categories of individuals for whom any levels of alcohol consumption may cause health risks. This information must appear as part of the specific health claim.

(iii) Health-related directional statements. A statement that directs consumers to a third party or other source for information regarding the effects on health of malt beverage or alcohol consumption is presumed misleading unless it—

(A) Directs consumers in a neutral or other non-misleading manner to a third party or other

source for balanced information regarding the effects on health of malt beverage or alcohol consumption; and

(B) (1) Includes as part of the health-related directional statement the following disclaimer: "This statement should not encourage you to drink or to increase your alcohol consumption for health reasons;" or

(2) Includes as part of the health-related directional statement some other qualifying statement that the appropriate TTB officer finds is sufficient to dispel any misleading impression conveyed by the health-related directional statement.

(f) Use of words "strong," "full strength," and similar words. Labels shall not contain the words "strong," "full strength," "extra strength," "high test," "high proof," "pre-war strength," "full oldtime alcoholic strength," or similar words or statements, likely to be considered as statements of alcoholic content, unless required by state law. This does not preclude use of the terms "low alcohol," "reduced alcohol," "non-alcoholic," and "alcohol-free," in accordance with §7.71 (d), (e), and (f), nor does it preclude labeling with the alcohol content in accordance with §7.71.

(g) Use of numerals. Labels shall not contain any statements, designs, or devices, whether in the form of numerals, letters, characters, figures, or otherwise, which are likely to be considered as statements of alcoholic content, unless required by state law, or as permitted by §7.71.

(h) Coverings, cartons, or cases. Individual coverings, cartons, cases, or other wrappers of containers of malt beverages, used for sale at retail, or any written, printed, graphic, or other matter accompanying the container shall not contain any statement or any graphic pictorial, or emblematic representation, or other matter, which is prohibited from appearing on any label or container of malt beverages.

These requirements and prohibitions are pretty straightforward and the plain meaning/reading of these regulations is probably sufficient to figure out what you should and shouldn't do.

Once you have designed the labels for your beverage, then you can submit for review/approval on the COLAsOnline System at https://www.ttb.gov/labeling/colas.shtml.

FORMULAS

As one might expect, there's a customer page for processing formulas online for the TTB as well. Formulas, depending on your perspective, may be becoming less and less important as more and more ingredients are being exempted from formula registration.

A beer needs formula approval if it incorporates ingredients or processes that are not "traditional" for beer. On a frequent if not regular basis, the TTB issues guidance on additional ingredients and processes that are exempt from formula registration. For example, in 2014, the TTB issued a ruling which declared the following traditional ingredients/processes (effectively exempting these from formula approval):

- "Sweeteners," including brown sugar, candy (candi) sugar, chili peppers, chocolate, coffee (beans or grounds), honey, maple sugar/syrup, molasses/blackstrap molasses, and lactose
- Fruits, including apples, apricots, blackberries, blueberries, cherries, cranberries, juniper berries, lemons, oranges, peaches, pumpkins, raspberries, and strawberries
- Spices, including allspice, anise, pepper/peppercorns, cardamom, cinnamon, clove, cocoa (powder or nibs), coriander, ginger, nutmeg, orange or lemon peel or zest, star anise, and vanilla
- Aging beer in barrels (or using wood from barrels) that were previously used to age wine or spirits, so long as the barrels do not contain a discernable quantity of wine or spirits

Between these recent exemptions and those already exempted (look at the TTB website), the brewer has a large palette of ingredients to play with which do not require formula approval. However, if the beer requires formula approval, the formula must be approved before a COLA may be issued for the product. As you might expect, there's a TTB website for that too: https://www.ttb.gov/foia/fonl.shtml.

TOP PERMITTING ISSUES

Like with real estate (where the three most important things are "location, location, and location"), the three most important issues with the TTB are documentation, documentation, and documentation. By far, this is the number one thing that will hold back your permit or get you in trouble from a permitting perspective.

DOCUMENTATION: PERMIT

Your documentation should be clear, consistent, and detailed. If your application in one part says "brewpub" and in another part says "brewery with a taproom and kitchen," it can cause problems because the TTB sees these two businesses as very different even if the words are interchangeable in your mind. It's better to ensure that you consistently use the same terminology throughout the application. If you refer to something as a brite tank, it better always be referred to as a brite tank, and not sometimes as a "brite tank," sometimes as a "serving tank," and sometimes as a "uni-tank." The same is true of your fermenters and filters, etc. Mind what you call your taproom. Is it a tavern? A taproom? A tasting room? These may all be very similar in our minds, but have very significant differences for the TTB. FYI—a taproom is a tavern where you sell beer made at the brewery. A tasting room is a place where you give away free samples of the product (and sometimes a consumer can buy product to consume offsite). Be very clear and consistent in your documentation and be sure you know precisely what the words mean for the TTB (which is not necessarily what you *think* they mean).

John Says: *"Do not skimp on documentation. Document document document. And, if you're not absolutely sure you know what they mean, double-check the meaning."*

DOCUMENTATION: TAXES

This should be simple: pay your taxes. But, often it is not so simple. The Brewer's Report of Operations is the place where you detail the production of the facility and determine how much tax is owed and for what product. The form may not be entirely intuitive. Be sure to study up (maybe even ask a fellow brewer for an example) and take a look at the hints and help on the TTB website at https://www.ttb.gov/forms/f51309i.pdf or at https://www.ttb.gov/forms/51309worksheet.pdf. If you have concerns about taxes, contact a Certified Public Accountant (CPA) with experience dealing with the TTB.

John Says: "I can't believe that I have to say this...pay your taxes."

DOCUMENTATION: REMEMBER TO ASK FOR APPROVAL

Remember that having a license to brew beer is a privilege and not a right. The TTB makes it very clear that as a brewery owner you must keep them informed of changes and that many of those changes require approval before they happen. Major changes require approval by the TTB before they are made and that application/approval comes in the form of an amendment to your Brewer's Notice. Amendments should be made whenever there is:

- A change in ownership of the brewery
- A new officer or manager of the LLC
- A new (or second) location
- A major change in equipment that affects capacity

John Says: "It's a lot easier to deal with stuff before it happens than after."

The TTB is unlikely to "shut you down" if you fail to notify them first, but they are very clear that the requirement is that you apply before you do anything. And, in general, the Amendment process is much less rigorous and time consuming than the initial application. This is *not* the situation to follow the hackneyed saying, "It's better to ask for forgiveness than to ask for permission."

EXPORTING

This tome will not spend too much time on exporting products to other countries, but there are a few points worth noting—at least from the federal perspective. The TTB (and a few other agencies) also governs the exporting of products to countries outside the U.S. The requirements for exporting are different and often easier to comply with than the requirements for domestic sales. The requirements also differ depending on whether the exporter is the producer or the wholesaler. §27 CFR 28 governs the exportation of malt beverages from the U.S.

In general, the regulations provide for removal of tax-paid beverages from the premises for:

- Exportation to a foreign country
- Use as supplies on vessels and aircraft (as specified in the regulations)
- Transfer to and deposit in a foreign-trade zone for exportation or storage, pending exportation

Alternatively, the regulations also provide for export of wine (just for your reference) without payment of tax from the premises for:

- Exportation to a foreign country
- Use as supplies on vessels and aircraft
- Transfer to a foreign-trade zone
- Transfer to a customs-bonded warehouse
- Transfer to a manufacturing bonded warehouse
- Shipment to the U.S. armed forces for use overseas

There are additional requirements for labeling for exportation and additional documentation needed. However, if this seems confusing or daunting, do not worry. The TTB's International Affairs Division (IAD) can assist with questions and a sub-group within the IAD is specifically tasked with helping U.S. producers export to other countries.

John Says: "The TTB actually has a group that will help you do this stuff!"

PENALTIES

Now comes the difficult conversation, starting with "what if I didn't..." The consequences of not complying with federal regulations can be severe. TTB fines can range into the tens of thousands of dollars if you have failed to comply for whatever reason. However, there may be an incentive to "turn yourself in" rather than waiting to be caught. The TTB generally looks more favorably on those who reach out and admit their mistake (hopefully it was a mistake and not intentional fraud). Penalties may be less severe or in some cases, may be eligible to be waived, if you are working with TTB to correct the issue(s).

CHAPTER NINE: STATE LICENSING

The Twenty First Amendment to the United States Constitution (a process begun with the Cullen-Harrison Act in 1933) repealed the Eighteenth Amendment (the Volstead Act) that banned the production and sale of alcohol. The Twenty First Amendment's text in its entirety reads:

> *Section 1. The Eighteenth Article of Amendment to the Constitution of the United States is hereby repealed.*
>
> *Section 2. The transportation or importation into any state, territory, or possession of the United States for delivery or use therein of intoxicating liquors, in violation of the laws thereof, is hereby prohibited.*
>
> *Section 3. This article shall be inoperative unless it shall have been ratified as an amendment to the Constitution by conventions in the several states, as provided in*

the Constitution, within seven years from the date of the submission hereof to the states by the Congress.
(https://www.law.cornell.edu/constitution/amendmentxxi)

That's it. That's all the Amendment says. As you can see, in Section 2, the vast majority of alcohol regulation is actually left to the states to implement as they see fit. So, state licensing of a brewery, or any alcohol business, is a touchy subject for two reasons:

1. The regulations and requirements vary widely across all fifty states (and U.S. Territories) and
2. Because so much regulation is left to the states, the regulations tend to reflect a very local approach or set of priorities.

By way of example for #2, consider the southeastern United States. Large swaths of this part of the U.S. are often (and aptly) characterized as the Bible Belt where the conservative/evangelical lens and pressures of an anti-alcohol stance lead to some unique, and downright bizarre, state and local regulations. In contrast, the much less evangelically influenced Pacific Northwest has its own unique regulations and quirks (like being unable to pump one's own gasoline in Oregon). With respect to #1 above, there is some ability to provide broad guidance on state laws and regulatory approaches. However, it is important to consult with a legal professional licensed to practice law in your state to get good guidance regarding your particular situation.

John Says: "*You wouldn't believe the trouble you can get into with the phrase 'I didn't know I couldn't do that.'*"

Before getting into the general rules or guidance of alcohol regulation, it's helpful to consider that not every state wanted to repeal Prohibition. Looking back, history teaches us that it was a grand celebration and merriment filled the streets. And, certainly, the beer industry saw the repeal of Prohibition as a sea change and return of important rights and privileges to the American citizen. But not all of the United States felt that way.

To get a flavor of how each state felt at the time, consider that Congress proposed the Amendment in February of 1933, but it took until December of 1933 for thirty-six states to ratify the Amendment. That's between nine to eleven months of deliberation for some of the thirty-six states that were the first to ratify the Amendment. The responses of the states were varied.

John Says: "*By the way, the Twenty-First Amendment made alcohol production legal again, but Prohibition for beer effectively ended in April 1933 by the Cullen-Harrison Act allowing production of beer up to 3.2% by weight (a level thought to be non-intoxicating). Signing the Cullen-Harrison Act prompted President Roosevelt to say, 'I think this would be a good time for a beer.'"*

The following states ratified the Amendment:

- Michigan (April 10, 1933)
- Wisconsin (April 25, 1933)
- Rhode Island (May 8, 1933)
- Wyoming (May 25, 1933)
- New Jersey (June 1, 1933)
- Delaware (June 24, 1933)
- Indiana (June 26, 1933)
- Massachusetts (June 26, 1933)
- New York (June 27, 1933)

- Illinois (July 10, 1933)
- Iowa (July 10, 1933)
- Connecticut (July 11, 1933)
- New Hampshire (July 11, 1933)
- California (July 24, 1933)
- West Virginia (July 25, 1933)
- Arkansas (August 1, 1933)
- Oregon (August 7, 1933)
- Alabama (August 8, 1933)
- Tennessee (August 11, 1933)
- Missouri (August 29, 1933)
- Arizona (September 5, 1933)
- Nevada (September 5, 1933)
- Vermont (September 23, 1933)
- Colorado (September 26, 1933)
- Washington (October 3, 1933)
- Minnesota (October 10, 1933)
- Idaho (October 17, 1933)
- Maryland (October 18, 1933)
- Virginia (October 25, 1933)
- New Mexico (November 2, 1933)
- Florida (November 14, 1933)
- Texas (November 24, 1933)
- Kentucky (November 27, 1933)
- Ohio (December 5, 1933)
- Pennsylvania (December 5, 1933)
- Utah (December 5, 1933)

Ratification was completed on December 5, 1933.

The amendment was subsequently ratified by conventions in the following states:
- Maine (December 6, 1933)
- Montana (August 6, 1934)

The amendment was rejected by the following state:
- South Carolina (December 4, 1933)

Voters in the following state rejected holding a convention to consider the amendment:
- North Carolina (November 7, 1933)

The following states took no action to consider the amendment:
- Georgia
- Kansas
- Louisiana
- Mississippi
- Nebraska
- North Dakota
- Oklahoma
- South Dakota

Think about that. North Carolina and South Carolina said a flat out "no." And a bunch of states did not even want to consider the question or put it to their citizens whether to repeal Prohibition. Plus, there is no real accounting for the distinctions. Some Southeastern U.S. states voted "yes," some "no." The same with the Midwest. But, even the very conservative (alcohol-wise) Utah, voted "yes" along with the first thirty-six states.

As a result, the regulatory schemes and systems are "all over the map" in terms of how they treat certain products or certain activities. This book will attempt to provide some general guidance. First, consider that there are generally two types of state regulatory systems: control states and license states.

John Says: "Of course, my home state of North Carolina had to be difficult about it."

CONTROL STATES

Control states are those states in which the state government itself maintains some amount of control over the production, distribution, or retail sales of alcohol. There are approximately nineteen states (as of 2015) that are control states. While the language of the general description alludes to the fact that states *could* control the entire alcohol chain, what actually happens is *somewhat* more benign.

In control states, generally, the state controls the wholesale and distribution of alcohol products, the retail sales of distilled spirits, and a certain amount of retail sales of wine/beer. For example, in North Carolina, beer and wine can be sold at convenience or grocery stores, but distilled spirits must be sold at North Carolina state-controlled ABC Stores (ABC, of course, standing for Alcohol Beverage Commission). Meanwhile in Idaho, the ABC stores are state run and must sell *anything* over 16% alcohol by volume ("ABV"). But in Michigan, the

ABC stores are privately run, but all *wholesale* or *distribution* of distilled spirits are controlled by the state. Pennsylvania has, perhaps, the most counterintuitive system: all wine and spirits are sold in Pennsylvania Liquor Control Board stores, known as "State Stores" and malt beverages are sold by the case by licensed beer retailers known as "distributors," and in smaller quantities by on-premises establishments.

So even in control states, who "controls" what varies widely depending on their regulatory scheme. For reference, the nineteen control states (as of the date of this writing) are:

- Alabama
- Idaho
- Iowa
- Maine
- Maryland (Montgomery County only)
- Michigan
- Mississippi
- Montana
- New Hampshire
- North Carolina
- Ohio
- Oregon
- Pennsylvania
- Utah
- Vermont
- Virginia
- Washington
- West Virginia
- Wyoming

And, by the way, these change from time to time as states loosen or tighten regulations to encourage growth or discourage the negative effects of alcohol consumption/over-consumption.

LICENSE STATES

The remaining thirty-one states plus the District of Columbia (other than the nineteen control states) are license states. License states have created licensing systems to allow private companies to distribute and sell alcohol to consumers. In license states, such as California, the type of license a retailer needs may depend on the location, whether the product is made onsite, whether they are also self-distributing, and whether or not they serve only their own product (for example, see https://www.abc.ca.gov/forms/abc616.pdf). It is often critical for a business to pursue precisely the correct license to be able to execute their business plan.

One issue with many license state systems is the complexity that can ensue when there are different types of licenses based on the combinations and permutations of producer, distributor, retailer, with and without food, etc. Additionally, some states allow licenses to be transferred when the business is sold or if the business changes location. Some license states do not allow licenses to be transferred. Perhaps more so than with control states, individuals starting alcohol businesses, especially new business models, should consult with a legal professional familiar with their state's processes.

For reference, the thirty-two license states, including the District of Columbia, (as of 2015) are:

Alaska

Arizona

Arkansas

California

Colorado

Connecticut

Delaware

District of Columbia

Florida

Georgia

Hawaii

Illinois

Indiana

Kansas

Kentucky

Louisiana

Maryland (except Montgomery County)

Massachusetts

Minnesota

Missouri

Nebraska

Nevada

New Jersey

New Mexico

New York

North Dakota

Oklahoma

Rhode Island

South Dakota

Tennessee

Texas

Wisconsin

CONSIDERATIONS FOR LOCAL/STATE LICENSING

In working with a state for licensing an alcohol production facility, wholesaler, or retail location, it is important to remember what interest the state has in the process. Generally speaking, a state is going to be interested in a few key factors:

- Collection of tax revenue
- Enforcement of the state's alcohol laws (and state administrative code)
- Protecting the public

One or more of these reasons may influence or inform the other when we are trying to interpret state statutes or regulations. For example, take the requirement to separate tax-paid and non-tax-paid beer. This is a federal requirement but also universally required by states as well. From an enforcement perspective, states want to ensure that it is clear what beer has had excise tax collected so non-tax-paid beer isn't served or removed from the brewery without paying the tax (that's the revenue collection part).

John Says: "*Sorry, I just can't get too specific with fifty plus different ways of doing things.*"

Another example: the brewery space has to be separate from the public taproom space. Why? To analyze the question, the state interest has to be identified. What is the state's interest in the separation? The state wants to make sure that the general public (who are hanging around in the taproom) are not injured by chemicals (like caustic cleaning solutions), equipment (hoses, hot tanks or pumps, etc.), or any of the other hazards of a production area. The state wants to protect the public. But, the state *also* has an interest in making sure that the general public does not wander into the production area and have ready access to non-tax paid beer (like bottles waiting to be shipped, or sampling off of a brite tank). That's the part of the state's interest in collecting tax revenue.

So, if you are asking, "How separate does it have to be?" the question should really be, "How can we demonstrate that we can address the concerns and show that we can keep the public safe and prevent them from drinking non-tax-paid beer on site?" From a brewer's perspective, the second question is a lot easier to understand and address in design and construction.

The vast majority of state laws and regulations addressing alcohol are seriously antiquated and do not reflect the current craft alcohol industry. That said, in many cases, the issues come down to interpreting the existing regulations based on the state's understanding. So, when thinking about how the regulation or law applies to the brewery, it is important to ask, "How or why

John Says: "It's a lot easier to solve a specific situation than to come up with rules and hope that you're not overlooking an exception."

is this important to the state?" and "How can we address the concerns the state would have?" Thinking about the regulations and laws through this lens will help most brewers anticipate state objections and address them ahead of time.

STATE AND FEDERAL INTERSECTION

This issue will be dealt with in detail in a later section, but it is worth mentioning here as well. The state has a tremendous amount of leeway in regulating alcohol within the state. The federal government has to license and approve certain activities (wherever they are), like producing alcohol, but the state's authority only extends to its borders. And, in many cases, federal authority only applies when state lines are crossed.

One of the most significant examples of this involves labeling. Brewers are typically familiar with the COLA (Certificate of Label Approval), issued by the TTB that approves the label for use in commerce. But, in many cases, no federal label approval is needed *if the product is not leaving the state* where it was produced. For example, if a beer was brewed in North Carolina and the brewer only distributes draft beer and only within their home county, the brewer *does not need federal approval for their labels*. The brewer *still has to register and receive approval from the state*, but not the federal government. Yet, that all changes as soon as a manufacturer or wholesaler sends product across state lines. On the other hand, some states do not have their own label approval process and, instead, rely on the TTB COLA to stand in for the state approval.

Additionally, states may have more stringent rules on certain things than the federal government. For example, while the federal government may require "adequate separation" between the taproom and the brewery space, the state may require a full wall. Or when the TTB requires a description of the property, the state may require a plat drawing *and* a description. Or, in some cases, the state may rely on the TTB requirements.

John Says: "We generally recommend that, if you're not sure, go ahead and file for federal COLA as well as your state label approval."

Other examples of state requirements differing from federal requirements have to do with labels. Two "famous" examples are:

- Flying Dog Brewery's Raging Bitch label (http://flyingdogbrewery.com/raging-bitch-freedom-speech/) and
- Founders Brewery's Breakfast Stout label (http://www.chicagotribune.com/news/weird/chi-beer-baby-label-20150115-story.html)

Lastly, states often have approval processes that do not line up with federal approval process. Some states want an independent application that the state reviews in parallel with the TTB. Some states want the TTB application to be completed before applying at the state level. It is critical to understand your own state's requirements and not to rely on the experience of other brewers in other states.

LOCAL REQUIREMENTS

Each state treats local governments differently. And, each state has different ideas of what authority governments have over the area. State regulations, county (or parish) ordinances, and city ordinances are not necessarily written to always comport with each other, particularly when it comes to alcohol regulation.

For example, it may surprise some to find out that there are still dry counties in the southeastern United States, particularly in the Bible Belt. There are also dry cities, where the county may be wet, but the city has decided to remain dry. Perhaps counter-intuitively, in some places, the opposite is true, where a county is dry and a city within that county is wet. So, in the case of the latter, one could operate a brewery in the county, but could sell the product only within the city limits.

John Says: "Can't tell you how often this happens. We've found situations where the town didn't even realize that they had elected to have different requirements."

While it is unusual for someone to start a brewery or any other alcohol business on a whim in a location far from where they have at least some passing familiarity with the local ordinances, it can happen as brewery owners look for expansion potential, more favorable demographics, and—particularly—for places where there is no "local" brewery to serve the population.

It would be impossible in this book to even to list all the kinds of variations in local ordinances, potential conflicts, and state regulatory schemes. But, as brewers-search for a location, it is absolutely critical to research and evaluate city and county rules and ordinances in addition to knowing the state regulations.

John Says: "Sometimes there's a reason why there are no breweries near you."

TOPICS TO RESEARCH AND UNDERSTAND IN ANY STATE

The following represent special topics that brewers and other alcohol business owners may not need to immediately consider, but still need to research and understand thoroughly as they may impact the viability of a business in a particular location:

- Historic Structures—Many breweries find themselves looking at historic structures or older buildings in need of revitalization. This situation often coincides with a desire to match the theme of the brewery itself, or the corporate culture the company wants to foster. Unfortunately, historic structures often come with significant challenges. While there may be incentives from local or state government to utilize some of these locations, it should be noted that they often require extensive upfits to make them viable alternatives for the needs of a production brewery. In addition to the upfits required, there may also be state or local regulations regarding the use, modification, or alteration of historic structures. Conflict often arises when the use of a structure is changed significantly, and what has been grandfathered into the existing building code now has to be retrofitted to include handicap access, new wiring, ingress and egress issues, and parking and other limiting factors. These regulations or requirements may significantly increase the cost of using such a location.

- Recycling—The need to "reduce, reuse, and recycle" has long been a topic of discussion and is often close to the heart of many brewers. However, many states and municipalities have begun to implement required recycling programs. These recycling programs can be counterintuitive. In many states, so called "self-haul" recycling (where the business hauls off its own recycling) is not permitted—that is, the business *must* have a contract with a service provider rather than being able to manage it themselves. Be sure that any recycling requirement, service, or option has been thoroughly investigated and possible contingencies identified.

- Zoning—Perhaps one of the biggest single issues with local and state regulation is land use for breweries. Large packaging breweries would, intuitively, be considered an "industrial" use and should be relegated to industrially zoned areas. However, with the burgeoning craft beer movement, brewers often rely heavily on foot traffic, taproom sales, and on-site events and festivals. Each state, county, and city has differing views on whether "brewing" is a "retail," "commercial," "manufacturing," or "industrial" use—the quotation marks are intentional as each state, county and city may have different and distinct definitions for each of these (as well as other land use classifications), and those definitions are often **not** intuitive. Identifying a location at the local level means diligent research into the local land-use and zoning code(s).

- Transportation—Relics of Prohibition-era regulations can be special regulations regarding the transportation of alcohol. Typically this is a state-level concern, through the state's Department of Transportation or equivalent agency. The concern may stem from the fact that alcohol, in sufficient concentration, is of course flammable. While this is clearly not an issue for beer, it may require a specific endorsement or permit from a state agency to avoid running afoul of regulations. This may be true even in states where self-distribution is allowed; it may be necessary to have special permitting or licenses to transport the alcohol that's separate from your permits to produce, distribute, and sell the product.

John Says: "DO NOT sign a lease or buy a building until you are absolutely sure that the zoning is right for what you want to do. If you find out something later, it's not the landlord's fault and it may not be reason enough to get out of a lease or purchase."

- Packaging—Each state has its own requirements and regulations regarding the size and attributes of packaging alcohol. For example, growlers (i.e. a 64 oz. re-sealable container) have become commonplace in most of the country. However, smaller growlers, such as 32 oz. re-sealable containers, are available in some states, but not others. State regulations also vary on what is required for on-demand filling of consumer packaging (such as filling a customer's growler for them to take home to consume); is this allowed versus pre-filling a package like a growler for purchase? Does the state follow the TTB distinction that pre-filled growlers are packaged beers while on-demand filled growlers are merely serving vessels? This can be further complicated by whether or not breweries are allowed to "trade-off" growlers (i.e. give a customer a new-filled growler in part exchange for their empty growler—which is then cleaned and re-used by the brewery). Additionally, technology is moving at a pace that those regulations cannot often keep up. The advent of on-demand filling and sealing of "crowlers" (i.e. typically a 32 oz. non-re-sealable metal/can container) has created a potentially new category for states to regulate. It is important to remember, when looking at state regulations with respect to new technology or packaging, that unfortunately, the alcohol beverage control laws are proscriptive—if it doesn't say that something *is* legal, then by default it is *illegal*.

- Environmental Impact, General—Each state, county, and city has different regulations regarding the environmental impact of manufacturing businesses (in most cases, brewing is considered manufacturing). While it may not normally seem like an issue to a brewer or small business owner, local and state governments are keenly interested in the environmental impact of businesses—even small breweries. For most breweries this is not a tremendous issue as there is little in the way of noxious products or by-products of brewing. But, there may be issues with the business in terms of the structure's watershed, water use, soil, etc., that should be explored in some depth before committing to a location.
- Environmental Impact, Wastewater—In many cases, the main concern in terms of environmental impact is the issue of waste-

water. Brewers are aware that breweries use a tremendous amount of water. Having a good quality water supply is normally of paramount concern. For most municipalities the concern with wastewater is the caustic or other cleaning chemicals that can sometimes come in a "slug" through the system. Consider that for a brewery most discharge is relatively free of cleaning chemicals. However, cleaning multiple tanks over the course of a day may result in a fairly concentrated discharge of caustic or other chemicals in a short period of time—a slug. Slugs of high concentration are a concern because most municipalities treat their water in a series of chemical and microbiological treatment steps. A slug of concentrated chemical wastewater can injure or—in some cases—entirely kill off some of the "bugs," which are beneficial bacteria used in wastewater treatment. In municipal systems that are at or near treatment capacity, a new brewery can cause issues with the ability to treat the rest of the area's wastewater. This should be addressed with the city or county development office.

CHAPTER TEN: LABELING

Arguably the single most influential piece of advertising for brewers, in terms of getting the consumer to see your beer brand on the shelf among all the competition, is making the actual label of the final package stand out.

Because consumers rely on package labeling to determine manufacturer, product attributes, and value, the government—both state and federal—is interested in ensuring some modicum of control over those labels. Both the federal government, as well as all the states, have implemented label requirements, limitations, and other do's and don'ts. The idea behind label regulations is to protect consumers from being deceived or being taken advantage of with respect to quantity, contents, and nature of the product. The regulations are designed to prevent false or misleading statements, anything that might confuse the consumer about the maker of the product, and anything that might be disparaging about competitors.

This book addresses mostly the federal requirements for two reasons:

1. State requirements vary widely and are too voluminous to address in each variation, and
2. Many states have simply adopted federal requirements or have based their states requirements on the federal versions.

But first, what is a label? A label includes anything printed, pasted, stenciled, ebbossed, or otherwise displayed on the outside of any container (like kegs, barrels, bottles, and cans) or promotional product.

MALT BEVERAGE LABELS—FEDERAL

Labels must be approved by the TTB before the product can be sold or distributed. Additionally, most states require copies of the federal approval before state approval can be granted.

But, first, you should understand the basic requirement for federal approval and the system for getting that approval: the Certificate of Label Approval (COLA).

COLAS

The COLA online application is fairly straightforward and is based on how closely you follow the required label information and regulations (http://www.ttb.gov/labeling/laws_and_regs.shtml). Most owners and operators complete this on their own applications. Specifically, the label approval step happens very frequently, every time a new beer is brought to market, so the owner/operator typically wants to have this capability in-house.

Also, once the application is received, planning is critical; the TTB has ninety days to approve or deny the application. This is important because a COLA must be obtained for the product before it may be bottled, packed or removed from the brewery since it's the means for the government to authorize the packaging of the product for consumer (or wholesale) consumption.

For beer, these requirements include making sure the label includes:

- Brand name
- Brewery name and address
- Net contents (in ounces and/or mL)
- Alcohol content
- Other specific requirements (like whether it's imported, the name and address of the importer, whether the product contains FD&C Yellow No. 5, etc.)

John Says: "Get comfortable with this process and the online system. This is one area where I advise clients that they really don't need an attorney's help. Besides, if you're making any real amount of beer, you want to bring this expertise in-house anyway."

And there are similar corresponding requirements for other alcohol products.

In addition to the above requirements, a copy of the label, copies of any lab analysis of the beer, and any formula approvals are also required. If, after review, the application is denied, the Notice of Denial will outline the reasons for that denial. After denial, the brewer may appeal the decision or may correct any deficiencies or issues that led to the denial.

However, even if the COLA is approved, the TTB has the opportunity to change its mind. At any time, with forty-five days' notice, the TTB may revoke a COLA if it finds that the label is not actually in compliance with the regulations or if there are substantial issues with the label. As with a COLA denial, a brewer may appeal the decision.

FEDERAL ALCOHOL ADMINISTRATION ACT (FAA ACT)

The FAA Act is the main source of authority for the federal government to regulate the labeling of alcohol beverages. Some requirements are simple—such as the requirement that kegs and barrels must be labeled with the brewery's name and address. Other requirements are more complex, but all labels for kegs, tap handles, barrels, and bottles must be approved.

All alcohol products sold, shopped, or delivered for sale must be marked, branded, or labeled in compliance with the federal labeling requirements. That is the general rule. However, in most cases, the federal requirement for approval only applies to interstate commerce. That is, if the product is brewed, distributed, and sold only within a single state, then federal approval may not be required. That is the exception to the general rule. On the other hand, many states require federal

John Says: "Even aside from the labeling aspect, read through the FAA Act. It's something you should have at least a passing familiarity with—even if you don't know it chapter and verse."

approval regardless of distribution in order to get state approval—meaning that in those states, even if the beer brewed and sold exclusively within the state, federal approval is still necessary. That is the exception to the exception.

MANDATORY STATEMENTS

The regulations recognize two different "types" of labels: the brand label and separate labels. Think of the brand label as the one with the trade and brand name on it, while the other labels may be ancillary, like on the back of the bottle or bottle neck. There must be a brand label, but separate labels are optional.

The items that must be on the brand label include:

- Brand name
- Class of beverage (beer, ale, porter, etc.)
- Brewery (name and address)
- Net contents in the package (must be fluid ounces, pints, quarts, or gallons—or their fractions—it cannot be listed only in the metric system)
- Alcohol content (if the malt beverage contains alcohol derived from non-beverage ingredients)

John Says: "Think you know what 'class' of beer you make? Think again. These are specific words that have specific meanings in the regulations. And some states' regulations don't always align with the federal terms."

Of this list of requirements for the brand label, "class of beverage" can be the most confusing. The regulation merely says:

> The class of the malt beverage shall be stated and, if desired, the type thereof may be stated. Statements of class and type shall conform to the designation of the product as known to the trade. If the product is not known to the trade under a particular designation, a distinctive or fanciful name, together with an adequate and truthful statement of the composition of the product, shall be stated, and such statement shall be deemed to be a statement of class and type for the purposes of this part. (§27 CFR 7.24a).

That means that class will be whatever the "trade" generally recognizes as correct. But, generally that means "Ale," "Lager," "Porter" or another designation. That is the general rule. However, there is a caveat to that general rule. Specifically, if the class or type is geographic in nature it must either actually conform to the type designated or it must include the term "type" or "American," such as "American Vienna Lager" or "Dortmund Type Lager." That is the exception to the rule. But, there are certain words such as Pilsen, Pilsener, or Pilsner that do not require the "type" or "American" designation; these have become generic and American made beers can be labeled with these without further modification.

The other items that must be included, but may be on any separate label, are:

- Government health warning
- Importer (name and address, if imported)
- Bottler or packer (name and address)
- Alcohol content (if required by state law, may be marked as "alcohol by volume" or as required by state law, but cannot be marked as "ABV")
- If the product contains one of these specific ingredients, then there needs to be a statement to that effect for
    - FD&C Yellow No. 5
    - Sulfites
    - Aspartame

For reference, the Government Health Warning, which must be included, is found at §27 CFR 16.21. It reads:

> **GOVERNMENT WARNING**: (1) According to the Surgeon General, women should not drink alcoholic beverages during pregnancy because of the risk of birth defects. (2) Consumption of alcoholic beverages impairs your ability to drive a car or operate machinery, and may cause health problems.

This warning must be on the label in a "conspicuous and prominent location" and must be shown on a contrasting background, with the first two words emboldened and capitalized. These requirements are very specific and depend on the size of container (see §27 CFR 16.22).

PROHIBITED STATEMENTS

Also, there are certain items that *cannot* be on the label. These include:

- Any misleading brand name
- Any statement that is disparaging of a competitor's products
- Any statement, design, device, or representation which is obscene or indecent
- Any statement, design, device, or representation of or relating to analyses, standards, or tests, irrespective of falsity, which the appropriate TTB officer finds to be likely to mislead the consumer
- Any statement, design, device, or representation of or relating to any guarantee, which the TTB finds to be likely to mislead the consumer
- A trade or brand name that is the name of any living individual of public prominence, or existing private or public organization (there are specifics and exceptions to this general prohibition)
- Any statement, design, device, or representation that tends to create a false or misleading impression that the malt beverage contains distilled spirits
- And many others…

The full list of requirements and prohibitions is located at §27 CFR 7.20-7.29 (https://www.law.cornell.edu/cfr/text/27/part-7/subpart-C). Additionally, and this is one that can cause folks confusion or—at the very least—make them correct a label, the label cannot use the words "strong," "full strength," "high proof," or other similar words to describe the product. But words like "low alcohol," "reduced alcohol," or similar are okay to include.

However, once known, these prohibitions are generally pretty easy and straightforward to avoid. The one that causes the most consternation, however, is the prohibition regarding "obscene or indecent." This particular prohibition is quite subjective and has led to several—often contradictory—pairs of approved labels and rejected labels. https://www.uschamber.com/blog/one-man-approves-every-beer-label-america

It is strongly recommended that anyone designing or submitting labels for federal approval carefully read through, *carefully*, the regulations at §27 CFR 7.1 through §27 CFR 7.81.

FDA AND OTHER LABEL ISSUES

There are also specific requirements and do's and don'ts for words like "organic" and "gluten-free." These have very specific meanings within the law and should be researched thoroughly before being included on a label. So far as the TTB is concerned, the term "organic," for beer is governed under §27 CFR 7.81.

Some alcoholic beverages are considered "beer" for tax purposes even though they may not be malt-based; these beverages may not be subject to TTB labeling jurisdiction. For example, the term "gluten free" may subject the brewery to FDA regulation

John Says: "Just when you think you 'get it'... well, there's more."

under the Federal Food, Drug, and Cosmetic Act, the Fair Packaging and Labeling Act, as well as other FDA regulations

John Says: *"There's a lot of talk about the nutrition information and additional label requirements. Stay tuned, some of this may change in the near future."*

regarding the truthfulness, accuracy, and required statements on labels and packaging. See http://www.fda.gov/Food/FoodIngredientsPackaging for more.

The Food and Drug Administration (FDA, http://www.fda.gov/) is often overlooked as a source of regulation for the alcohol industry. However, because alcohol enters the food supply, the FDA does have a regulatory interest. See http://www.fda.gov/iceci/inspections/iom/ucm122519.htm (section 3.2.8.1) for one example. Additionally, in terms of the FDA, the Food Safety Modernization Act (http://www.fda.gov/Food/GuidanceRegulation/FSMA/default.htm) came very close to having a significant impact on breweries and distillers by requiring spent grain to carry certain risk plans and controls—because the grain entered the food supply when it was sold to farmers as cattle feed. This potential hazard was stemmed by serious industry pressure, but it is likely not the last time that the FDA will have an impact on alcohol production. For example, the FDA has promulgated rules on caffeinated alcohol and beer labeling/menus. So, the FDA is an agency to watch as a place that will have an increasing effect on the regulation of the alcohol industry.

The number of people suffering from celiac disease (sometimes also referred to as gluten intolerance) is such that gluten content in beer has become a significant topic among beer drinkers. So much so that on February 11, 2014, the TTB issued a ruling governing labeling for "gluten-free" beers. Pending a final rule from the FDA, the TTB has indicated that they will not approve a label which is marked "gluten-free" if it has been made from products which initially contained gluten (such as barley, wheat, and rye). They would however allow the phrase

> "[Processed or Treated or Crafted] to remove gluten," together with a qualifying statement to inform consumers that: (1) the product was fermented or distilled from a grain that contains gluten; (2) the gluten content of the product cannot be verified; and (3) the product may contain gluten. TTB believed that the qualifying statement was necessary to avoid misleading consumers and because of the serious health consequences associated with the consumption of gluten by individuals with celiac disease. http://www.ttb.gov/rulings/2014-2.pdf

Also the TTB issued a recent interim guidance (pending a final rule) governing the listing of Nutritional Information on your beer. The TTB is still evaluating the rule they want to propose long term, but in the meantime, they've broadened what's allowable on labels in terms of serving size, alcohol content, and other nutritional information. The TTB is also continuing their stance that

> …any caloric or carbohydrate statement or representation in the labeling and advertising of wines, distilled spirits, and malt beverages will continue to be viewed by the TTB as misleading unless it provides complete information about the calorie, carbohydrate, protein, and fat content of the product http://www.ttb.gov/rulings/2013-2.pdf

Miller64 was the first brand to offer the additional nutritional information in compliance with the guidance from the TTB. Keep in mind that the nutritional information label information is voluntary, not mandatory. So, be on the lookout for more beers to offer additional information about their nutrition.

If the brewery is creating innovative "beers" which may use non-traditional ingredients or wants to make claims regarding certain "loaded" words, the impact of those words and the requirements for labeling should be thoroughly researched and evaluated before committing to those brands, labels, and products.

MALT BEVERAGE LABELS – STATE

As a general rule, all alcohol products must be registered with the state in which they are sold. This registration can take the form of product approval, label approval, or both. States such as North Carolina require that the product itself be approved; that is the trade or brand name, the brewery, and an analysis of the product. And the label must be approved, that is, the actual image of the bottle label or keg ring. Whether the product, the label, or both are required to be approved in the brewery's state, the main issues come from the fact that the state(s) may have different requirements from the TTB. Merely because the TTB has approved the label as meeting the federal label requirements does not mean that the state will approve the same label.

Generally speaking, state requirements cannot be more lenient than federal government requirements, but they can be different in nature or more strict. For example, there have been multiple cases of labels being approved by the TTB and neighboring states, only to be rejected in one state. The most famous examples of this are those where the brewery sued the state (and in some cases won) or have taken action to get the laws or standards changed in the state. Recent examples include:

- Founders Breakfast Stout: http://www.mlive.com/business/west-michigan/index.ssf/2015/08/breakfast_stout_label_michigan.html
- Flying Dog Raging Bitch: http://reason.com/archives/2016/05/23/how-raging-bitch-and-dirty-bastard-escap

These differences between state and federal regulations are often based on a couple of critical distinctions, such as images or words that

- "might appeal to minors" (Alabama)
- "undignified, immodest, or in bad taste" (North Carolina)
- "promotes overconsumption" (Washington)
- "depicts a child or other underage person" (Washington)
- "detrimental to public health, safety and welfare" (Michigan)

First, it is important to understand and comply with federal labeling requirements and regulations—that is a given. Second, the brewery must understand and comply with the brewery's home state labeling requirements and regulations. However, as the world of commerce makes it easier and easier to transcend state borders, it is important to identify those state requirements which are different for neighboring states or for those states where the brewery may ship product.

ADVERTISING

Advertising and labeling are tied closely together in terms of federal and state regulations. Both advertising and labeling regulations at federal and state levels have requirements ("you *must* do these things") and prohibitions ("you *must not* do these things"). This chapter will focus on the federal issues but will also give some state examples or general rules, as appropriate.

One thing to consider when thinking about advertising for alcohol is the entire background of the framework for post-Prohibition alcohol laws. Specifically, when Prohibition was repealed, there was still a strong desire to ensure that manufacturers didn't have too much power over retail sales. At that time, manufacturers were seen as the large economic powerhouse that had far more resources and backing than either wholesalers or retailers. As a result, the laws were structured to restrict the abilities of the manufacturer to wield influence over the retail outlets. Side note: reducing that influence was the major driver in inserting a required "middle tier" in the three-tier system, so wholesalers could act as an intermediary between the "large and powerful" manufacturers and the "small and independent" retailers.

When talking about influence, more than mere ownership is at stake. The post-Prohibition laws and regulations explicitly prevent a manufacturer from owning a retailer, with some exceptions carved out for small breweries, etc. Everyone is familiar with the idea that you cannot have a "tied house" in the U.S., i.e. where a brewery like MillerCoors would own a chain of MillerCoors bars. But in post-Prohibition America, the legislators, regulators, and lobbyists had other worries about "influence," as well. In addition to ownership, regulators were concerned about manufacturers leveraging economic, social, or marketing influence to pressure retailers (or wholesalers) into an unfair advantage. As a result, there are a whole host of regulations about what manufacturers, and to some extent retailers, can and can't do in the marketplace. These regulations are all aimed at "leveling the playing field" between manufacturers (of any size) and retailers (of any size).

John Says: "If you don't know where you've been, it's hard to figure out where you're going. So, it's important to understand why things (especially laws) are as they are."

In trying to "level the playing field," legislators look beyond the "tied-house" prohibition to areas of economic influence, such as advertising. With respect to advertising, we see prohibitions on manufacturers paying for advertising for retailers and manufacturers paying for giveaways to be used by retailers, etc. These activities are captured under the umbrella of Commercial Bribery. I always thought "Commercial Bribery" was very mobster, Al Capone, sorta sounding. But really, beer distributors do this all the time (and are regularly caught and fined).

COMMERCIAL BRIBERY

It may seem odd to discuss Commercial Bribery as part of advertising, but this portion of the industry is where most violations occur. The issue is when a manufacturer (or a wholesaler for that matter) provides something of value to the retailer in exchange for consideration or purchasing of product. Examples of Commercial Bribery include when a manufacturer or wholesaler:

- Loans a jockey-box to a retailer for a festival
- Purchases a kegerator for a bar so their beer can be sold
- Sponsors a giveaway for a restaurant
- Provides t-shirts or promotional materials for a retailer
- Performs services that the retailer would otherwise have to pay for themselves *line cleaning etc,*

All of these tend to create a competitive advantage for the brewer or wholesaler. Any of them can create an incentive for the retailer to favor one product over another.

Commercial Bribery is prohibited and generally applies to transactions between "industry members" (such as manufacturers or wholesalers) and "trade buyers" (such as retailers or, in some cases, wholesalers). The industry member cannot give "something of value" to trade buyers in exchange for the purchase of products. Specifically, §27 CFR 10.21 says (quoting directly here):

John Says: "The federal (and most states) call it 'Commercial Bribery,' but most people know it as 'Pay to Play.'"

> It is unlawful for an industry member, directly or indirectly or through an affiliate, to induce a trade buyer to purchase the industry member's products, to the complete or partial exclusion of products sold or offered for sale by other persons in interstate or foreign commerce, by offering or giving a bonus, premium, compensation, or other thing of value to any officer, employee, or representative of the trade buyer. The bonus, premium, compensation, or other thing of value need not be offered or given for the purpose

of directly inducing a trade buyer to purchase from the seller, but rather is applicable if an industry member induces officers, employees or representatives of the trade buyer to promote sales of the industry member's products and thereby indirectly induces the trade buyer to purchase from the industry member.

In plain English this means at both the federal and local level, there are a slew of exceptions to this general prohibition. For example, if someone came into a retail grocery store and offered to rearrange the shelves or provide a shelf layout that showcases all the beer, that would be something that a grocery store employee would otherwise have to do, so it's a cost savings to the grocery store and "something of value." And, remember, "something of value" = "commercial bribery" if you're not careful. However, there are several specific exceptions carved out for this type of activity. What about when a wholesaler pays for a restaurant's beer tap lines to be cleaned? Again, it is a cost savings so it is "something of value," but again there is an exception carved out for this activity—meaning it's okay and not considered "commercial bribery."

Why is this discussed under "Advertising?" Because this is often where the issues creep up. As a manufacturer, can you loan one of your customers a jockey-box for their event? Can you promote a "tap takeover" on social media or with flyers? Can you sponsor a tournament at a restaurant? Can you give your local bar glassware with your brewery's logo on it? When the you're aggressively trying to promote your product, it can be easy to trigger Commercial Bribery without intending to do so.

It is critically important to know what sorts of activities and items are allowed at the federal and state level so as not to cross the line to create an issue with Commercial Bribery or appear to unduly influence or risk retailer independence.

FEDERAL ADVERTISING REGULATIONS—FAA ACT

The types and content of advertising that work for marketing and selling most goods and services are sometimes not allowed for marketing and selling alcohol. What can and cannot be said about the manufacturer or the product is heavily regulated at both the federal and state levels. The Federal Alcohol Administration Act ("FAA Act") starts to lay the groundwork for many of the specific prohibitions and requirements that are currently part of the U.S. alcohol regulation scheme. In §27 USC 205(f), the FAA Act prohibits any publishing or dissemination of any advertisement for alcohol beverages that deceives the consumer as to the nature, content, or identity of the product being advertised. Misleading, false, or otherwise deceitful statements are prohibited from any alcohol advertising. So, to make a claim in advertising an alcohol product, the claim must be either (a) objectively true and provable or (b) "mere puffery."

Here, "mere puffery" are statements meant to "puff up" or sell the product without making a specific claim. For example, a used car salesperson might say, "This here is the best used car in the entire state!" Now, no reasonable person would actually believe that that particular car can be shown to be the "best" car in the entire state. The salesperson is just "puffing," and his statement is "mere puffery." If you later found a better car, you couldn't go back and sue him because he was lying.

So, a brewery might say they've got the "best IPA on the planet," and that would not be illegal; it is "mere puffery" in its advertising. However, if a brewery advertised that it had the "lowest calorie IPA in the country," that claim would be either demonstrably true or illegal.

In addition, under the FAA Act, disparaging statements about competitors are prohibited. So a brewery could say that your "macro lagers don't have a lot of flavor," and they'd be okay. But a brewery could not say, "Budweiser tastes like horse piss," and still be okay. Pretty sure they'd get in trouble with the FAA, the FTC, and AB-InBev too.

John Says: "What's the difference between a 'claim' and 'mere puffery' for advertising purposes? It's tough to say. It depends on each case's specific circumstances. It depends on whether a reasonable person would believe the statement—not a beer-geek-reasonable-person but your average-consumer-reasonable-person."

The FAA Act also prohibits any advertising that includes obscene or indecent statements or images, though the definition of "obscene" or "indecent" is subjective and can shift over time. Specifically, there are also shades of this issue cropping up from time to time at the state level where states vary in what's allowed in advertising even if their respective statutes and regulations are written very similarly.

MANDATORY STATEMENTS

To a large extent, this is covered under Labeling, but for any advertising, the advertisement must include the name and address of the brewery (or bottler, packer, wholesaler, or importer—whoever is responsible for the advertisement) and the class of product (which matches the class on the product label). Details on this are at §27 CFR 7.52, including the exception quoted here:

> If an advertisement refers to a general malt beverage line or all of the malt beverage products of one company, whether by the company name or by the brand name common to all the malt beverages in the line, the only mandatory information necessary is the name and address of the responsible advertiser. This exception does not apply where only one type of malt beverage is marketed under the specific brand name advertised. §27 CFR 7.52(c)(1).

Oh, and because it is the government, it gets specific about how it should be written (§27 CFR 7.53), quoting again:

> (a) Statements required under [these sections] of this part that appear in any written, printed, or graphic advertisement shall be in lettering or type size sufficient to be conspicuous and readily legible.
> (b) In the case of signs, billboards, and displays, the name and address of the permittee responsible for the advertisement may appear in type size of lettering smaller than the other mandatory information, provided such information can be ascertained upon closer examination of the sign or billboard.
> (c) Mandatory information shall be so stated as to be clearly a part of the advertisement and shall not be separated in any manner from the remainder of the advertisement.

(d) Mandatory information for two or more products shall not be stated unless clearly separated.

(e) Mandatory information shall be so stated in both the print and audiovisual media that it will be readily apparent to the persons viewing the advertisement.

Generally, mandatory statements are easy to comply with. The issue for these—and the regulators—is that it is very clear who is doing the advertising and who is benefiting from the advertising. This limits the ability of a large company to pay for advertising of other people's products or for the advertising of brand names that do not readily identify the manufacturer (think about "ShockTop" versus "AB-InBev").

PROHIBITED STATEMENTS

Prohibited statements are more challenging to comply with. Unless the advertiser is intimately aware of these regulations and how they are interpreted, it can be easy to run afoul of them. §27 CFR 7.54 contains the list of federally prohibited statements. It is an extensive list. Here's a quick summary of the type of statements that are prohibited:

John Says: "Believe it or not, this is the shortened 'quick' list."

- False statements ("false or untrue in any material particular, or that, irrespective of falsity, directly, or by ambiguity, omission, or inference, or by the addition of irrelevant, scientific or technical matter, tend to create a misleading impression")

- Statements disparaging of a competitor or their products
- Statements, devices, designs, or representations that are obscene or indecent
- Any guarantee which the TTB has found to be "likely to mislead the consumer"
- Any implication that the product is "approved" or in compliance with any federal, state, or municipal authorization, law, or regulation
- "The words 'bonded,' 'bottled in bond,' 'aged in bond,' 'bonded age,' 'bottled under customs supervision,' or phrases containing these or synonymous terms which imply governmental supervision over production, bottling, or packing"
- Statements that tend to create a false or misleading impression that the malt beverage contains distilled spirits (there are a couple of exceptions to this)
- Statements inconsistent with labeling
- Any statement including the words "strong," "full strength," "high proof" or other similar words where that statement tends to relate to the alcohol strength of the product
- Statements which relate to health or health claims of the product
- Statements that could create confusion between brands among consumers
- Any representation of flags, seals, coats of arms, crests, or other insignia of the United States, the armed forces, or other group such that the use of that representation would lead consumers to believe that the product was produced in accordance with the specifications or approval of that government, group, family, organization, or person

- *Per se* deceptive statements—specifically "subliminal or similar techniques"

This is a condensed and paraphrased version of the code, and it is strongly recommended that anyone creating advertising material read the code for themselves and look at the way different agencies and courts have interpreted these prohibitions.

The key with the prohibited statements is to remember that these apply to all advertising, including coasters, promotional giveaways, labels, websites, posters, etc. And, these apply whether the product crosses state lines or not. Owners often forget to be mindful of these prohibitions when creating a new website, or a new growler look, or an advertisement in their local paper.

There is an "upside." If the advertisement is in question as to whether it is "okay" as far as the requirements and prohibitions go, the TTB can "pre-approve" the advertisement. The TTB, on request, will "clear" an advertisement after reviewing it against the statutes. This process, however, is on request. Ordinarily, the TTB does not have to approve advertising.

SOCIAL MEDIA

There are additional topics with respect to advertising do's and don'ts, and those will be discussed shortly, but the above section is a good segue to a growing issue: social media as advertising.

The TTB provides guidance to the alcohol industry through "Industry Circulars." Industry Circulars provide insight on how the TTB views certain situations, upcoming issues, and how recent court decisions or laws will be implemented. In

Industry Circular 2013-1, the TTB stated unequivocally that social media is advertising as far as the TTB and alcohol beverages are concerned. Here's one of the few times your author will use an equation:

Social Media = Advertising

Regarding social networking, specifically platforms like Facebook and LinkedIn, the TTB says:

John Says: *"I hope you can follow me on this technical, engineering equation."*

A social network service is a service, platform, or site where users communicate with one another and share media, such as pictures, videos, music, and blogs, with other users. Many industry members have created pages on social network services for their company and/or a particular brand. These are sometimes referred to as "pages" or "fan pages," and users of the social network service can become "fans" of the company or brand and creating a link between their own page and the fan page. The purpose of fan pages is to increase brand awareness and loyalty by allowing industry members to communicate with consumers in an interactive manner. TTB considers fan pages for alcohol beverage products or companies and any content regarding alcohol beverage products posted to the pages by the industry member to fall under the category of "any other media" in TTB's regulatory definition of advertisement, and therefore the fan pages are subject to the provisions of the FAA Act and TTB regulations.

And, (it gets better!):

Because TTB considers industry member fan pages for alcohol beverages to be advertisements, all mandatory statements required by the regulations (in §§ 4.62, 5.63, and 7.52) must be included on them. TTB views the entire fan page (i.e., the "home" page and all sub or tabbed pages directly associated with the "home" page) as one advertisement, so mandatory statements need only appear once on the fan page, either on the "home" page or on any sub or tabbed pages directly associated with the "home" page.

John Says: "Social media is advertising. Don't just type stuff without thinking about it first. Anything you say on social media…well, would you say it to your state regulator?"

The circular goes on to address video sharing websites (i.e. YouTube and the like), blogs, "microblogs" (such as Twitter and Tumblr), mobile apps, and Quick Response (or "QR") codes. In every case, the TTB has determined that these sources of social media interactions meet the threshold of "advertising." That means that the mandatory statements above, must be included somewhere in the "advertisement." In Circular 2013-1, the TTB does provide guidance on where and how the statements should be included based on each type of social media, but these are merely guidelines. Not all social media is addressed in the document (Vine, SnapChat, etc.). The circular is included in the supplemental

John Says: "Wait a minute. Vine's dead now, right? MySpace? I can't keep up with all these fancy interweb things."

material, but every brewery owner, brewer, marketer, salesperson, and manager should read it for themselves.

Some states are also considering guidelines on social media as advertising. As these develop around the country, breweries should make sure to pay attention to those in their own jurisdiction, but also in neighboring jurisdictions as they seek to expand distribution or marketing. Additionally, because state focus on advertising can be somewhat different—or can impose additional requirements on the manufacturer—state guidance on social media use will be particularly important.

FEDERAL ADVERTISING REGULATIONS—FTC

The Federal Trade Commission (FTC) also has an interest in protecting consumers. Primarily, the FTC is concerned with unfair and deceptive advertising and trade practices. And, any manufacturer must comply with both the FAA Act (i.e. the TTB) and the FTC regulations. Also, the FTC maintains what is called "concurrent jurisdiction" with the TTB on advertising—meaning that the FTC can independently investigate or prosecute regarding an advertisement even if the TTB believes there to be no violation, and vice versa.

An additional area of focus for the FTC relates to the target of the advertising. Any advertisement which may encourage underage drinking or irresponsible behavior is prohibited by the enabling statutes for the FTC. So any advertisement that looks like it could potentially encourage underage drinking or irresponsible behavior will receive heightened scrutiny.

Unlike the TTB, the FTC does not issue opinions or approve

advertisements. The FTC is strictly reactionary in this respect. They will only notify the advertiser in the event of a violation.

STATE ADVERTISING REGULATIONS

As with labeling, state advertising regulations are often related to, but not exactly congruent with federal regulations. For example, in addition to the federal prohibited statements, North Carolina also imposes a prohibition on any advertisement that depicts "nudity or is obscene or indecent," and any picture or illustration "depicting the use of alcoholic beverages in a scene which is undignified, immodest or in bad taste" as well as others. These additions are clearly above and beyond the federal requirements and are, often times, much more subjective. States tend to reflect, much more so than the federal government, the prevailing public opinion regarding alcohol, vice, advertising, and government control.

Additionally, whereas advertising does not have to be pre-approved by the TTB, some states require that advertising be pre-approved by the state authority (typically the ABC) for any use in the state. The general rule is that, if the advertisement complies with the applicable state regulations, then it will likely comply with federal requirements. State requirements tend to be more stringent than federal requirements, if they differ at all.

VOLUNTARY ADVERTISING REGULATIONS

The industry, as a whole, has a history of working cooperatively with respect to major industry issues. Advertising is just such an issue. At a national level, both the Brewers Association and the Brewers Institute have adopted voluntary guidelines for advertising. These guidelines address issues like not condoning drinking and driving, excessive consumption, etc. These guidelines are not, in and of themselves, sufficient to ensure that advertisements are within the letter of the law, but they are good places to start for best practices and advisory examples.

Additionally, more and more state brewing guilds are taking an active role with state ABCs to identify ambiguities and provide guidance to state manufacturers and retailers.

CHAPTER ELEVEN: DISTRIBUTION AGREEMENTS AND FRANCHISE LAW

Distribution agreements and franchise law (and its reform) are hot topics right now in the craft beverage industry. To understand alcohol distribution and franchise laws, you need to understand the genesis of the three-tier system (http://www.nbwa.org/about/what-beer-distributor). The three-tier system applies equally to beer, wine, and distilled spirits. This book has already provided an overview of the three-tier system, so please refer to Chapter Seven for more detail on how the pieces interact. For the purposes of this discussion,

John Says: "I've said it before, take all you've learned about the law and throw it away when it comes to alcohol. Franchise law, especially for a has special rules."

we'll focus on beer. But, be aware that the principles are the same for wine and spirits, though the actors (like the state in the case of the distribution and retail sales of distilled spirits) may be different and vary from state to state.

QUICK SUMMARY OF THE THREE-TIER SYSTEM

The three-tier system was implemented by states after Prohibition. Prior to Prohibition, a manufacturer could produce the alcohol, distribute it, and sell it anywhere they wanted. There are pictures, stories, and anecdotes of going to the local Schlitz bar and ordering beer (not much of a choice as they only carried Schlitz beer). See http://forgottenchicago.com/features/tied-houses/ for an example. These tied houses would also offer lunches, hot meals, entertainment—almost anything to draw in patrons. This led some bars (and breweries) to develop the reputation for drunkenness, debauchery, brawls, and rowdiness—all before two in the afternoon.

John Says: "Is the three-tier system still relevant? Some say yes, some say no. But, when we look at how large some corporate conglomerates are—there's a good argument that the public still needs some level of protection."

The tied-house bars could compete on price and had a huge impact on the local market, starving out smaller, independent bars or breweries. After Prohibition, the states wanted to ensure that the large beer manufacturers could not wield the local economic power that they used to. Enter the three-tier system. It requires that manufacturers sell their product to distributors (wholesalers) who distribute and sell the product to retailers (bars, etc.) who sell to the public. The idea being that no tier member can own a business in another tier. So, places like Schlitz would have to sell their beer to a local or regional distributor who then would sell the product to whichever account (retailers) would pay for it, regardless of the other beers sold there. It's one of the reasons why you can go into your local pub and see Miller, Budweiser, and other brands all served side by side.

WHY FRANCHISE LAWS?

One of the real issues in the three-tier system is that the distributor does most of the "sales" for a brewery. The large international breweries don't have the infrastructure to send sales representatives to each bar to sell their beer. Even if they tried, the practice would not be sustainable. One can imagine a bar getting visited by a rep from AB-InBev, then another from MillerCoors, then another from Yuengling, another from Sam Adams, another from Sierra Nevada, another from Pabst, another from Mike's Hard Lemonade, another from … each asking for that week's keg orders, case orders, and wanting to talk about the latest promotion for their brand? No, it's simpler and far easier for one or two distributor reps to visit a bar and take orders for multiple brands and breweries (a portfolio of represented brands).

John Says: "There is a place and value for the wholesale tier—even just from a business perspective."

So, the expectation of distributors is to invest time and money in equipment (trucks and cold storage) and sales (people, training, promotions and events) to sell someone else's brand for them. Sure, they receive a fairly significant return in the form of the wholesaler's markup, but they run the risk of investing a lot in building a brand only to have it yanked away from them by a fickle manufacturer. Against large brewery-manufacturers, the local beer distributor was at a serious economic disadvantage. So, the beer and alcohol franchise laws began to take shape.

Just like McDonald's or other national franchises, the distributor takes on the brand of another (the brewery in this case) and builds the brand and sells the brand's product. But, unlike a McDonald's franchise, the alcohol franchise laws put a system in place to protect the franchisee outside of the franchise or license agreement—even overwriting the franchise agreement terms. This type of regulation is seen in only three industries—most notably, oil/gas, automobiles, and alcohol. For example, think of a local Chevrolet car dealership. Now think about what would happen if GMC decided that they wanted a different dealer to have that franchise, effective in sixty days. The dealership would be nearly ruined between inventory, service, and not having the same brand that they have built their community reputation on. The same analysis was applied to beer distributors and gas station owners.

SHIFTS IN INDUSTRY ECONOMICS

However, post-Prohibition also saw industry consolidation among the breweries and distributors. Bigger breweries bought up smaller breweries and got even bigger. National and international brands became commonplace. At the same time, distributors also starting expanding and buying up adjacent distributors, creating large regional distribution networks with multiple warehouses, fleets of trucks, and armies of salespeople. Distributors grew so large there are several that are worth far in excess of their flagship brand/brewery (like AB-InBev). For the most part, there is a serious question as to whether there is any significant economic power or bargaining position disparity between manufacturers and distributors—and hence no need for the franchise law framework. In fact, there's good evidence that for the vast majority of breweries (by number, not by volume), the bargaining and economic power is much stronger for the multimillion dollar regional distributor than for the two-to-five person local brewery. What I mean is, any one distributor is probably larger and has more market power than most small breweries they work with.

John Says: "Beer distribution and franchise lawsuits regularly involve multimillion dollar settlements or verdicts and billion dollar companies."

DISTRIBUTION RIGHTS

The general rule in the U.S. is that a manufacturer cannot distribute its product to retailers, nor sell it as a retailer to customers. That is, the U.S. does not allow tied houses. By way of contrast, the UK still allows tied houses (http://en.wikipedia.org/wiki/Tied_house), but also has independent bars.

The general rule means that for a manufacturer to sell its product to anyone, it must sell to a distributor. Exceptions to the general rule have been carved out over time. For example, in

North Carolina, breweries may self-distribute their beer and may operate a retail outlet. Each state determines its own approach to this issue. Some states require a brewery to always use a beer distributor, others allow for some self-distribution, and some states even regulate the sales of beer at the brewery differently from the rest of the brewery's sales.

A key item to remember when thinking about distribution rights is the underlying relationship. A brewery owns a brand. The distributor represents and sells that brand to other accounts. The relationship is essentially a trademark licensing agreement. A brewery allows a distributor a limited right to use the brewery's mark (i.e. the brand) to sell the product to additional accounts. So, distribution rights are basically the rights to use the mark and sell the product (and have the brewery produce enough to satisfy the created demand).

John Says: "Most states have enacted some exemption or 'carve-out' to allow breweries to sell their own product at least at their location. Many (or most?) allow some level of self-distribution."

Based on that analysis, distributors often see distribution rights (to a portfolio of products) as portable. One brewery or brand may be traded between distributors or sold off to another distributor to balance a portfolio or to further sales figures. Although the agreement is based on the use of the mark/brand and selling the product, the laws are designed to protect the marketer/seller (distributor) rather than the manufacturer (brewery).

SELF-DISTRIBUTION

As mentioned above, some states allow self-distribution. Some, like North Carolina, place a cap on the amount of beer a brewery can self-distribute. In North Carolina, a brewery may self-distribute only if they produce fewer than 25,000 BBLs annually (~788,000 gallons). To sell any amount above that cap, the brewery must engage a distributor. See http://www.ncleg.net/EnactedLegislation/Statutes/HTML/BySection/Chapter_18B/GS_18B-1104.html

Self-distribution caps, in most states that allow self distribution, are under attack. These caps are viewed as one of the items of franchise and alcohol laws that are anachronistic from post-Prohibition.

Remember too that any brewery that is self-distributing is also subject to the limitations and prohibitions imposed on wholesalers as well as breweries. This means that the self-distributing brewery may not violate state statutes for:

- Credit: how are late invoices addressed? Is there an impermissible relationship created by one of you "extending credit" to the other?
- Transporting beer: does the state have limitations on when/how beer can be delivered or to whom?
- Returns: does the state have restrictions on when, where, or how returns can be taken back from retailers?
- Storage: is non-tax-paid beer stored correctly (at the brewery or at a bonded warehouse)?

Also, in terms of self-distribution, understand that this means that the more production and distribution the company takes on, the less the company looks like a brewery and more it begins to look like a trucking company. To adequately self-distribute substantial amounts of beer (for example, beyond 8,000-10,000 BBLs/year) requires a substantial investment in vehicles, maintenance, and people, as well as additional insurance/liability. Though the margins are better for self-distributing, because the costs are kept in-house, it can also be a distraction from the main business of making beer.

SELF-DISTRIBUTION AND FRANCHISE LAWS

The interplay between self-distribution and franchise laws is complex. Those states that allow some self-distribution have statutory and regulatory schemes in place to carve out exceptions from the general three-tier system to allow for breweries to self-distribute. The problem often arises when a brewery signs up with a distributor then decides they want their distribution rights back. In general, distribution agreements are extremely difficult to get out of. Some state schemes allow for a brewery to "buy back" their distribution rights, but short of some special procedure in the statutes, generally the distribution rights belong to the distributor after a relationship is formed.

John Says: "If you don't deal with this stuff for a living, it can quickly make your head hurt."

Additionally, it does not take a lot to form an agreement with a distributor. Forget almost all you thought you knew about contracts—that knowledge doesn't apply with franchise laws. In some cases, a written agreement is not necessary at all. The statutory framework in some states almost completely overwrites any written agreement between the parties. There are some distributors who use a single sheet of paper for the distribution agreement—an agreement that represents potentially millions of dollars of revenue and the lifeblood of the brewery. In some cases, the mere fact that a distributor is allowed to distribute the brewery's product may be enough to show that the brewery has entered into a distributor relationship and is now subject to all the laws that come with that relationship.

John Says: "Some folks get indignant very quickly and talk about how small breweries are 'kept down' by franchise laws. Well, that may be true, but they're also protected by franchise laws from undue influence of larger (big $) breweries."

THE UNEXPECTED ROLE OF THE DISTRIBUTOR

The sales role of the distributor was addressed in the first discussion of the three-tier system in Chapter Seven. But there is another aspect of the distributor relationship that is not intuitive to the uninitiated. Specifically, distributors routinely trade, buy, or sell brands between themselves on a regular basis. Generally speaking, distributors will have a flagship brand or brewery (like AB-InBev or MillerCoors) and then will buy and sell brands around that flagship to their best business advantage.

As a retailer, this means that instead of buying Yuengling from Jimmy at XYZ Distributor like last month, this month the retailer is buying Yuengling from Joyce at LMNO Distributor. This can be unsettling and sometimes confusing for the retailers. But it is far worse for the brand owners.

If you're a brand owner whose product has recently been sold by a distributor, the brewery no longer has the sales representative you have spent time training on the beer and going to events and festivals with to promote the beer. The brewery now has a new sales representative for the beer with a new distributor who may or may not have the same focus or investment in the brand as the previous distributor. The brewery then has to start over getting a new sales rep trained on the beer and "pumped up" about selling the brand (as opposed to the other eighteen brands that that sales rep sells).

John Says: "A good motto to keep in mind: don't piss off your distributor. They are often the first exposure a brewery has to a retailer."

In some cases, there is a saving grace in this buying-and-selling-of-brands arrangement in that a distributor cannot sell the brewery's brand to another distributor without the brewery's consent, but that requirement varies from state to state. The bad news is that it may not be a good business practice to withhold consent—a brewery does not want to be in a relationship with a distributor that wants to get rid of them but is forced to keep them. That sort of situation can lead to negative brand treatment, lack of sales and brand support, and overall dismal brand representation in the market.

STATUTORY FRAMEWORK

The North Carolina alcohol franchise laws can be found at NCGS §18B-1300 through 1309 (http://www.ncga.state.nc.us/EnactedLegislation/Statutes/PDF/ByArticle/Chapter_18B/Article_13.pdf). For the purposes of this discussion, the North Carolina statue will be used. Some states are much more lenient, and some are more strict. The hope is that within these pages it will be obvious the types of issues that come up with a distribution agreement. The basic structure of the statute is (paraphrased and emphasis added):

- A franchise agreement is a commercial relationship between a wholesaler and supplier of a definite or *indefinite duration*, whether written or *oral*, including:
    - where a wholesaler is granted the right to offer and sell the brands of malt beverages offered by the supplier; or
    - where a supplier grants to a wholesaler a license to use a trade name, trademark, service mark or related characteristic and in which there is a community of interest in the marking of the products of the supplier by lease or otherwise.
- A franchise agreement *exists* when:
    - The supplier *has shipped malt beverages to a wholesaler or accepted an order* for malt beverages from the wholesaler;
    - A wholesaler has paid or the supplier has accepted payment for an order of malt beverages intended for sale within this state;

John Says: "Do you see how easy it is to form a distributor agreement (i.e. a franchise agreement) without even meaning to?"

- The supplier and wholesaler have filed with the commission a distribution agreement as required by G.S. 18B-1303; or
- A supplier acquires the right to manufacture a malt beverage product, or the trade name for such product, or the right to distribute a product, for which a wholesaler has a franchise agreement.

- No supplier may provide by a distribution agreement for the distribution of a brand to more than one wholesaler for the same territory. A wholesaler shall not distribute any brand of malt beverage to a retailer whose premises are located outside the territory specified in the wholesaler's distribution agreement for that brand.

John Says: "That's a pretty low standard for performance. So, it can be hard to prove that the distributor is treating you worse than they should."

- A wholesaler *shall service all retail permit holders within his designated territory without discrimination* and shall make a *good faith effort to make available* to each retail permit holder in the territory each brand of malt beverage which the wholesaler has been authorized to distribute in that area.
- A franchise agreement shall not, either expressly or by implication or in its operation, establish or maintain the resale price of any brand of malt beverages by a wholesaler.

- A supplier cannot:
    - Coerce or attempt to coerce or persuade a wholesaler to violate any laws.

- Unless authorized by 18B-1305(a1), *alter in a material way, terminate, fail to renew, or cause a wholesaler to resign from, a franchise agreement with a wholesaler except for good cause* and with the notice required by G.S. 18B-1305.

John Says: "So, you're also not allowed to end or alter the agreement after you have (accidentally) created it."

- Withdraw money from or otherwise access a wholesaler's bank accounts without the wholesaler's consent.
- Present a franchise agreement, amendment, or renewal to a wholesaler *that attempts to waive compliance with any provision of this article* or that requires a wholesaler to waive compliance with any provision of this article. A wholesaler entering into *a franchise agreement containing provisions in conflict with this article shall not be deemed to waive rights* protected by, or in compliance with, any provision of this article.
- Induce or coerce, or attempt to induce or coerce, any wholesaler to assent to any franchise agreement, amendment, or renewal that does not comply with this Article and the laws of this state.

John Says: "AND you can't even agree NOT to be bound by the statute."

- Coerce or attempt to coerce a wholesaler, or its designated or anticipated successor, to sign a franchise agreement, amendment, or renewal to a franchise agreement by threatening to refuse to approve or delay issuing an approval for the sale, transfer, or merger of a wholesaler's business.

- Terminate, cancel, or non-renew or attempt to terminate, cancel, or non-renew a franchise agreement on the basis that the wholesaler fails to agree or consent to an amendment to the franchise agreement.
- *Prohibit a wholesaler from distributing the product of any other supplier,* except that a supplier may prohibit a wholesaler from distributing the product of another supplier if reasonable grounds exist for prohibiting the wholesaler's acquisition of the product and the acquisition would result in the wholesaler acquiring 80% or more by volume of all malt beverage products sold in the territory being acquired at the time of the acquisition.
- *Refuse to approve or require a wholesaler to terminate a brand manager or successor manager without good cause.* A supplier has good cause only if the person designated for approval by the wholesaler fails to meet reasonable standards and qualifications.
- Discriminate in price, allowance, rebate, refund, payment term, commission, discount, or service between wholesalers licensed in North Carolina.

John Says: "So, you also have to treat all wholesalers equally. Statutes like this take away a LOT of your freedom to contract."

- Good cause means the wholesaler fails to comply with provisions of the agreement which are reasonable, material, not unconscionable, and which are not discriminatory when compared with the provisions imposed, by their terms or in the manner of enforcement, on other similarly situated wholesalers by the supplier.
- A "small" brewery's authorization to distribute its own malt

beverage products shall revert back to the brewery, *in the absence of good cause*, following the fifth business day after confirmed receipt of written notice of such reversion by the brewery to the wholesaler. *The brewery shall pay the wholesaler fair market value for the distribution rights for the affected brand. For purposes of this subsection, "fair market value" means the highest dollar amount* at which a seller would be willing to sell and a buyer willing to buy at the time the self-distribution rights revert back to the brewery, after each party has been provided all information relevant to the transaction.

- Good cause does not include:
    - The failure or refusal of the wholesaler to engage in any trade practice, conduct or activity which would violate federal or state law.
    - The failure or refusal of the wholesaler to take any action which would be contrary to the provisions of this article.
    - *A change in the ownership of the supplier* or the acquisition by another supplier of the brewery, brand or trade name or trademark, or acquisition of the right to distribute a product, from the original supplier.
    - *Sale or transfer of the rights to manufacture, distribute, or use the trade name of the brand to a successor supplier.*
    - *Failure of the wholesaler to meet standards of operation or performance* that have been imposed or revised unilaterally by the supplier without a fair opportunity for the individual wholesaler to bargain as to the terms, unless the supplier has implemented the standards on a national basis and those standards are consistently applied to all similarly situated North Carolina

wholesalers in a nondiscriminatory manner.
- The establishment of a franchise *agreement between a wholesaler and another supplier*, or similar acquisition by a wholesaler of the right to distribute a brand of another supplier.
- The desire of a supplier to consolidate its franchises.

- NCGS §18B-1306 & 1307 deal with remedies and mergers of wholesale businesses, respectively.
- The provisions of this article *shall be part of all franchise agreements* as defined in NCGS §18B-1302 and *may not be altered by the parties*. A wholesaler's rights under this article *may not be waived or superseded by the provisions of a written franchise agreement* prepared by a supplier that are in any way inconsistent with or contrary to any part of this article. The rights of a wholesaler under this article shall remain in effect regardless of a provision in a written franchise agreement prepared by a supplier that purports to require arbitration of a franchise dispute or that purports to require legal remedies to be sought in a different jurisdiction.

John Says: "The worst reason for screwing up is that you didn't bother to look up the law."

So, these items/terms are incorporated in the agreement between the brewery and the distributor whether they want them there or not. Additionally, if there's a conflict between the agreement and these terms—these terms overwrite the agreement. Almost nowhere else in American law is this type of economic and contractual freedom stripped from the transaction parties. And, if the deal that was made is a bad one, there is almost no way for the brewery to get out of the agreement unless the distributor meets one of the "for cause" termination provisions—which are really difficult to do or prove.

Again, this is only an example (based on North Carolina's statutes), but each state has some variation on this plan. It is vitally important that a brewery understand its state's franchise laws before contemplating a distributorship agreement.

DEVELOPING A FRANCHISE/DISTRIBUTOR AGREEMENT

As is clear from the emphasis added above, sections of this statutory framework are wholly unique and would—in many cases—shock the conscience of traditional transactional attorneys. "What do you mean you can't contract for rights or their waiver?" "What do you mean I have to buy back my own trademark rights?" "What do you mean that I can't ever terminate my contract without good cause?"

It is critically important that a distribution agreement be drafted carefully and with a copy of the statute in hand for reference. Most state statutes point to "reasonableness" at several points. What is reasonable is often not clear under the statutes. But, the terms of a contract agreed to at the initiation of the agreement are probably a good indicator of reasonableness between the parties. Therefore, some points to consider when evaluating a distribution or "franchise" agreement include:

- Quality Requirements. Be sure to incorporate any quality requirements that are critical to the client. Examples include:
  - How often does the distributor do periodic shelf audits or staling reports to ensure freshness?
  - What happens when product is returned?
  - How are complaints investigated?
  - Who has the responsibility (or ability) to manage the retailer or end customer interaction?
- Service Requirements. Examples of potentially reasonable requirements might include:
  - First In First Out (FIFO) inventory management
  - Temperature maintenance (cold chain) requirements
  - Critical accounts and customers (for example, the bar next to the brewery or bars at the beach)—any account that may be especially important to the brewery.
  - Specific activity or support (such as beer dinners, festivals, or other promotional events)
- "For Cause" Termination. While the specific items or reasons that a brewery can terminate for cause are specified by statute, the degree to which those items are issues may be up for negotiation in an agreement. For example:
  - Are more than a threshold number of customer, product, or service complaints attributable to the wholesaler sufficient to show failure to comply with a reasonable standard of the agreement?

John Says: "Just because it might not be enforceable, or you hope you won't need it, doesn't mean that you shouldn't make those terms clear in the written agreement."

- Is material misrepresentation or severely bad planning (i.e. can't make their sales forecasts) sufficient? It would put the supplier at a serious economic disadvantage if they produced 2500 BBLs a month based on the distributor's forecast, but the distributor could only sell 1000 BBLs a month.

These are a couple of possibilities and, though terms like these have not been tested in court in North Carolina, they are showing up more and more as suppliers become more sophisticated in their negotiation (and have some additional power based on the growing public demand for craft beer).

SELECTING A DISTRIBUTOR

Because distribution relationships are so complex and can last a very long time, it is critical that a brewery is careful and thoughtful about selecting a distributor. Some points to consider include:
- Larger Distributors
    - Most cities or counties have one or two "larger" distributors that represent the larger brand and are distributing several other smaller brands.
    - There are several distributors that cover an entire state or sometimes large portions of several states.
    - For these distributors, a small volume brewery might get to take advantage of robust infrastructure, but might also be a small fish in a big pond.
- Smaller Distributors
    - Many new distributors just starting up or just entering

the beer industry tend to have a "craft" or "niche-market" mindset.
    - Sometimes smaller distributors do not have the infrastructure (such as cold-chain capacity) to be able to meet the sometimes higher standards of craft brands.
- Relationships
    - Talk to retailers about their experience with distributors; signing up with a distributor that is not well-liked or is known to be difficult to work with may hinder your growth and cause other issues.
- Education and Brand Support
    - The distributor will likely be the face of the brand to many retail accounts and customers, so be sure that the distributor's goals, style, and values line up with the brewery's.
    - Be aware that this may not matter if the brewery's brand is sold to another distributor. But, if the brewery lines up with the distributor's core values and portfolio, it's probably less likely to be sold to another distributor.
    - The brewery needs to educate the distributor on the beer (the product), the brand (the trademark), and the story (how the brewery wants to market itself). Without commitment and alignment from both sides, the overall success of the marketing effort might not meet expectations.
- Terms and Service
    - Understand the distributor's processes, goals, and the way they do business.
    - Identify any deficiencies in the distributor's process

versus expectations on how the product is handled.
- Identify the reporting that the distributor does to suppliers (quality, sales, complaints, etc.)

CHAPTER TWELVE: TAXES

There are, as a general rule, lots of different kinds of taxes. There are taxes on value, use, and income to name just a few. Any business is likely to owe taxes in some form, but for a highly regulated business like brewing, there are a plethora of taxes and ways to run afoul of them. Additionally, there are several different layers of taxes: is the tax owed to the federal or state government? What about local taxes? City or county taxes? I do not purport to be a tax expert, but we will review some of the basics. I strongly recommend, however, that anyone thinking about starting a brewery consult with a competent licensed professional such as a CPA or licensed tax attorney with experience in alcohol taxation. Most of this section will be focused on excise tax, but other common forms of tax will also be discussed.

EXCISE TAX

This is the tax most think of when thinking about alcohol. Excise taxes are taxes that are paid on the purchase of certain goods. For example, gasoline at the local convenience store includes a federal excise tax, but it is often buried in the total price of the fuel. The same is true of alcohol production and purchases. When an individual purchases a pint at their local pub, the receipt is not itemized to show the amount of excise tax paid by the consumer; that tax is subsumed in the price of the beer. The manufacturer is taxed directly on the production (for sale) of the product.

As of writing, the standard rate for federal excise tax on beer is $18 per barrel (a barrel being 31 gallons for tax purposes). However, if producing less than 2,000,000 BBLs annually, the first 60,000 BBLs is taxed at $7 per BBL and $18 per BBL after 60,000 BBLs.

Several competing acts are being debated at the federal level that both aim to reduce the effective federal excise tax on beer. The Small BREW Act is favored by the Brewers Association (https://www.brewersassociation.org/) and many of the "smaller" and craft breweries. The Small BREW Act stands for "Small Brewer Reinvestment and Expanding Workforce Act." The BEER Act, technically referred to as the Fair BEER Act is favored by the Beer Institute (http://www.beerinstitute.org/) and most of the "larger" and more "macro" beer companies. The Fair BEER Act stands for "Fair Brewers Excise and Economic Relief Act." Recently, the Craft Beverage Modernization and Tax Reform Act (https://www.brewersassociation.org/government-affairs/

craft-beverage-modernization-and-tax-reform-act/talking-points-and-resources/) has also been put forth as a compromise and seems to be gaining widespread support.

Distributors and retailers have no real interest in the ongoing debate. Retailers do not expect change in the final price of the product and, in fact, demand no change. And distributors simply pass any reduced profit or additional cost back to the manufacturer.

John Says: "Which one will win? Who knows? But it looks pretty good that sometime in the next few years there will be some tax reform that will likely benefit smaller brewers."

All three acts—the Small BREW, BEER, and Craft Beverage Modernization and Tax Reform Acts—seek to adjust the excise tax rate on alcohol produced. The acts want the tax to be tiered based on production volume. Here's a brief comparison:

Current Tax Rate		Small BREW		Fair BEER		Craft Bev Modernization	
Volume	$/BBL	Volume	$/BBL	Volume	$/BBL	Volume	$/BBL
0-60k	$7.00	0-60k	$3.50	0-7,143	No excise tax	0-60k	$3.50
60k-2M+	$18.00	60k-2M	$16.00	7,144-60k	$3.50	60k-6M	$16.00
		2M+	$18.00	60,001-2M	$16.00	>6M	$18.00
				>2M	$18.00		

Here are a couple additional resources to read up on the detailed differences:

https://www.brewersassociation.org/wp-content/uploads/2015/01/Excise-Tax-Impact-Small-BREW-Act.pdf

https://www.brewersassociation.org/government-affairs/excise-taxes/small-brew-act-vs-beer-act/

http://www.beerinstitute.org/assets/uploads/Fair_BEER_Act_One_Pager_HOUSE.pdf

http://www.craftbrewingbusiness.com/news/the-beer-act-vs-the-small-brew-act-whats-the-difference/

When the average price for a keg (1/2 BBL) for beer is between $100 (macro lager) and $175 (craft beer), excise tax can make up a substantial amount of the overall cost of the product. Reducing the federal excise tax on beer is one way to reduce the burden on brewers and, hopefully, engender additional spending and capital improvements.

HOW IS EXCISE TAX COLLECTED?

Federal excise tax is collected on beer that is produced for sale to consumers. More specifically, the term in the regulations is beer that is "removed for consumption or sale." This means that the beer is either sold to a consumer or someone who is going to sell it to a consumer after the beer is removed from the place of production for sale. That means if the beer leaves the premises in someone's stomach or in a vehicle, then tax is owed on the beer.

According to ss26 USC 5053 and ss27 CFR 25, tax is not owed on beer that is

- Produced for export outside the United States
- Sour or otherwise damaged*
- Sent for laboratory analysis
- Used for research and development and testing
- Later distilled in a distilled spirits plant
- For use at a foreign embassy if removed to a customs warehouse
- Destroyed
- Delivered to certain vessels and aircraft
- Delivered to another brewery owned by the same brewer

John Says: "You know that they're going to get their money, but there are some times when it's okay to let someone else collect it."

There's one other nuance for taxes that are not owed. It is not an intuitive leap. The issue is whether you operate a "tasting room" or a "taproom." In the industry, the terms are used interchangeably or, more commonly, just referred to as a taproom. However, for tax purposes, they are very different things. A "tasting room" to the TTB is a place where customers (or potential customers) may sample, for free, your beer. A great example of a "tasting room" is at somewhere like the St. Louis plant for ABInBev. After taking a tour of the St. Louis plant, one is invited to stop by the tasting room (dressed up to

John Says: "This is another one of those times when the words they use have very specific meanings; not the ordinary meaning that you would think of in normal conversation."

look like an old pub) and receive a sample of one or two beers at no cost. The tasting room doesn't sell alcohol. It only provides samples post-tour.

Contrast that with a "tavern." A tavern, for the TTB, is a place where alcohol is sold. So the brewery with a taproom serving customers is more often a brewery operating a tavern (because the brewery is selling pints to customers at the taproom) rather than a tasting room. It is a key difference for licensing purposes. Tasting room samples are not taxed if the tasting room is on the premises and customers are not charged for the samples—even if they are charged for parking, tour fees, tasting glasses, etc.

The TTB relies on a brewery's report of operations or Brewer's Report to determine what tax that is due and when.

REPORTING BEER FOR TAX PURPOSES

The Brewer's Report of Operations is a standard form that must be filled out by the brewery on a periodic basis. Depending on the amount of beer produced, tax must be paid either monthly or quarterly. For most small breweries, tax is due quarterly. However, regardless of production, the Brewer's Report of Operations is due. After licensing, the TTB expects to start seeing the Brewer's Report of Operations coming from the brewery—even if the report just says "no production." Failure to send in a Brewer's Report will throw up red flags at the TTB at a certain point. An example of a Brewer's Report of Operations is attached in the Supplemental Material.

The Brewer's Report of Operations is available through the TTB and identifies the beer produced, removed, destroyed, lost in process (such as QA/QC testing or yield issues), as well as losses in the tasting room or due to sampling. The brewery must keep records of all transactions and any data used to compile or fill in the Brewer's Report of Operations. Daily records should include:

- Beer produced
- Beer transferred (to another tank)
- Beer bottled, canned or packaged
- Materials received (including raw materials, yeast, packaging materials, and returned kegs)
- Beer removed from the brewery (including amount, package size, and destination)
- Materials removed from the brewery (including yeast and materials that are "dumped")
- Gravity of wort produced or beer in process
- Amount and gravity of unsellable beer
- All other records associated with the operations of the brewery

The brewery must also keep accurate inventory records along with a physical inventory reconciliation every month. Inventory reports and reconciliation should be signed by the person taking the inventory and must be filed with the TTB.

The TTB cares about all the beer produced, not just the beer sold. Therefore, there are restrictions on when and how beer can be destroyed (or "dumped"). For example, if the beer is going to be destroyed on site, the beer must be recorded as produced and destroyed for the Brewer's Report. But, if the

John Says: "Recordkeeping is critical. Don't skimp on keeping good records."

beer is going to shipped off site to be destroyed, then the brewery must provide the TTB twelve days' prior written notice of the destruction and must provide details about quantities, methods, and other details about the actual destruction.

Beer which was initially identified as for sale, but is later returned, destroyed, sent to a distilled spirits plant, or exported outside of the U.S., may be eligible for an excise tax refund. If the product is eligible for an excise tax refund, that claim must be filed with the TTB within six months.

The brewery must retain all records for brewery operations for at least three years.

STATE EXCISE TAX

The above discussion has really centered on the federal excise tax, collected through the TTB. Additionally, each state has a state excise tax which will be collected through a state agency. Some states will require a separate form while others may rely on the TTB Brewer's Report of Operations for calculating tax due. In either event, the system and application are similar in terms of reporting, recordkeeping, and notice to the government agencies.

TTB AUDITS—COMMON ERRORS AND PENALTIES

Understand and remember, the TTB is—above all else—a tax collection agency. The primary concern of the TTB is the proper payment of taxes on regulated industries (including alcohol, but also firearms and tobacco). Issues to keep in mind when preparing for a TTB audit include:

- Critical recordkeeping, production and inventory mistakes: the brewery must document thoroughly and consistently every fractional gallon of product coming from the brewhouse and going into and out of the fermentation process. Once fermentation is complete, remember that there are still process losses due to sampling, barrel aging, or distilling (for spirits). There should be procedures and systems in place to ensure that the weights, measures, and samples are cataloged consistently and accurately. Don't forget, too, that process losses also include having to "dump a batch." All destroyed or "drained" product needs to be accounted for as well. Note: if a batch is "dumped," you may want to let your local sewer/wastewater processor know—a large volume (or "plug") of alcohol and live yeast could have an adverse impact on the town's water treatment facility—and it is not good business practice to be responsible for shutting down the local sewage plant! Additionally, frequent recordkeeping issues include:
    - Failure to keep records such as bills of lading;
    - Not keeping records for the required time period; and
    - Not properly explaining shortages or discrepancies.
- Frequent mishaps: this goes again to consistency. Be sure to establish procedures, policies, and systems to deal with doing the same task and documentation the same way every time. For the TTB, the major issue of tankage is whether or not the brewery is serving beer from tanks or kegs. If serving from tanks, the tanks must be tax-determined tanks (http://www.ttb.gov/pdf/brewery_industry_compliance_training.pdf). Serving off a non-tax-determined tank is a real no-no, other than for Quality Assurance or Quality Control,

i.e. QA/QC sampling purposes. Don't forget that measurement devices need to be properly calibrated. The brewery should have a calibration program where instruments are regularly calibrated to a trusted standard (usually done at the manufacturer or a metrology lab). Failure to ensure accurate readings is not a defense to when failing to pay taxes due. In addition to calibrating the appropriate equipment, it is also important to keep records demonstrating appropriate calibration.

- Excise Returns, Computation of Tax and Determination Mistakes: commonly, errors in these include:
  - Failure to pay tax on promotional events and samplings (even if free to the consumer, excise tax may be owed),
  - Incorrect conversion factors,
  - Simple computation errors,
  - One best practice on excise reports is to have a second person independently re-complete the forms and calculations to ensure that the same results are achieved.
- Brewer's Report of Operations Top Blunders and Tips: the actual form causes no end of frustration to both the TTB and the brewers/operators. Frequent issues arise around:
  - The brewer's daily "beer and cereal beverage produced" records do not match or support the amount entered under "beer produced by fermentation."
  - Brewers misinterpret "beer that is received in bond from other breweries and pilot brewing plants of same ownership." Breweries bring beer in bond onto

John Says: "There is a lot of information available on the TTB website and online about how to avoid common pitfalls. But, once something happens, get professional help."

their premises from breweries NOT under the same ownership and mistakenly record that transfer of beer. Beer under bond from another brewery or a pilot brewery may not be brought onto a brewery's premises unless all parties are under the same ownership.
- Exporting: "removed without payment of tax for export" should reflect the amount of beer the brewer exported that month. Many brewers ask whether exported beer counts toward the 60,000-barrel threshold for the reduced rate of tax. Only domestic removals for consumption or sale count toward the 60,000-barrel threshold.
- "Removed without payment of tax for use in research, development and testing." Brewers must support such removals by their daily operational records.
- "Beer consumed on premises." Brewers may not consider beer "removed tax determined for use at tavern on brewery premises" as beer "consumed on premises." Remember, "beer consumed on premises" has no charge of any type.

More detail, insight, and lists of penalties can be found at:

http://www.ttb.gov/beer/beer-tutorial.shtml

http://www.ttb.gov/spirits/common_compliance_tax_issues-during-audits-ds.shtml

http://www.ttb.gov/pdf/brewery_industry_compliance_training.pdf

http://www.ttb.gov/alcohol/penalty_alcohol.shtml

PAYROLL TAXES AND INCOME TAX

Excise tax is the elephant in the room for alcohol producers. However, excise tax may not be the largest source of taxes that a brewery pays. Another significant portion of total tax burden to the brewery are the taxes associated with payroll. Depending on the type of employee (versus independent contractor), taxes and withholding must be paid on

- Federal income tax withholding
- State income tax withholding (except Florida, South Dakota, Washington, Texas, and Alabama)
- Social Security and Medicare
- Federal unemployment tax
- State unemployment tax

REAL ESTATE AND PROPERTY TAX

Generally speaking, the federal government does not exact a federal property tax on real property or personal property. However, most states do. And the state tax rate for real property and personal property varies widely from state to state and even within the state at different counties or cities.

Almost all property taxes are assessed on real property. Real property includes land, buildings, or other immovable improvements to land that increases the value of the land. If leasing the premises for a brewery, it is key to understand who is responsible for paying the property tax on the premises. Generally, for leased space, the property tax is paid by the landlord.

Personal property, i.e. movable property, is sometimes taxed based on its value or use. For example, in North Carolina, personal vehicles are taxed based on their current fair market value each year. Some states also tax certain types of property used in a business (again, a North Carolina example: North Carolina Mill and Machinery tax).

Whether addressing a real estate property tax or a personal property tax, the brewery needs to work with a qualified public accountant to identify the taxes that the brewery may be subject to.

John Says: "Don't forget you're probably an employer, even if you're just employing yourself. Failing to pay these taxes is an easy way to dig a giant hole for yourself."

SALES TAX

Sales tax is a subject that most are familiar with from their experience as consumers. Sales tax is collected by the seller at the point of purchase and is a tax on the goods or services purchased. There is no federal general sales tax, though alcohol excise tax is a form of sales tax. Sales tax is especially important for breweries operating a tavern or taproom, particularly if the taproom sells brewery merchandise outside of the beer itself.

Each state determines its own sales tax rate, and counties and municipalities often add sales taxes based on the location or type of goods or services.

USE TAX

Use tax is very similar to sales tax in that it is applied based on goods or services. But unlike sales tax, use tax is typically collected on the use, storage, enjoyment, or other consumption in the state of tangible personal property that has not been subjected to a sales tax (for example, where sales tax was not paid in the state where the property was purchased). That is, use tax may be applied to purchases from out-of-state vendors that are not required to collect tax on their sales within the state. The use tax imposes a compensating tax equal in amount to the sales tax that would have been imposed on the sale of the property if the sale had occurred within the state's taxing jurisdiction.

Generally speaking, use tax is not a huge issue for breweries, but in those cases where it is an issue, it is usually substantial. For example, purchase of equipment may trigger a use tax depending on whether or not sales tax was originally paid on the equipment and where that tax was paid (on purchase or on delivery, for example).

Work with a competent CPA to ensure that the brewery is planning appropriately for potential tax burdens in this area.

EVERYTHING ELSE

All the taxes referenced here are just the most common taxes that tend to influence a brewery. In addition there are personal taxes to worry about (depending on the corporate structure), tax credits that may apply, and other industrial or state taxes. At the very least, a consultation with a qualified tax expert in *your area with experience with alcohol production/sales* is well worth the fee.

John Says: "Bottom line? Get help from a tax professional."

CHAPTER THIRTEEN: BUYING AND SELLING A BREWERY

Whether a brewery owner chooses to believe it or not, the beer business is highly regulated at multiple levels. Owning a brewery is like no other business, as is hopefully explained in this book. Yet another way that the alcohol business is regulated is in the transfer of business interests.

John Says: "Sometimes taking on the liability isn't too bad. For example, if it's a pretty new company, it might not have had much time to rack up 'hidden' liability."

BUSINESS PURCHASE BASICS

What may not be intuitive to the average person is that there are several ways to buy or sell a "business." For the purposes of this discussion, we will focus on "buying," but the inverse (i.e. selling) can be thought of as the "other hand" in a right-hand/left-hand pair. The three major types of purchases are buying the business, buying the assets, and mergers.

BUYING THE BUSINESS

People often say they "have bought a business," or "own the business now," without really understanding what it is that they now own. The idea can be illustrated in a short chart:

```
            Owners of the Legal Entity
               (receive the profits)
                       ↕
          Legal Entity that is Responsible
    (owns the equipment, pays the employees, leases the space)
                       ↕
  Day to Day Running of "the business" – Products, Employees, Inventory, Sales, etc.
```

So, legally, if someone "buys the business," are they buying the legal entity? Are they buying the stuff that the legal entity uses?

Well, if they buy the legal entity, they actually change places with the owners. Instead of Owner A, now Owner B owns the legal entity.

Additionally, note that the term "legal entity" is used here. The chart above works no matter whether the legal entity is an LLC, a corporation, a partnership, or a sole proprietorship (which really isn't *much* of a legal entity).

In the situation where the legal entity is an LLC, buying the business would be the equivalent of buying the membership interests of the owners of the LLC. For example, if the company is Third Street Brewery LLC, that is owned by Artie Angel, Bill Brass, and Cassie Cee, and they're selling the business to Dave Duquesne, then Dave has to buy the membership interests of Artie, Bill, and Cassie—all three of them—to be the full owner of Third Street Brewery LLC.

John Says: "You would be surprised to know how many people buy something without knowing what it is that they bought."

Advantages to buying the business (i.e. the legal entity)

- There are minimum changes in terms of lease assignment, bank accounts, vendor and supplier agreements, etc.
- This is a simple transaction between the owners even if the owners are themselves legal entities (like LLCs, corporations, etc.).
- New owners inherit the track and credit record of the company, "Established in 1973" or the like. Additionally, new owners inherit the credit history of the company which can be more advantageous than starting a company with no credit history.

Disadvantages of buying the business

- With the business comes the business liability—the new owner also inherits all the liability that the company may have incurred previously (product problems, worker's compensation and injury claims, etc.)

BUYING THE ASSETS

In contrast to buying the business, if one buys the assets of the business, the original owner *and* the original legal entity stay intact and can be closed down.

> That is, continuing with the example from above: Artie, Bill, and Cassie are the owners of Third Street Brewery LLC. Dave is going to buy the assets of Third Street Brewery LLC (the equipment, the lease, the inventory, the raw materials, *even the trademark or name of "Third Street Brewery."*), but he doesn't *buy the company*. So, Dave starts a new business 3rd Street Brewing LLC that now owns all the assets that used to belong to Third Street Brewery LLC. Then he can file a "doing business as" certificate (i.e. a "dba") for Th3rd Street Brewing LLC dba Third Street Brewery, and keep right on operating the business with the same beer, the same labels, etc. Meanwhile, Artie, Bill, and Cassie still own Third Street Brewery LLC, which now has no assets but has a bunch of cash to give out to its owners. After the profits are distributed, the company is wound up and closed down.

Advantages to buying the assets
(i.e. the stuff the legal entity owns)

- Simple transaction between two companies—merely buying and selling assets.
- New company gets to shed most of the liability that had built up with the previous company/owners.

Disadvantages of buying the assets

- Significant changes to "all the other" incidence of ownership (i.e. for the new company); the lease has to be re-assigned, all the utility services have to be updated, all the contracts have to be assigned or rewritten, bank accounts have to be changed, etc.)
- The new company does not inherit the track and credit record of the original company. This can often mean greater requirements for personal guarantees or security deposits for contracts or leases.
- Some items are not assets, and so don't transfer to the new company. For example, the biggest concern is human resources. Essentially the new company either needs to hire all new staff or re-hire some or all of the existing staff.

John Says: "With buying the assets, you have to be very clear on what it is that you're buying. If it's not listed in the agreement, you don't get it. Think about it, there's not a 'title' to a tank or pump the way there is with a car or a house. So, sometimes it can be hard to prove who actually owns that piece of equipment if there's a dispute."

MERGERS

Mergers are different beasts. Mergers essentially consist of two different transactions: one transaction involves two companies giving up their assets to another new company and the other transaction is the destruction of the two previous companies leaving one surviving (new) company.

> In the example, instead of buying outright, Dave proposes a merger. If Dave has a smaller brewery (D-Dog Brewing LLC) and wants to merge it with Third Street Brewery LLC, here's how it might go: if Artie, Bill and Casie each own one-third of Third Street Brewery LLC, maybe Dave gives them $300k along with an interest in the merged company. So that D-Dog Brewing LLC and Third Street Brewery LLC transfer all their assets to a new company, Th3rd Street Brewing LLC, that's owned 70% by Dave, and 10% each to Artie, Bill, and Cassie. Then they close and destroy D-Dog Brewing LLC and Third Street Brewery LLC, leaving Th3rd Street Brewing LLC as the surviving entity with all the assets and able to run the two businesses as one.

Advantages to mergers (i.e. one surviving legal entity)

- New company gets to shed most of the liability that had built up with the previous company/owners.

- New company inherits some of the track and credit record of the company (such as reputation, goodwill, etc.), but not all (such as credit history).

Disadvantages of mergers

- Complex transaction from a legal standpoint involving companies and owners of three different entities (though they overlap). Of particular concern here are tax consequences depending on the amount of interest carried over by the original owners into the new company.
- Significant changes to "all the other" incidence of ownership (i.e. for the new company, the lease has to be assigned, all the utility services have to be updated, all the contracts have to be assigned or rewritten, bank accounts have to be changed, etc.).
- Some items are not assets, and so don't transfer to the new company. For example, the biggest concern is human resources. Essentially the new company either needs to hire all new staff or re-hire some or all of the existing staff.

John Says: "*Mergers are actually really complicated. Don't think that this is something that you can do from some pre-printed form on a website.*"

In general, these are the main paradigms that the purchase of a business can be viewed through. And, as one might expect, the relative advantages and disadvantages are different for each party depending on whether they are buying or selling.

BREWERY OWNERSHIP

However, the regulatory framework that governs alcohol production in the United States makes this paradigm somewhat more complex. For example, in most if not all states, *any* change in ownership must be approved by the applicable regulatory authorities before that transaction can take place.

John Says: "Hang there with me, this example is getting pretty deep!"

For example, instead of buying the entire business, if Dave merely wanted to buy into the company, that purchase might have to be approved by the state and/or federal government before the sale of that ownership interest could happen. Recall the federal government treats LLCs like partnerships for ownership purposes.

*If the company is Third Street Brewery LLC, then the federal government needs to approve **any** ownership change in the LLC, even if Dave only buys 1% of the LLC. On the other hand, if the company is Third Street Brewery Inc. (i.e. a corporation), the federal government doesn't care about ownership or changes of ownership where the result will have the shareholder own less than 10% of the outstanding shares. However, if Dave will own 9% or less of the corporation but will be an officer or director, he would still have to be approved because the TTB wants to approve any shareholder (of more than 10%) who is a member, officer, or director.*

In addition, each state handles this somewhat differently. As noted earlier, North Carolina treats LLCs like corporations for ownership purposes—so for LLCs only, ownership changes above a certain threshold are important, rather than any ownership changes.

APPROVAL

At the federal level, approval of ownership changes, including outright purchases of a business, are done through an amendment to the brewery's Brewer's Notice through the TTB. This amendment process has traditionally been somewhat quicker than a new Brewer's Notice, so this may appeal to some individuals looking to shorten the time until they can produce and sell beer.

If the deal involves a new company purchasing the assets of an existing brewery, then a new original application must be placed with the TTB for the new company. This application can take a substantial amount of time and must be coordinated with the existing brewery's cessation of operations. That is, the new company needs to submit a Brewer's Notice Application with all of its pertinent documentation and reference the brewery whose assets are being purchased. Then the brewery that is being purchased must file an amendment to show cessation of operations and reference the purchasing company. In general, the old company's Amendment and the new company's Brewer's Notice will be approved at the same time, effectively transferring legal brewery operations from one company to the other.

But no matter how the deal is structured, federal and state

approval must happen before the deal closes or the business/assets change hands. Otherwise, the new ownership may find itself in possession of a business or assets that is/are not legally allowed to produce beer. There are alternatives to this nightmare scenario, but it is critical to involve experienced legal help in this process early and remember that this is not a fast process.

So far, this section has focused on buying a brewery. This portion will shift focus to the person considering selling their brewery. This is a growing concern and question for many entrepreneurs in this industry as part of an exit strategy for either retirement or return on investment.

John Says: "This is one of those areas where it is better to seek permission rather than forgiveness."

The "big boys" have been buying craft breweries like crazy the last several years. Even with the "review provision" of the AB-InBev/SABMiller acquisition deal, the larger breweries are still going to move to acquire additional craft breweries. In fact, most of the larger breweries have said that the majority of their profitability growth is coming from the "super-premium" or "craft beer" segments. Large breweries know how to purchase and integrate smaller breweries—it's been the game for several years now—so it is unlikely that it will change in a fundamental way for some time. Meanwhile, there are more and more consolidation and purchases among craft breweries as well.

That said, it's important that brewers and brewery owners understand the mechanics and what to look for if they're thinking about selling their brewery or buying someone else's.

NO. 1: WHAT ARE THEY BUYING?

The first question the owner has to answer is: *What* is being bought or sold? That may seem like a "duh" question, but there is a reason that it is important. The two major ways that a purchase can be structured are that either the buyer purchases the assets or the buyer purchases the business. See the discussion above.

If the assets are being sold, that normally means more than just the equipment. It also means the trademarks, the "goodwill," the reputation, the digital assets and accounts, the customer and marketing information, etc. When purchasing a brewery by purchasing the assets, it should include purchasing all the stuff that makes the business *that* business.

On the other hand, if the business is being purchased, the business or company as a whole is being sold. If purchasing the business, the seller is/are the owners of the company and they are selling their shares/interest in the company to the purchaser who will be the new owner of the company (i.e. the same business owned by the same company, which is owned by someone new).

Why care? Well, one major reason is that—in most cases—the liability or debt follows the company, not the assets. If a brewery is run for ten years, it has accumulated ten years of potential liability ("Tonight on Nightline: John's Brewery Causes Cancer. Millions drank Cancer Beer. Details at Eleven."). If the company sells the assets of the business to a purchaser (who purchases the assets, but not the business), all those people are going to sue the original brewery,

John Says: "No matter what they say—just like with a lease—there is no 'standard purchase agreement.'"

not the new owner of the assets of the old brewery.

Know what is being bought or sold and negotiate accordingly.

NO. 2: CONTRACT FOR PURCHASE—REGULATORY

Buyer and seller can make an agreement to sell or purchase. Then what? There had better be a written agreement that outlines the terms of the sale, what transfers and what doesn't and what happens between the agreement and "closing."

Two major issues in this period: regulatory approval and "risk of loss."

In terms of regulatory approval, you will have to contend with two sub-issues: 1) TTB approval of the ownership change and 2) the local ABC approval of the ownership change.

The TTB is very clear on this point: the redemdant amendment to change ownership needs to be submitted and approved before the transaction takes place. Does this always happen? No. Does the TTB like it when they are the last to know? No.

And, each state is different in how it handles ownership changes. So you need to research and plan for whatever hurdles you have to cross in your particular situation.

John Says: "Make sure that you write in provisions for these 'what if' scenarios. After the deal goes south is not the time to try and figure out what to do and who owes what."

The point is that you need a purchase agreement that takes into consideration these issues, the time it takes to get the necessary approvals, and a contingency plan if there are unforeseen problems, such as an inability to get the approvals, or the financing does not work out, etc. Is there a way to escape the agreement without enormous penalties?

NO. 3. CONTRACT FOR PURCHASE—RISK OF LOSS

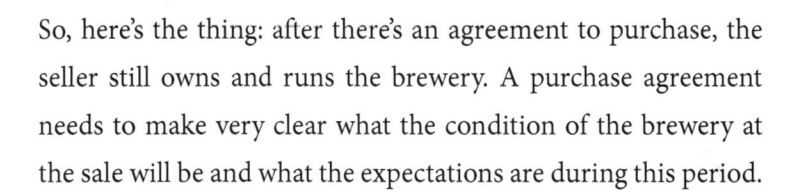

So, here's the thing: after there's an agreement to purchase, the seller still owns and runs the brewery. A purchase agreement needs to make very clear what the condition of the brewery at the sale will be and what the expectations are during this period.

> *For example: Mollie agrees to buy John's Brewery in ninety days. We have a purchase agreement, but the agreement doesn't say anything about risk of loss. Thirty days before the closing, the brewery burns to the ground and the equipment is a total loss. John receives a check from his insurance company for $1,000,000. Does Mollie still have to buy the not-a-brewery? The answer is two-fold: a) "maybe" depending on the agreement, and b) no one wants to litigate to find out. So, be sure that these items are addressed in the purchase agreement.*

> *Another example: Mollie agrees to buy John's Brewery in ninety days. The agreement doesn't name the precise assets that transfer. John immediately starts selling off excess equipment. Mollie's left buying a brewhouse, one fermenter, and two kegs. Could John do this? Same answers: a) "maybe" depending on the agreement and b) no one wants to litigate to find out.*

Last example here: Mollie agrees to buy John's Brewery in ninety days. The agreement does not say anything about how the business is to be run until the closing. John proceeds to take a two-month vacation financed by a huge loan he just took out on the equipment Mollie thinks she just bought. The business goes down because the taproom isn't open for two months and Mollie takes possession of a brewery with no customers and a ton of debt she didn't agree to.

John Says: "I tell clients 'it's about managing the risk' a lot. It doesn't have to be a forty-page contract for a $10,000 purchase. But a $1,000,000 brewery purchase shouldn't have a one-page agreement. The degree of care, rigor, and diligence should be proportionate to the risk involved."

There are some general rules about who is responsible for what in these pendant periods, but those general rules were not written for the specific buyer, seller, and brewery in this transaction. The general rules are the best that judges or legislators could come up with after the businesses imploded. It is better to be proactive and address these risks in the agreement itself.

NO. 4. CLOSING

Ever bought a house? Remember the pages and pages and pages of documents that had to be signed? Documents that described every aspect of the transaction, the title, the financing, the pre-sale, the post-sale, the warranties, etc.? Those documents are there to safeguard both parties and to make very clear the extent of the transaction.

It is surprising that people spending a significant amount of money on a business, perhaps $500,000-$1,000,000, often think it can/should be done with one or two signatures or a couple of pieces of paper. People often don't think that they need the same level of protection for buying a $1,000,000 business as when you buy a $150,000 house.

The closing is important; it is the actual handoff of ownership from one person/company to another. That means this is the time to make sure that all of the documents line up, that all of the keys and access to premises or digital assets are handed over, that all the leases or contracts have been updated, that all the approving people have been approved, etc. This is the time to make sure that all the "i's" are dotted and "t's" are crossed. After handing over a big check, it is a lot harder to pressure the seller to help with things that still aren't done, especially if it is a really big check and they have fled to a country without an extradition treaty.

John Says: "Don't overlook the importance of the closing and make sure that everything is in place to protect the parties and the transaction before marking things as 'done.'"

There are, obviously, lots of other questions, nuances, and details that come up as the parties complete the due diligence process (non-compete agreements, non-disclosure agreements, trademark assignments, etc.). There are (what seem like) hundreds of tiny moving parts—purchasing or selling something that dictates one's livelihood is not the place to skimp on attention to detail or diligence. If you are considering being a buyer or a seller, get professional legal help.

CHAPTER FOURTEEN: HUMAN RESOURCES AND EMPLOYMENT LAW FOR BREWERS

This section will cover some of the most common human resource topics that alcohol producers run into, but this is by no means an exhaustive treatise on employment law, employer requirements, or even on human resource issues. This will give you some general guidance, but there are many and significant nuances that vary from state to state.

BASICS OF EMPLOYMENT LAW

Hiring and managing employees is more than just picking good people and knowing how to yell at them. There are federal and state requirements for fair treatment and protection of employees because the employer is in a position of power and authority. As an employer you need to know some basic pieces of do's and don'ts and where to look for deeper answers.

John Says: "Employment law and how you treat employees is serious stuff, and the rules aren't always intuitive."

WHO MAKES THE RULES

The main folks that you need to worry about:

- State Regulators—there are likely several separate agencies, so look it up for your state, but they should (at least) cover the following topics:

    - Unemployment—manages the unemployment benefits for the state and ensures that employers are acting appropriately with respect to firing/laying off workers
    - Labor—sets some minimum rules (like minimum wage) and may manage one or more of the other areas
    - Workers' Compensation—ensures the employers are treating accidents in the workplace and the employees involved are treated fairly

John Says: "These are things that are easy to overlook early on. But, if you don't spend the time up front to get this right... well, what's the likelihood that you'll have more time later to come back and fix it? Not good."

- Occupational Safety—ensures that employers are not creating unnecessary risks for employees
- Revenue—the tax people
• Federal Regulators—these you've heard of before
    - Internal Revenue Service—the federal tax people
    - U.S. Immigration and Customs Enforcement—ensuring that employees are legal workers and that employers are not hiring illegal workers
    - Equal Employment Opportunity Commission—ensuring that employers are not discriminating on the basis of impermissible considerations (sex, race, religion, etc.)

A word on federal and state regulators: these folks are two things: (1) serious and (2) vindictive. I say vindictive somewhat facetiously, but the reason is that—unlike many areas of law—these labor areas carry fines and retroactive payment. That means if they find you're doing something wrong, you not only have to correct it for the future and pay a fine, you may also have to go back and pay all the delinquent wages (or whatever) since you started doing it. In some cases, even good faith mistakes can cost companies thousands, if not tens or hundreds of thousands. Be sure that you understand your specific state's requirements and consider getting help from a local labor attorney on this one. This section will focus mainly on federal rules, which are still substantial.

John Says: "These fines, fees, and back pay rack up big numbers fast. So, be on the lookout to act quickly if you find an issue."

HIRING

Here we will focus mainly on hiring employees, but there are other "quasi" employees. In this group the biggest concerns for brewers are interns and independent contractors which will be discussed separately.

There should be a defined process for hiring employees, including a written job description. A job description should include:

- Job title
- Hours
- Salary or hourly wage range
- Physical requirements of the job
- Requirements of the position (degree, experience, age, etc.)
- Responsibilities of the job
- Manager or supervisor of the person/position
- Special requirements of position (like security clearance, certifications, etc.)

If advertising for a position, the job posting should be based on the written description. Additionally, the job description is integral to managing the performance of the individual—especially if the individual is not meeting expectations. The job description begins the paper trail for rewarding or disciplining the employee.

When drafting a job posting, avoid using loaded or targeted words that implicate religious beliefs, age (for ages forty-five plus), race, and nationality. Also, avoid requesting resumes with headshots or pictures which could be construed as a way to discriminate without asking about it. Criminal history and convictions are discussed later.

Background checks are an open question. Some states disfavor background checks unless there is a specific reason or doing so such as handling money. Some business owners, however, prefer to run background checks on nearly all employees. The issue here is that your diligence should be proportional to the risk or the trust you are putting in the employee. Recall that alcohol production is considered (by the federal government and most states) akin to pharmaceutical production in terms of its potential for abuse (addiction and tax dodges). So, depending on where the employee will work in the process or in the cash chain, it may be prudent to invest in a detailed background check.

On selecting a candidate to be an employee, there should be an onboarding process with a checklist that includes:

- Review and signing up for benefits
- Completing federal and state employment forms
    - Especially Form I-9 (eligible to work in the U.S.) and Form W-4 (withholding)
- Employee receiving copies of the appropriate procedures or training
- Review of job description
- Employee receiving employee handbook including company policies (see on next page)

John Says: "*Don't skimp on documentation.*"

PAYING AND COMPENSATING EMPLOYEES

As far as compensation goes, employees fall into three categories:

- Hourly, Nonexempt
- Salaried, Nonexempt
- Salaried, Exempt

I tend to think of the whole "exempt/non-exempt" question in terms of being "exempt from overtime" or not. That is, if you're nonexempt, then you are eligible to receive compensation for overtime work. If you are exempt, then some amount of overtime is just expected for your position—you are considered a "professional" for the purposes of employment law.

So an hourly, nonexempt employee receives an hourly wage and is paid overtime for their work over a certain threshold, i.e. forty hours/week.

A salaried, nonexempt employee receives a flat wage per week, regardless of hours worked *except* that if they work more than forty hours in any seven-day period they are eligible to receive overtime pay in addition.

Salaried, exempt personnel are not eligible to receive overtime pay, regardless of how much time they work.

Overtime is almost universally required to be paid at 1.5 times the hourly wage/rate.

John Says: "Employment law is one of those areas where you cannot 'contract' for less than the statutory protections. Even if you have a contract that says they don't get overtime. If they otherwise qualify for overtime, you still owe them overtime unless there's a statutory exemption."

The default setting is that employees are nonexempt—that is, they are entitled to overtime pay unless an exemption exists. Exemptions are defined by law that cannot be amended or changed based on an agreement between the employer and the employee.

Lots of employers want to hire salary, exempt personnel because then "overtime is free." So, regulators have been very particular about who can qualify for salary, exempt positions and what it takes to show that someone is a "professional" for these purposes. Certain jobs are specifically exempted (doctors, lawyers, and many other jobs that require an advanced degree). "Brewer" is not one of them. So the company must identify whether or not the employee—whatever their title—meets the exempt threshold requirements before designating the employee as meeting the salary payment threshold for exempt employees. For many years, this number was approximately $23,000. That is, if the employee was making more than about $23,000, they could be safely classified as an exempt employee except in special circumstances. However, there have been recent changes to that threshold, moving that number up to over $47,000. At the time of writing, that move (to $47,000) has been enjoined by a federal judge, but it is likely that it will at some point increase beyond $23,000.

John Says: "They call out lawyers and doctors in particular. Essentially saying, 'no matter how little you get paid, they still never have to give you overtime.' Bastards."

The numbers above are really just the most common exemption used in designating an employee salaried, exempt. In truth, the exemption for "exempt" employees is that the employee

John Says: *"Just like the salary numbers above, these numbers tend to change. Always check for the latest numbers with the federal or state government."*

must either be classified as "Administrative," "Executive," or "Professional." Each classification has a test based on the job's duties and a test based on the salary. The job must pass *both* tests to be exempt.

If the employee makes less than the threshold amount (whatever it is) and they are paid a salary (rather than an hourly wage), then they are automatically salaried, nonexempt. This is where employers can get in trouble very quickly. If an employee is actually salaried, nonexempt but the company treats them as salaried, exempt, the company could potentially be liable for the difference in income back to the hire date based on the hours worked—and those are overtime hours! That can quickly add up to thousands of dollars in back wages due the employee.

Additionally, as one would expect, hourly employees (and salaried employees for that matter) must be paid at least minimum wage, $7.25, federally mandated at the time of this writing. Some states allow "tips" to supplement minimum wage requirements. How your company deals with tips is important in two ways for (1) how much the employee actually earns for their labor, i.e. this is a tax question, and (2) reporting and owner liability.

With regard to tips and #1 above, tips are generally given directly to the employee or the company establishes a "tip-pool" that all employees (or at least those employees dealing with retail sales) join in on. In either case, the employee needs to report the tips for income tax purposes. If the employee retains the tips directly given to them by customers, then they need to report those as wages on their own tax returns. If the company takes in the tips and then distributes them to the employees, the company should report those tips as wages on the individual's W-2.

As far as #2—reporting and owner liability—the question comes up when an owner or employee/owner is working in the retail aspect (pouring beers at the taproom for instance) and receives a tip. Is that tip coming to the individual like wages (like an employee) or like a distribution (just because they are an owner)? These two are taxed differently and may impact how the owner is seen as acting at the time. For example, if the employee just served to an underage person, does it change the company's liability if they were acting as an employee or as an owner?

It's critically important for the company to manage employees and regulatory risk so that employees are classified correctly and paid appropriately.

BENEFITS

It is almost universally required for employers to maintain workers' compensation insurance. How this is administered and whom it applies to vary from state to state.

However, withholding and paying payroll taxes are not only universally required, the administration is largely similar for all states and the federal government. And while it is possible for employers to manage their own payroll deductions, processing, and payments, it is often more cost-(and time-) effective to outsource payroll services to companies that specialize in that area.

John Says: "Most of the time this is not an 'automatic thing.' You have to intentionally get a workers' comp policy. Be honest, you probably didn't know that."

Time off, vacation time, "comp time," Paid Time Off ("PTO"), holidays, and "sick time" requirements or offerings are also regulated (or not) state by state. Some states require minimum offerings or compensation, while other states have no requirement to give any employees any time off. The important thing here is that you understand your state's requirements and that—however you implement those requirements—you do it consistently with an enforceable and enforced policy.

With respect to health insurance and retirement plans, there are a myriad of requirements that are in flux (such as the Patient Protection and Affordable Care Act, i.e. "Obamacare") and requirements that are complex and long-standing (such as Employee Retirement Income Security Act, i.e. ERISA). The general rule is that if you offer the benefit to one employee, you must offer it equally to all employees. There are, as you would guess, exceptions to this general rule. So, if you are entertaining implementing one or more complex benefit programs (IRAs, 401(k)s, health insurance, Health Savings Accounts, etc.), you should seek assistance from specialists and professionals with experience in implementing and administering these programs for your size business (small business versus larger organizations).

Additionally, you should ensure you look at your state's requirements (if any) for mandatory breaks, rests, or meals.

PERFORMANCE MANAGEMENT

In addition, your company should have a documented performance management process. While many flee the "corporate" world to work in the "artisanal" craft beer industry, some "corporate" vestiges tag along. Performance management is one of those. A performance management process is a tool for the company and should have the following goals:

- Reward high-performing employees
- Identify growth and employee development opportunities (such as promotions or next steps in their job)
- Improve underperforming employees
- Discipline and remove employees who are chronically underperforming or who commit serious violations of the law or company policy.

Often, the question comes up when firing an employee for a serious infraction or for a series of minor infractions. It is important that the company has a documented trail of identifying the issue with the employee while giving the employee an opportunity to correct the behavior or issue. When an employee has egregiously violated a policy, immediate termination may be appropriate; however, in most cases, only after the employee fails to improve is it appropriate to fire the employee versus "laying them off." Laying off an employee carries with it the requirement of paying unemployment for a period of time, which can cost a small company significantly. Firing, on the other hand, does not carry such financial obligations for the

John Says: "If you don't have a performance management process, you'll eventually regret it."

employer. But differentiating between "firing" and "laying off" has been the subject of much litigation, and the company's best defense is good documentation.

A robust performance management process should include procedures (which are followed!) and

- Job descriptions that are reviewed at least annually and updated appropriately
- Review of job description with the employee(s)
- Periodic documented performance reviews (at least annually)
- Documentation of "verbal" warnings and informal employee counseling for policy or discipline issues
- Written warning(s) prior to termination
- (Optional) Exit Interviews, so the company can improve

EMPLOYEE OR INDEPENDENT CONTRACTOR?

I won't go into why you might want to designate someone an "independent contractor" as opposed to an "employee," but rather what you have to do to make that designation stick. Often, businesses want to avoid generating an employer-employee relationship and would prefer to have an independent contractor perform certain tasks or jobs. Great. That's totally okay. But what makes a person an independent contractor as opposed to an employee?

EMPLOYEES

Employees are regular workers for the employer. Employees perform work for the employer at the direction of the employer. The employee's labor and activity benefit the employer, and the employee is subject to the direct supervision of the employer as to the manner and results of the work to be performed. Hmmm… by that definition, my dad was my employer for a whole bunch of weekends working on his old car. But the idea here is that the employee is paid and is responsible to the employer for the work and how it's done.

John Says: "Just because you call them an independent contractor that does not mean they are an independent contractor."

INDEPENDENT CONTRACTORS

Independent contractors, by contrast, have a defined scope of work to complete and are, generally, free to determine the means and manner of getting the work done.

Maybe an analogy would help: me helping my dad work on his car, where he's telling me what wrench to use and where to put it when I'm done ("For Pete's sake! Wipe the grease off before you put it back in the tool box!") —that's more like an employee. If my dad took the car to a mechanic and said, "I need a new water pump installed." And then he goes away and picks the car up a few days later—that's

John Says: "This level of detail is one of the reasons I never worked with my dad much."

John Says: "Of course, maybe if I didn't write books about beer, he'd think I had a 'real' lawyer job."

more like an independent contractor.

In my analogy with the mechanic, my dad doesn't care what wrench the mechanic uses, how he treats his tools (or employees for that matter), or what it takes to get it done. They made an agreement for certain results or for certain things to be done.

Independent contractors run their own business and work for another person or business to complete an agreed-to scope of work. If you've got an "independent contractor" who's not doing that, then you've really got an employee.

HOW DO I ENSURE THAT THEY'RE REALLY AN INDEPENDENT CONTRACTOR?

Generally, whether a person is an independent contractor or an employee hinges on the degree of control exercised over them versus the independence of the work. Specifically, the IRS looks at factors it identifies as:

1. Behavior control—does the employer have a right to control the manner and method of the work?
2. Financial control—does the worker have the right to control the economic aspects of his or her job (tools, profit/loss, etc.)?
3. Type of relationship—how do the parties perceive their relationship?

It's best to be sure that there isn't any confusion in these factors or in the relationship at all. I advise clients that independent contractors should have:

- Written agreement for services
- Defined scope of work
- Work requirements, in writing, if there are any—but any requirements shouldn't be unreasonably detailed
- Defined milestones which are measurable
- Measurable deliverables (so it can be easily seen whether the work is "complete")

For independent contractors, the business should not

- Dictate how the work is done
- Let independent contractors supervise employees
- Allow the independent contractor to make decisions for the business
- "Over" supervise the work—be sure to give the independent contractor latitude to do the work as they see fit

John Says: "When the IRS finds independent contractors who should have been employees, that's another place that fees, fines, and back pay can add up before you know it."

CONCLUSION

Okay, so this section wasn't so brief. But the point is that, if you've made the decision that you want an independent contractor rather than an employee, make sure you take the steps necessary to ensure that the classification is accurate and holds up to scrutiny.

WHO NEEDS COMPANY POLICIES? YOU DO!

Many people start their own business to get away from the bureaucracy of large corporations, procedures, policies, and paperwork. But, there is a critical purpose to some of those trappings of Corporate America.

> *For example, as a business owner, if you or one of your employees discriminate against a minority or sexually harass an employee, you and your company could be on the hook for a lawsuit from the employee and/or action by the government for violating someone's civil rights.*

How do you protect yourself and your business from these types of issues? How do you prove that something didn't or couldn't happen? It's hard to prove a negative. You have to show that you've taken reasonable steps to ensure that these sorts of violations do not take place in your business. Documented policies, procedures, and training go a long way toward showing a court that you (or the business) didn't condone the behavior and, therefore, are not at fault.

Company policies should prescribe specific behavior that you either *want* or *don't want*. They should spell out the behavior as well as the consequences of the behavior (such as termination). Each and every employee should be trained on the policy or policies and the training should be documented and kept in your employee files.

John Says: "Spend the time up front to do this right. Trying to make time later to go back and do it is extremely hard to do. And, if you don't do it at all, you have a huge risk as you hire more and more employees."

So what policies should you have? You should have a company policy against, at minimum:

- Discrimination (race, gender, or national origin)
- Sexual harassment
- Workplace violence
- Substance abuse
- Theft

Consider having the employee fill out, sign, and date a form indicating that they received a copy of the policy(ies).

That way if you or your employee(s) are accused of, for example, sexual harassment, you can point to your company policy(ies) and training to show that this conduct was specifically prohibited by the company and the responsibility is on the individual employee, not the business.

Also, you can't just "have" policies, you need to make sure

that you're following and enforcing them. When you learn of an issue, you should immediately address the issue and document the violation as well as the consequences of the violation.

Lastly, make sure that as policies change or are updated, you update and train your employees on the changes too! Protecting yourself and your business isn't a one-time thing; it's an ongoing process.

WHY DO I NEED AN EMPLOYEE HANDBOOK AND HOW DO I GET ONE?

First, the "why."

As every business owner knows, or should know, when you take on employees (as opposed to owners), your world changes quite a bit. All of a sudden you have to worry about payroll, tax payments, withholding, etc. Additionally, you're also now covered by a myriad of federal and state laws that protect employees and their rights. Among your now applicable laws are such intimidating topics are the Fair Labor Standards Act, the Civil Rights Act of 1964, and the Americans with Disabilities Act, along with oversight by agencies such as the National Labor Relations Board, the Occupational Safety and Health Administration, and the Equal Employment Opportunity Commission. Plus all your state requirements and laws!

A lot of headache and potential risk can be avoided by a well-written and up-to-date employee handbook. An employee handbook should contain your company's policies and procedures on many of the topics that are covered by the various laws and regulations. An employee handbook creates a documented, shared understanding of what is and what is not appropriate and expected behavior at the company. This places the onus, or at least some of it, back on the employee and takes away their argument of "I didn't know."

HOW DO I GET AN EMPLOYEE HANDBOOK FOR MY COMPANY?

Several online companies offer a "comprehensive employee handbook" for a small fee. While this may be an option for you and your company, I generally recommend against it.

You need to have an employee handbook that is geared toward your business and your specific needs. For example, if the handbook includes a "zero tolerance" for drinking on the job, but you're a winery...well, the Quality Assurance department may have some issues doing their job properly.

In terms of "getting" an employee handbook, you've got a few options:

1. Buy a generic one online
2. Write one yourself
3. Have one written for you

The first option, as I've said, I don't recommend. The handbook should be set up for you and your company, which also makes it easier to follow, update, and rely on.

Next, you can write your own. Which is a great option to have something that is specific to your needs and your business. But there are a lot of ways to run afoul of the law or the regulations or missed opportunities to protect yourself from potential litigation. Even if you write your own employee handbook, I'd strongly suggest at least having an attorney review it before you finalize it.

Finally, and probably the most expensive option, is to have one written and developed for you. The upside is that you'll get something that covers the regulations, laws, and requirements. Also, you'll gain the benefit of others' experiences and best practices. Just be sure that, if you have it developed for you, the person or company doing the work for you has experience in employment law, small businesses, and/or human resources…and, ideally, the craft beer industry.

John Says: "These are the minimums. You can add more, but if you have less than this, you better have a good reason."

In any event, whether you're writing it yourself or buying one, the following is a very good start for a list of topics/contents that should be included in any employee handbook:

- Purpose
- Definitions/Glossary
- Policies
    - Employment at Will (if applicable)
    - Equal Employment Opportunity
    - Americans with Disabilities Act
    - Drug Free Workplace
    - Personnel Records
    - Anti-Harassment Policy
    - Anti-Impairment Policy
    - Alcohol Consumption Policy

- Employee Code of Conduct
- Use of Computers/Social Media
    - Company Computers and Social Media
    - Personal Social Media and Email on Company Time
    - Company Devices or "Bring Your Own Device" Policy
- Attendance/ Leave of Absence
- Health and Safety
    - Safety Guidelines
    - Workplace Violence Prevention
    - Smoking
    - Security
- Employee Performance
    - Performance Appraisal Process
    - Employee Discipline
- Separation from Employment
    - Termination Process
- Employee Acknowledgement

CONCLUSION AND WORDS OF WARNING

Which brings us to the "word of warning" about employee handbooks. You should be sure to keep your employee handbook up to date. That means reviewing it for changes and possible updates at least annually. Be sure to document any updates or changes that you provide to employees. You also want to make sure your employee handout is accessible either in hard copy or online to all of your employees.

And—this is critical—be sure to follow whatever employee handbook you have. It's almost worse to have a handbook that you don't follow than to have no handbook at all. But, don't get me wrong, you should *really* have an employee handbook. If you have any questions about your current handbook or if you need assistance developing a handbook, give my office a call or contact other legal counsel.

UNPAID INTERNSHIPS – IT'S A BUYER'S MARKET, RIGHT?

Many growing companies and businesses want an intern. Especially if, by intern, you mean "slave labor." Unfortunately, this isn't always a good idea. And, in certain situations, it can turn to disaster.

John Says: "There is no free labor."

THE SLIPPERY SLOPE

The economy is not that great. It's better than a few years ago, but not *that* much better. So many people are looking for jobs and would be happy to have jobs making much less than they were making five plus years ago. Sophisticated, educated, and experienced folks are competing for the same jobs as fresh university graduates. The effect is to drive down the price of skilled or semi-skilled labor in the modern office. So, it only stands to reason that some folks would be willing to work for free, just for the experience. Right?

EMPLOYMENT LAW BASICS

See, here's the thing: a basic tenet of employment law is that people deserve to be paid fairly for their work. Even the most bizarre and erudite employment laws have some tangential relation to that idea. So the argument goes, "Well, sure. The [unpaid] intern gets experience as their pay."

Not Enough

More and more unpaid interns are bringing suit against the companies that they work for to secure reasonable pay for their work. The disparate bargaining positions between the employer and the desirous intern/employee has often been abused. Cases where unpaid interns were worked extended hours without a break, used to replace full-time employees, and otherwise exploited by businesses are rampant. The most egregious cases have resulted in significant monetary verdicts in favor of the intern.

What Do We Learn?

What we find out from the courts is that a general, hand-waving excuse of "experience" in lieu of pay is not enough. Courts are carving out the requirement that, if the intern is not paid, they must get substantive training, advancement opportunities, or other development commensurate with the work performed.

OKAY. WHAT DOES THAT MEAN?

What that means, is that, if you have an unpaid intern, to avoid running afoul of the Fair Labor Standards Act and other employment laws, you need to be sure to meet certain requirements. I advise clients that unpaid interns must receive:

- Substantive training
- Learning and practice opportunities
- A defined development plan
- And that you (i.e. the business) must not:
    - Receive any substantial benefit from having the intern "on staff"
    - Replace any existing employee with an unpaid intern
    - Assign the intern any work not already being done by existing staff (that is, you can't get more work done with an unpaid intern than you can without them)

John Says: "Brewing is one of the few industries where people will actually volunteer to work for you for free. Even volunteers come with concerns. Make sure they know it is a 'volunteer' position and unpaid—it's not an internship or a try-out for employment. And get it in writing."

The idea here is that the unpaid intern should be seen as a development opportunity for the intern, not for the business. The business should not receive a benefit at the expense of the unpaid intern.

WOW. WHY WOULD I GET AN UNPAID INTERN AT ALL THEN?

Exactly. Unpaid interns should be seen as way to give back or contribute to the education or development of the intern, not as a means to get work done for free. I advise clients that, given the requirements and the (typical) limitations of small businesses, you're better off paying for your intern or administrative staff. Avoid the risk of potential lawsuits or regulatory action by paying your staff what they are worth and don't take the "buyer's market" too far.

CRIMINAL BACKGROUND CHECKS

I sometimes get questions about how a criminal history would affect hiring decisions. Now, as I'm almost exclusively practicing small business law, I get the same sort of questions, but from a different angle: can I *not* hire this person?

Here's the thing: you've got several moving parts, and you need to understand how they fit together whether you're the employer or the potential employee.

CIVIL RIGHTS ACT OF 1964 AND THE EEOC

I think we all understand that there are certain things you can't do as an employer or, rather that an employer cannot hold against you. Title VII of the Civil Rights Act of 1964 has a lot to say on hiring decisions and is the basis for the rest of this discussion. Specifically, the U.S. Equal Employment Opportunity

Commission ("EEOC") ensures that how businesses employ others complies with the act. In April of 2013, the EEOC promulgated (or "implemented" in non-lawyer-speak) a new Regulatory Guidance for enforcing the regulations, especially as related to race and national origin. With good intentions, the EEOC wanted to ensure protection of individuals from discrimination on these protected classes (race and national origin) that they felt were particularly susceptible to abuse in the private sector. But, it did open up the proverbial "can of worms."

WHAT DOES RACE AND NATIONAL ORIGIN HAVE TO DO WITH CRIMINAL HISTORY?

Well, the EEOC believes, probably rightly, that criminal history issues impact some races or national origins more than others. And that filtering potential employees on that basis would create unlawful discrimination in effect, if not in words.

And, now, with the guidance in place, employers often find themselves between a rock and a hard place. If they ignore the guidance, they could be open to action from the EEOC for disparate impact. If they don't look at criminal background at all, they could expose the business to serious issues with employee theft, fraud, and perhaps negligent hiring.

John Says: "In general, you should not be asking—in a job interview or application—if they've ever been charged with a crime. You can and should ask if they've ever been convicted of a crime."

What's an employer to do? Let's look at the guidance:

EEOC GUIDANCE

Here is the high-level view on how this can impact a hiring decision (I'm paraphrasing the regs here):

1. Arrest Records
    a. What they mean generally:
        i. Arrest records do not, in themselves, prove any bad act, crime, or conduct.
        ii. Arrests and arrest reports may include inaccuracies and may continue to be reported even after they hsve been "expunged" or "sealed."
        iii. The accused is presumed innocent until proven guilty.
    b. What it means for an employer:
        i. You should probably not ask about arrests in interviews, applications, or questionnaires.
        ii. An arrest is not a "fact" of criminal conduct and can be seen as too prejudicial to allow objective review of other qualifications of the person.
2. Convictions
    a. What they mean generally:
        i. A conviction means that a court of competent jurisdiction has determined that a crime was committed and the person in question committed the crime.
        ii. This is seen, legally, as a fact despite all the hoopla we hear on television and movies about

wrongful convictions. Until proven otherwise or overturned by a higher court, a conviction is proof of the fact.

    iii. Unfortunately, convictions can also continue to be reported after they have allegedly been expunged.

b. What they mean for an employer:

    i. You can ask about convictions, but only within reason.

    ii. For example, it may be unreasonable to refuse to hire someone for a job as a bank teller based on the sole fact that she was convicted of speeding.

    iii. On the other hand, it may be reasonable to refuse to hire someone for a job as a bank teller based on the sole fact that he was convicted of fraud or theft.

To determine if you or your business is complying with the law, the EEOC will look at the text of your policy (you have a policy now, right?), any associated documentation, and how that policy was implemented (especially training). Additionally, the EEOC will look at

- what types of charges/convictions were reported or evaluated by the employer
- how much time has passed since the charge/conviction
- the job being considered
- the reputation of the business (used for determining whether the conviction was relevant to the business)

In short, the EEOC looks at all the pertinent circumstances for the hiring decision, as related to the criminal history or background. The EEOC then compares that with national data regarding disparate impact of criminal records and hiring.

HOW DO I DO IT RIGHT?

As an employer, you're probably getting a little concerned (or "terrified" in non-lawyer-speak). It's really not that bad. The EEOC offers guidance on how to stay compliant with respect to the above in the form of two options:

1. Ensure that any criminal screening done for hiring purposes meets the Uniform Guidelines on Employee Selection Procedure standards OR
2. Develop a screening procedure that considers the nature of the crime, time elapsed, nature of the job, and the individual candidate(s).

If you opt for #2, which certainly *sounds* simpler, you should have:

- A written policy describing your approach to job applicants who have a criminal history
- A procedure for documenting the candidate review process and how the candidate or the facts stack up against the policy in the critical areas (i.e. nature of the crime, time elapsed, and nature of the job).

The critical aspect of either of the two compliance options above is that you need to think about these (and act accordingly) before you hire or refuse to hire someone. Also, be sure that you're in compliance with your state laws and regulations as well!

IMMIGRATION FOR THE BUSINESS OWNER

I had a question come up recently from a client, and I had to learn a lot more about immigration law than I had ever intended. I thought I'd try and share what I learned as a sort of primer for businesses to think about when addressing non-native labor issues.

The issue that came up with my client was related to a visa. If you're like me, when you hear "visa" you think about how much Best Buy charged for that new Star Wars Blu-ray boxed set you bought someone for their birthday about thirty days ago. But for many, the term "visa" brings worry, consternation, and a mountain of work.

John Says: "This may be important for your company formation too. If you want to qualify as an S-Corp, the owners must meet certain citizenship requirements."

IMMIGRATION

For many people in the U.S., we take our citizenship for granted. For a large part of the rest of the world, citizenship—particularly U.S. citizenship—is a big deal. For someone from another country, the path to citizenship generally goes like this: non-immigrant visa → immigrant visa →

naturalization → citizen. So, let's take a look at what each of those concepts mean.

NON-IMMIGRANT VISA

A non-immigrant visa is a limited residency document. It covers a broad swath of circumstances but focuses on one main principle: the holder of the visa is in the country for a limited time. With a non-immigrant visa, the holder can visit the U.S. for work, recreation, school/study, or one of a (very) long list of possible categories of visit (visa classes start with "A" and go through "U"). The holder can apply for a non-immigrant visa at the U.S. consulate in the country of origin.

IMMIGRANT VISA

This is the really popular topic. An immigrant visa is colloquially referred to as a "green card." The term comes from the fact that the wallet-sized cards used to have a green background. A better description of the immigrant visa would be "lawful permanent residence" application or permit. This visa allows foreign nationals to live and work in the U.S. without an expiration date. The rights and privileges are similar to the non-immigrant status, except that they continue indefinitely.

NATURALIZATION

A foreign national can become a "naturalized" U.S. citizen. Naturalization is no joke. For many, this is the culmination of years of hard effort, work, and frustration. To become a U.S. citizen, a foreign national must have spent a specific time as a permanent resident (see immigrant visa), apply for citizenship, show good moral character, and demonstrate knowledge of English and civics. I've heard some of the questions on the civics test—there are a lot of natural-born U.S. citizens who don't know that much about our government!

ASYLUM

This one is always in the movies or the news. What is "asylum?" Well, in short, it's when the individual is granted limited residency to protect them from persecution they would otherwise receive. Julian Assange and Edward Snowden have been in the news of late on this front. But the more ordinary, and often more meaningful, more typical situation is the refugee. People persecuted for their religion, nationality, race, social group, political opinion, or gender (in certain limited cases) can seek asylum (or "refugee status") if they're already in the U.S. To qualify, the individual must apply within a year of entry or when their circumstances qualify them for asylum, and they must appear for a hearing on the matter before an asylum officer.

TEMPORARY PROTECTED STATUS

The U.S. has developed this category for individuals who cannot return to their home countries because of calamities (such as natural disasters, civil unrest, or political upheaval). This temporary status, as the name implies, is temporary but can also be quite lengthy. I read that some foreign nationals of El Salvador had been granted Temporary Protected Status in 2001. These same El Salvador nationals have recently had their status extended until at least March 2018, as of this writing. However long the temporary protected status lasts, it does not in itself provide a path to citizenship.

VISA WAIVERS

If the categories weren't complicated enough, there's also a subset of countries (thirty-seven of them) whose citizens do not need a visa to enter the U.S., as long as they are visiting for pleasure and for no more than ninety days.

EXECUTIVE OFFICE FOR IMMIGRATION REVIEW

Also known as "Immigration Court," the EOIR deals with all the various interfaces of the above classes and addresses all the "in between" and "gray areas" that aren't accounted for elsewhere. This is an administrative court, not a court of law. Yet this court is designed to adjudicate the issues that immigration status raises, though cases may be transferred to other federal courts in certain circumstances.

BEWARE SCAMS

If you or one of your employees has an immigration issue or concern, beware of scams set up specifically to take advantage of immigrants and small businesses. Both have been victimized by individuals who claim to be "immigration experts." If you have an immigration concern, seek out a licensed attorney with experience in immigration. (By the way, that's not me. I can spot the issues, but I don't know that I'd be best person to help you navigate the system). Specifically, be aware that there are very important differences between the legal profession (and the practice of law) in the U.S. compared to other countries. For example, a Notario Publico in Mexico is not the same as a notary public in the U.S. (the Texas Secretary of State has published a good comparison between the two). As a consequence, many people have gone to a notary public thinking that they can provide services that, in the U.S., only a lawyer can provide. Additionally, the ABA (American Bar Association) has initiated the Fight Notario Fraud Project specifically to combat this issue.

If you have any concern whether the person you're talking to is a licensed attorney, look them up at the State Bar—Lawyer Directory. If they're not on it, they're not a licensed attorney.

By the way, I found this really useful chart on the different types of non-immigrant visas (http://www.norbachegoff.com/immigration/non-immigrant-visa-chart.html).

STUDENT VISAS

Generally, student visas (F visas) ONLY allow the student in the country to study—not to work. Employing a person in the U.S. on a student visa may expose you to liability and certainly exposes them to potential revocation of their visa (and, therefore deportation).

Some student visas (F-1 visas) do allow for an optional

practical training period. However, both the student and the work/employment must qualify for Optional Practical Training ("OPT") Period approval. Be sure that the student you're hiring is approved to work doing the kind of work you're hiring them to do.

WORK STATUS VERIFICATION

All employers in the US are required to verify the employment status of all employees hired since 1986. This means completing an "I-9" form and keeping those records up-to-date as necessary. I know some companies which, as a matter of policy, make their employees update their I-9s every year. It's not a bad "best practice."

Also, employers in many states are required to use E-Verify to verify the employment status of all employees. Additionally, *all* federal contractors must participate in E-Verify. But, keep in mind that E-Verify *does not* replace the required I-9 verification process. E-Verify is an "in addition to" not an "instead of."

John Says: "This should be one of the items identified in your hiring procedures—when onboarding a new employee, don't forget to fill out all the required paperwork."

BUSINESS STRUCTURE AND ORGANIZATION

The immigration status of owners and/or employees can also have an effect on how best to organize the business. For example, some general principles include:

- Non-resident aliens may not be shareholders in an S-Corp.
- Companies owned (51% control or more) by American citizens or greencard holders cannot sponsor E1/E2 (treaty trader/treaty investor) visas.
- If a company sponsoring E1/E2 visas is acquired by a company which is owned (51% control or more) by American citizens or greencard holders, the E1/E2 Visa(s) can be revoked.
- Companies owned (51% control or more) by American citizens or greencard holders cannot sponsor L-1 visas (managers assigned U.S. positions by a foreign-owned company).

So be aware of these (and other, more nuanced) limitations as you look at starting or organizing a business where you're a visa holder or if you're looking to sponsor individuals needing work visas.

BUSINESS PURCHASE

If you're looking to purchase an existing business, be sure to make employment status verification part of your "due diligence" (business opportunity evaluation) process. Otherwise you could cause yourself some significant headaches depending on whether you have employees holding visas.

CONCLUSION

So:

- If you're starting a business and looking to hire visa holders, non-resident aliens, or other non-U.S. citizens, be sure you know the requirements for your specific situation.
- If you're a business owner looking to sponsor visas for workers, be sure you understand the limitations of your business.
- If you're *any kind* of business owner, be sure to make I-9 Employment Status Verification part of your standard procedure.

Immigration is a complex and highly technical area of federal law. If you have concerns or issues, be sure to consult a licensed attorney with experience in immigration law.

SUPPLEMENTAL MATERIAL. LEGAL BASICS: HOW THE LAW REALLY WORKS

Okay, so we're going to go over some pretty basic information about the U.S. legal system and how it applies to the different situations you may be facing. Sorry if these terms are too basic, but let's make sure that we're all on the same page as far as the concepts and issues are concerned.

CIVIL VS. CRIMINAL

In the United States, there are two basic different sets of law. Civil law is the group of law that deals with the relationship between private citizens, citizens and businesses, businesses and other businesses, and businesses, citizens and the government. One way to think about it is that civil law regulates "wrongs" between two "people." A "wrong" in this case, means someone or something was injured in a non-criminal way, or maybe think of it as an "offense against a person." This will make more sense after the next paragraph.

Criminal law is the group of laws that deal with "offenses against society (at large)."

> *For example, mugging someone is an offense against a person, but it's also an offense against society itself—it's a crime.*

We have laws that say what we believe is an offense, not just against one of us, but against all of us.

So, a civil wrong is an offense against "me" (as an individual). A criminal wrong is an offense against "us" (as a society).

Some actions give rise to both a criminal and a civil issue.

> *For example, for those old enough to remember the O.J. Simpson trial, he was acquitted of murder (a criminal charge), but found liable for wrongful death (a civil charge). Why? Well, along with being different sets of law, they also have different standards of guilt/liability.*

For criminal law, the standard is guilty "beyond a reasonable doubt," we've all heard that on TV before. But, for civil charges, the standard is a "preponderance of the evidence."

"Beyond a reasonable doubt," doesn't mean beyond *any* doubt, but does mean that there's no other logical and reasonable explanation other than the person having committed the crime. A "preponderance of the evidence" is a much lower (easier to prove) standard. A "preponderance of the evidence" simply means that the crime was more likely than not to have occurred. So, going back to the O.J. Simpson trials, the jury in the criminal trial couldn't say that beyond a reasonable doubt that O.J. did it. But in the civil trial, the jury found that it was more likely than not that O.J. was responsible for the death. Generally, the remedy in criminal actions is incarceration—i.e. loss of freedom. In civil actions, the remedy is generally money/compensation called damages or money damages or doing (or not doing) a certain thing, often called specific performance.

FEDERAL, STATE, AND LOCAL

Next, let's think about where our laws come from. First, understand that there is no one "government." Our lives are regulated by a matrix of governments, from international treaties down to local ordinances and infractions; there are layers of interaction we have with governmental authorities everyday that we don't often realize.

Think of "the law" as an overlapping Venn diagram. The U.S. Constitution gives the federal government "enumerated powers." That means that the federal government only has the powers that the states specifically give to the federal government. Alternatively, the states have all the power not specifically given to the federal government. And then, the states delegate some powers to counties, cities, towns, or other municipalities.

Most of the specifics and "everyday" interaction we have has to do with state law rather than federal law.

For example, even though there are federal crimes and criminal courts, the vast majority of crimes are prosecuted in state courts and are violations of state laws.

So, here's how they interact (generally):

- Federal law, where it exists, always overrides state law
- State law can offer more protection to the individual than federal law, but never less

Additionally, there are federal courts and there are state courts. Generally speaking, there are no "local" courts to handle municipal, county, or town issues. Don't get misled. Even though there are courts (generally) in each county that handle civil and criminal issues, those are state courts.

Federal courts are established to resolve issues between people of different states (if they meet certain requirements). Violations of federal laws can also be heard or resolved in state court. And violations of state laws can be heard in federal courts if they meet certain requirements. It's not quite as simple as state laws equals state courts, but that's one way to think of it.

Courts are divided into jurisdictions. Jurisdiction is the name for the sphere of authority of that court. All lower courts in a certain jurisdiction must follow the precedents of the higher court for that jurisdiction (that's called "mandatory authority"). Courts in a different jurisdiction, can follow the precedent, but don't have to (that's referred to as "persuasive authority").

LAWS AND THEIR SOURCES

Laws in the U.S. come from a few different sources. How they're treated often depends on where they come from.

COMMON LAW

Common Law is the collected sum of all legal cases identifying the law and requirements of the law. That is, Common Law is what courts agree what the law is. When we hear the term "legal precedent," this is generally what we're talking about. Additionally, there are some laws which have, through the centuries, come down to us as a general understanding of the way things work.

> *For example, the Common Law definition of burglary is "the breaking and entering the house of another in the night time, with intent to commit a felony therein." Now, most states have a statute that specifically defines burglary and, generally, the state statutes reflects/mimics the Common Law definition.*

Common Law also incorporates all the previous legal decisions and interpretations. So, when you hear that the U.S. Supreme Court has decided that something has to happen (or not happen), unless Congress enacts a statute that covers it, that decision is part of the Common Law and we all have to live with it.

Is there a written set that includes all "The Common Law?" No. Common Law is more fluid than that and is generally just what we all agree/think it is (plus all the published court decisions of your jurisdiction). You see why there can be arguments about what the law is, huh?

STATUTES

Statutes are generally what people think of as "the law." Statutes are the written laws of the jurisdiction whether it's federal or state. That means that there is a physical book that you can go to and read what the law says. Well, when we say "book," what we really mean is book-ish, as more and more states move to electronic publication or collections.

Statutes, whether federal or state, are passed by legislatures and are "the law" as far as the legislature is concerned. Also, keep in mind that international treaties that are ratified by the U.S. Senate carry the same weight as federal statutes.

Ultimately the courts get to decide what the law means.

For example, if the law says an individual "shall" do something, the court decides whether that "shall" means every time, sometimes, or if there are acceptable excuses for not doing it.

Generally, though, statutes describe behavior that should be done or should not be done. And, statutes can be civil or criminal in nature.

Federal statutes are generally referred to as Codes. So, if you're looking for specific laws, search for the applicable "U.S. Code," or USC.

For example, the Lanham Act which defines the trademark registration plan at the federal level has a definitions section at

15 USC §1141. This is also a good example, because this section (§1141) is the definitions section for the "Madrid Protocol." This shows how sometimes international treaties are incorporated into U.S. laws.

REGULATIONS

Statutes are the laws passed by the legislature. Regulations can be thought of as how those statutes are implemented.

> *For example, a single statute can create an agency like the Food and Drug Administration (FDA), but there is way too much about the science, the procedures, or the expectations of the FDA to include in statutes. So the FDA creates regulations to define those pieces that aren't covered in the statute(s).*

Regulations can be either federal or state in nature, and they carry the full force and weight of statutes, but don't necessarily get the approval of the legislatures. Regulations, generally, are very detailed and often have public or industrial input before being "promulgated." Promulgated is the fancy lawyer/government word for "published" or "effective."

Regulations are almost exclusively the result or purview of administrative agencies or regulatory bodies. For almost anything but the most serious issues or violations, the regulations are "where the rubber meets the road" around how businesses are run or what they can or can't do within their industry or within the confines of any regulatory body such as an Alcohol Beverage Commission, or ABC. Regulations are generally described as Administrative Law, and are often and initially resolved in special courts or procedures set up by the regulations.

For example, for an ABC regulation violation, you will likely face some sort of ABC process, procedure, or tribunal to address it.

GUIDANCE

Many agencies, particularly at the federal level, issue guidances to help individuals or industries follow the regulations. Think of it sort of like saying, "Yeah, but what we mean is…"

Guidances are not "law" per se, but can help you avoid issues so you know what to do or how to get it done. Guidances are really "suggestions" from the agency. Some industries or industrial/trade groups issue guidances as well. Again, these are suggestions, generally not requirements, and often fit better into the next category.

Guidances have persuasive authority, meaning they're a good idea and recognized as important, but are not mandatory authority, meaning they don't have to be followed.

PRACTICES

Practices are merely standards that are created by an agency or industry/trade group. Practices are suggestions, not requirements. But you may hear them used like they're regulations or guidances.

Practices can be written, unwritten, published, or unpublished. Often, the only way to identify practices of the regulatory or administrative agency is to call or work with them repeatedly over time.

SUPPLEMENTAL MATERIAL. ZONING AND LAND USE

AUTHORITY

Your state's statutes and regulations will define how land can be used. This is often delegated to the county and city where the land is located.

USE

Use of land or buildings can generally be broken into one of a few different categories:
- Residential (often multiple classes defined by resident density)
- Retail (shops and businesses)
- Commercial (businesses)

- Industrial or manufacturing (production and assembly)
- Agricultural (farming and livestock)
- Mixed use

And there may be combinations of these such as "Retail/Commercial" or "Commercial/Light Industrial" and the like.

Each of the uses, or subcategories of uses is the basis for a zone of that use.

Each zone will have its own requirements and prohibitions. Additionally, many municipalities offer the ability to get a zoning variance. In this case, a specific piece of property may be exempted from the local requirements for the zone or apply different requirements belonging to another zone. These are sometimes called conditional use or special user permits.

WHERE DOES A BREWERY FIT IN?

How the property is used will identify what type of zone or use the property has to be qualified for. Depending on your state, county, and city definitions, a brewer can be retail, commercial, or industrial. Be sure to check on these before signing a lease for a space.

Many states' municipalities allow for exceptions from the general rule that "only residences can be in a residential zone." For example, in some cases a brewery can be located on the same piece of property as a residence or on a farm (sometimes referred to as a "farm brewery"). But in those cases, there may be other considerations as well. No homeowners' association is going to allow a brewery in a gated, manicured subdivision. Real property covenants or local agricultural rules may also apply.

CONCEPTS BREWERIES NEED TO UNDERSTAND

CONCURRENT JURISDICTION

Concurrent jurisdiction is when two or more sets of regulations apply. A good example of this is in those cases where the city's zoning and regulations are in addition to, rather than instead of, the county's zoning and regulations. In these cases, if the brewery is located in the city, you may have to comply with county zoning requirements and city zoning requirements.

EXTRATERRITORIAL JURISDICTION (ETJ)

Sometimes, even if the brewery is not within city limits, the city may have something to say about the zoning and use of land near their city. Generally, if this right exists, it's granted by a state statute and gives the city the right to enforce its zoning and regulations a certain distance around its borders (for example, "one mile outside city limits"). In a case like this, the brewery needs to comply with both the county's and the city's requirements even if the brewery is outside city limits.

LEVELS OF RESTRICTION / RESTRICTIVENESS

It's worth noting that the state is less restrictive than the county and that the county is less restrictive than the city.

LEGAL NON-CONFORMING USE

A legal non-conforming use is a use that was legal and conforming, but no longer meets current zoning requirements. Buildings can become non-conforming because the zoning requirements change or because a new set of zoning requirements has been imposed (i.e. when a city or town has annexed an area or extends it with an ETJ). If a building or use is legal and nonconforming, it can often cause issues for a brewery because the expansion of or construction on the building can trigger new zoning requirements resulting in additional expense. However, sometimes these buildings can be "grandfathered in" because the use has not changed substantially.

CONDEMNATION / PUBLIC TAKING

Property can be condemned or taken by the state or municipal government, even if it is not in disrepair. Public condemnation or taking is generally the result of a public "need" and often has to go through extensive public hearing and notice processes. Most states require that the property owner is justly compensated for their taking. However, this may not provide any comfort for the lessee of a property.

TITLE REPORTS AND TITLE INSURANCE

Title is the means to convey ownership from one person (or company) to another. Title insurance is available to protect one or more people from mistakes in the title or chain of title. The idea is to protect the new purchaser against any mistakes in the title or chain of ownership of the property or against any defects in the deed. What is a deed defect? Well, if the deed says something like "... extending to coordinates 95 degrees 7 minutes 23 seconds West, 35 degrees 8 minutes 48 seconds North..." but it should really say "... extending to coordinates 95 degrees 7 minutes 32 seconds West, 35 degrees 8 minutes 48 seconds North..." that could mean the difference of several hundred feet being included or excluded from the piece of property. Title insurance helps to protect the parties from mistakes or to cover the cost of fixing the mistake in the title.

Generally there are two types of coverage: coverage for lenders and coverage for owners. The difference is how much is covered. As one would expect, a lender cares about the amount of money loaned and a lender policy covers this amount. An owner, on the other hand, has broader concerns, so an owner policy has broader protection, up to and beyond the purchase price (depending on the policy).

TYPES OF DEEDS

There are, for the most part, two types of deeds that breweries need to be aware of when it comes to real estate: warranty deeds and quitclaim deeds. Warranty deeds are called that because the seller "warrants" (or provides a warranty) that the title is good. The seller is essentially saying, "I guarantee that this deed is good and that I have the right to convey this property to you." Warranty deeds are generally backed up by a title insurance policy and the seller is "on the hook" if there's a problem with the title. A quitclaim deed is quicker, easier, and much less reliable. A quitclaim deed transfers the interest of the grantor ("seller"), if any, to the grantee ("buyer"). The grantor/seller of a quitclaim deed is saying, "I'm not saying that I own the property—heck, I'm not saying I have any interest in the property at all! But if I have any interest or ownership in the property, I'm giving that interest or ownership to you." It's pretty clear how this can cause problems if the brewery thinks it's paying for a warranty deed, but only gets a quitclaim deed.

SURVEYS

Surveys are a critical part of property, zoning, and deeds. In years past, survey technology was approximate at best. In the distant past and for large tracts of land, a survey was considered accurate if it got within several feet of the actual boundary line.

Imagine, if you will, George Washington (who started his career as a surveyor) treading un-trodden trails, bush-whacking through the Virginia countryside to carve out a few hundred acres with no distinct and permanent landmarks and sighting with a surveyor's transit over a couple miles to where the person holding the flag is standing and then trying to tell the flagman, "no, a little to the left." Surveys were notoriously inaccurate, but were the best thing available. Surveys in states that included the original thirteen colonies often included language like "…up to the large oak tree east of McCullers' field"— a less than desirable description 200 plus years later by which time the oak tree may well have died.

As such, an accurate, up-to-date survey is important for a

brewery to identify the actual property that is in question. In surveys, look for

- Access—how is the property accessed? Is there a deeded title to access roads or ingress/egress?
- Acreage—how much property is enclosed by the "metes and bounds" description?
- Waterfront—if there is water involved, whose water is it? Are there "riparian rights" (having to do with water access and use)? Or is the water or waterfront owned by the municipality? Or another landowner?
- Utilities—are there hidden or latent utility right-of-ways or easements? Are there buried water, sewer, electrical, or other utilities on the property? What about overhead utilities or power poles?

MOVING A BREWERY INTO A HISTORIC BUILDING? THINK TWICE.

I'm not saying you shouldn't do it. In fact, I'm all for revitalizing derelict structures or repurposing really cool old buildings into breweries, distilleries, brewpubs, whatever. But there are some serious considerations if you're going to do it. I've outlined some of my concerns (some legal issues, some not-so-legal) 114-117 and 243-244.

CAN YOU DO IT AT ALL?

I had a client who was looking to locate a nanobrewery in a really nice, historic, just-off-the-beaten-path town. In fact they were looking to remodel the 1950s-era gas station that's been abandoned for twenty plus years to turn the garage area into a brewery and the shop into taproom (pretty neat idea, huh?). Well, the town told them, "No way, we don't want a brewery in our town. Breweries are like bars and we don't want a bar in the [historic] downtown." The client tried to explain, "Hey, we'll refurbish that vacant eyesore over there and bring you foot traffic, festivals…" The town just flat shut them down. The nano moved down the road to a different (more friendly) downtown area. Town's loss.

The point is, whether it's zoning issues, political issues, or whatever, make sure that you've identified the issues you're going to face and know what you're up against. In the case above, even if money were no object, the town was going to throw up every barrier they could to make it harder for the brewery because that wasn't the vision the town had for itself. Make sure your vision is shared by the town.

INFRASTRUCTURE (REFER TO CHAPTER FOUR FOR MORE DETAILS)

Remember to check for electrical issues, if your floor can stand your equipment weight, incoming water and making sure you aren't polluting your town's water.

In the South, even the old/historic construction is fairly

new. Heck, most of Florida wasn't built until after the invention of central air conditioning. But whether it's recently-old or old-old, be wary of the infrastructure that you might have to deal with.

Most brewers can immediately spot electrical issues (requiring rewiring), substandard/inadequate electrical service (doesn't have 220 or the panel isn't big enough), or even roofing or structural issues. But, what about what you can't see? Are the drains sufficient? How long have they been building up sediment? Do you even know where the drains/plumbing lead to? This is especially an issue in buildings built in the early 1900s and before. You might have a great space in this really nice building, but do you know where the hole in floor drains to?

What about the incoming water? I talked to a client a while back who was looking to start a nanobrewery on a farm he had just acquired. "Great idea," I said. "Where are you getting your water?" "Oh, from the well." Uh … maybe not a great idea. If you're using a well, do you know if the well can meet your water demand? Remember, even *super* conservation-minded breweries are still using upwards of three plus gallons of water for each gallon of beer produced. If the well can meet your demand, do you know what's in the well? In many rural areas, you may have groundwater contaminated by heavy metals, pesticides, or other chemicals that may be below the threshold values for residential purposes, but may be above it when you're pulling a lot of water out of the ground.

The same thought process goes for streams or surface water sources. Oh, and make sure that when you start pulling your water, you don't adversely affect your neighbor's wells, streams, etc.

Finally on the subject of infrastructure, something not so easy to gauge from a simple visual inspection, can the floor stand the weight? Remember, you're going to be putting several tons of grain, liquid, and equipment on that floor. And, just because it's concrete, doesn't mean it can stand the strain. You really don't want to explain to the landlord that your fermenter just broke his foundation.

RETROFITTING (REFER TO CHAPTER FOUR FOR MORE DETAILS)

Remember that without appropriate waivers when you're retrofitting, you generally have to bring the building up to standard code regardless of what your requirements are.

SUPPLEMENTAL MATERIAL. GLOSSARY

Alcohol Beverage Control (ABC)—Most states have a department or agency that is tasked with taxing, regulating, and/or enforcing alcohol laws. The regulatory authority for the state is generically referred to as the ABC.

Accredited Investor—Defined by the Securities and Exchange Commission (SEC). Accredited investors are those who are of sufficient sophistication and net worth that they can accept the risk of investing in potentially risky businesses or endeavors. Specifically, accredited investors are those that

- Earn an individual income of >$200k per year, or >$300k as joint incomes with a spouse, and reasonably expect to maintain that level of income OR
- Have a net worth of >$1MM, individually or jointly OR

- Are a general partner, executive, or director (or a combination of these or equivalent offices) of the business being offered

Alternating Proprietorship—A federally recognized relationship between two companies which share brewing or alcohol production equipment. The ownership of the equipment "alternates" between the companies, allowing both companies to share the equipment but still produce different brands of alcohol. To be an alternating proprietorship, the companies must be licensed as such and must have an alternating proprietorship agreement on file with (at least) the TTB.

Alternative Dispute Resolution—A group of collaborative or alternative means to settle a dispute. Alternative dispute resolution is named as such because it is used as an alternative to legal action, which can be uncertain and expensive. Alternative dispute resolution processes include arbitration, mediation, and collaborative law. Of these, arbitration and mediation are the most common.

Angel—A single individual (or company) that invests in companies, typically during startup, often for exchange for equity or a loan that could be converted to equity. Often referred to as an Angel Investor.

Arbitration—An alternative dispute resolution procedure where the parties with the dispute submit the dispute to a neutral third party who decides the dispute based on the merits of the case. Arbitration is essentially an informal trial between the parties where the arbitrator acts as a "judge" in the matter. Arbitration can be a formal process, with rules of evidence and detailed and technical procedures. Arbitration should not be seen as an "easy" or "simple" process. Individuals looking toward arbitration should get legal assistance to understand their options and the process—even if they want to avoid a lawsuit. See also Mediation.

Articles of Incorporation—The basic terms of the existence of a corporation. Articles of incorporation in most states have been boiled down to a form (or series of forms) that need to be filed with the state's Secretary of State to create the legal entity in that jurisdiction.

Articles of Organization—The equivalent of articles of incorporation, but for limited liability companies (LLCs). See also *Articles Of Incorporation.*

Assignment—The giving of the rights, privileges, responsibilities, and obligations of one party to a separate party. Assignment is most commonly seen in contracts (where one party—like a buyer—assigns their part to a third party, a different buyer, called an assignee so the assignee steps into the shoes of the person doing the assigning, i.e. the assignor). Assignment is also seen in leases (similar to subleasing, but can have different legal nuances or liability on the lease) and intellectual property rights (for example, where a person assigns the ownership of their invention to another or to their employer).

Brewer's Notice—The actual license (or permit) given to the brewery when it has been approved by the TTB for the production and sale of malt beverages.

Brewpub—A brewery located inside or attached to a restaurant. However, this definition is likely misleading. There are differences in state and federal definitions of "brewpub" that may be significant, depending on the business strategy and structure. For example, in some states a "brewpub" is not allowed to distribute beer off site. In these cases the same business might be better termed a brewery operating a tavern (or taproom) which may allow distribution off site.

Bylaws—The "rules" that a corporation is run by. Bylaws identify important aspects of the operation of the corporation such as rights and responsibilities of shareholders, the board of directors, and corporate officers. Bylaws are to corporations what an operating agreement is to a limited liability company (LLC).

Corporation—A separate legal entity, like a person, that can act, take on liability, and earn income—just like any individual person. A corporation is one way that individual business owners can manage their risk, liability, profits, and the business overall. It is important to stress that a corporation is a separate legal entity, almost a separate legal person. A corporation is one way to limit an owner's liability in the event of significant debt, judgment, or an accident. A corporation is created by the state; there is no "federal registration" for corporations. States create a corporation and, to do business in the state, a corporation must be registered with the state's Secretary of State. Corporate formation is an act by a state. Designation as an S-Corp or C-Corp is an IRS designation. Therefore the statement "I formed an S-Corp at the Secretary of State" doesn't make a lot of sense, legally speaking.

- C-Corp—A corporation in the traditional sense. Because it is a separate legal entity, its income can be taxed by the IRS. A C-Corp's income is taxed as the corporation receives

the income and then when the corporation pays its shareholders (technically a "distribution," but sometimes called a "dividend"). The shareholders then pay income tax on that income as they receive it. This is the so-called "double taxation" of C-corps and corporations generally.
- S-Corp—A corporation that qualifies for a special designation as "small" by the IRS. An S-Corp is exempted from income tax on the corporation itself; the shareholders only pay income tax on the value they receive from the corporation. S-Corp is an IRS designation and the corporation must meet several requirements to qualify for this designation/exemption.

Certificate of Label Approval (COLA)—The approval, by the TTB, of a label or malt beverage (or other alcohol) package for transportation across state lines. COLA is the federal approval of the label or package to ensure that it meets federal requirements. COLA does not necessarily mean that the label meets state requirements.

Clearance (Trademark Clearance)—Term used to describe the process to determine whether any person or company has prior rights in a trademark based on use of the mark.

Common Law—The sum of all prior precedents and generally accepted laws. Common law is distinct from statutes, which are laws specifically enacted by state or federal legislatures to codify the law. Some statutes specifically state the common law as it applies to that jurisdiction, but the common law generally supplements the statutes of a given jurisdiction.

Common Law Protection (trademark)—This is based on inherent rights of a trademark owner and stems from use of the mark in commerce. The general rule is that there is common law protection available for trademark holders who have (1) used the mark (2) in commerce, (3) exclusively (4) for a period of time (5) in a geographic area. The extent of protections depends on the numbered variables (which have to be proved in a court) and the common law of the state.

Confidential Disclosure Agreement (CDA)—An agreement between two or more parties that allows for the parties to disclose information to each other for mutual advantage. A CDA also imposes requirements for safeguarding confidential/shared information and penalties for breach of confidentiality. A CDA can and should also specify nondisclosure of information to parties outside the agreement. A CDA is also referred to as a Nondisclosure Agreement (NDA).

Copyright—The exclusive ownership of a work, given to the creator of the work (or the creator's assignee). Works are creations of print, performance, film, music, art, literature, or other creation which can be reduced to a tangible media. Copyright includes the right to prevent or authorize others to reproduce or publish the work.

Craft Beer (Brewery)—There is no legally accepted definition of "craft beer" or "craft brewery." There are multiple definitions depending on the use, but the Brewers Association has the most robust and most widely accepted definition of "craft beer." The Brewers Association changes or updates the definition from time to time, potentially including or excluding businesses that meet or fail to meet the definition as it changes.

Discrimination—The disparate treatment of people or things. Discrimination can be "legal," but when used in causal conversation and most instances, discrimination is intended to mean unjust, illegal, or prejudicial treatment of people based on characteristics such as race, religion, gender, age, sexual orientation, or other discriminatory differentiation.

Easement—A license to use the property, or portions of the property, for ingress, egress, maintenance or other proper purposes. An easement is typically used with respect to these entities and granted to utilities, municipalities, neighbors, or users of real property.

Employee—A person who performs or provides services to a person or business for wages. An employee is subject to direct supervision by the employer as to how work is done.

Employment Retirement Income Security Act (ERISA)—The federal law that creates minimum standards for retirement plans and retirement savings/investment accounts provided by employers. ERISA creates a complex and extensive set of requirements for taxation, distribution, and disposition of retirement assets.

Equity—Ownership in a business. Equity is the general term for any ownership interest. Equity is, by definition, a Security subject to the Securities Act of 1933, the same act that establishes the Securities and Exchange Commission).

Fixture—An item of personal property that has become affixed or attached to a piece of real property (and is not easily removed without damaging the real property).

FAA—Federal Alcohol Administration Act

Franchise Law—The body of law, established at the state level, that determines how brands are bought and sold in certain industries. Franchise Law is generally limited to the gasoline/petroleum, automotive, and alcohol industries. For alcohol producers, franchise law defines the relationship and interaction between manufacturers, distributors, and (to a lesser extent) retailers.

Guarantee/Guaranty—A formal promise or agreement that certain conditions will be fulfilled. A guarantee is the general term for the promise to fulfill certain conditions. A guaranty is narrower in meaning and is almost exclusively referring to financial conditions. Generally, the term guaranty is only used in banking, bonds, and legal contexts.

Guarantee/Guaranty (Personal)—A personal guarantee/guaranty is a promise that an individual will be personally liable for the fulfillment of a particular promise. A lease, as an example, may often be in the name of a company or legal entity but may be accompanied by a personal guarantee that one or more of the owners will be personally liable for the lease.

Independent Contractor—A person or business hired to perform services but who has significant discretion as to how the work is completed. Relationship as an independent contractor is typically defined in a contract or agreement.

Intern—A student or trainee working for a person or business to gain work experience. Under limited conditions, interns sometimes work for no pay.

Limited Liability Company (LLC)—A special form of legal entity. It combines aspects of partnerships (such as "pass through taxation") with aspects of corporations (such as limited liability). LLCs have a limited legal history, as the first law in the United States allowing LLCs was enacted in 1997. LLCs are creatures of the state and very flexible legal structures, largely defined by their Operating Agreement.

Mark—A symbol or word(s) used to identify a brand or

source of goods or services for the purposes of marketing or selling those goods or services. See *also trademark.*

Mediation—An alternative dispute resolution procedure. Mediation is a collaborative process where a neutral party attempts to help the parties come to an agreement between themselves. The neutral party does not "decide" a dispute between the parties, but facilitates the parties to resolve the dispute. See also Arbitration.

Member (Industry member)—A participant in the industry as either a producer of alcohol or distributor of alcohol. Industry member is the term used to identify parties that are regulated by the Federal Alcohol Administration (FFA) Act and often state regulations regarding permitted or prohibited actions by producers or distributors.

Member (LLC)—An owner of an LLC. Member interest can be identified in several ways and can be divided up into the different types of ownership rights.

Nondisclosure Agreement (NDA)—See Confidential Disclosure Agreement.

Operating Agreement—The basis of the "rules" for how an LLC operates. An Operating Agreement determines the rights and responsibilities of owners (called members), managers, and officers. Operating Agreements are to LLCs what bylaws are to corporations.

Partnership—A legal structure where two or more parties intend to conduct business together. A partnership can be formed without any registration or written agreement. In a general partnership, each partner bears all the liability of the entire business—even the actions of the other partners.

Patent—A federally recognized registration of ownership of an invention or thing for a set period of time. A patent allows a person to control the reproduction and use of their invention or thing. A patent is to things as a copyright is to a work. Generally, to be eligible for patent protection, an invention must be "new," "novel," and "useful"—all of which have specific legal, term-of-art definitions.

Private Placement Memo (PPM)—A highly structured and specific document which identifies the risks and potentials associated with a securities offering. A PPM is designed to meet the requirements of an SEC exemption for registration of security sales. A PPM generally details a debt or equity sale offering by a small business to raise funds. A PPM is often used to establish the exemption outlined in Regulation D.

Regulation D (Reg D)—The SEC regulation that outlines the exemptions from the general requirement that all securities for sale must be registered with the SEC.

Trade Secret—A process, information, or procedure that is not generally known and creates an advantage for the one(s) who know the trade secret.

Trademark (generally)—A symbol or word(s) which is known to represent a particular source of goods or services for the purposes of marketing or selling those goods or services. It is sometimes used interchangeably with the term "brand." See also Mark.

Trademark (registration)—The process of identifying and registering a trademark with a government entity. Registration can be done at the federal and state levels. Registration does not in itself prevent the infringement or use of the registered mark by another. Even with registration, the mark owner is responsible for policing the mark. Registration merely shifts the burden for proving appropriate (or inappropriate) use of the mark.

- Federal Registration—Administered by the United States Patent and Trademark Office (USPTO). Federal registration is typically what people mean when they refer to "trademark registration." Federal registration sanctions the use of "circle-R" (i.e. ®) mark.
- State Registration—Each state has its own process for registration. Enforcement and recognition of state registration rights ends at the state borders. Because of a more global economy and the Internet, state registration is becoming less and less important.

INDEX

A

acceptance 86–96
Accredited Investor 70, 387
advertising 66–397
Alternating Proprietorships 98
Amendment
  Eighteenth Amendment 188, 229

B

boilerplate 86, 96, 112
Brewers Association 276, 300, 392
Brewer's Notice 203–225, 323, 389
brewpub 24, 127, 224, 383, 389
bylaws 19, 29, 51, 390

C

capital 53, 67, 73, 74
Certificate of Label Approval 98, 189, 213, 240, 250, 391
Civil law 369
Confidentiality Agreements 132–134
contract
  Contract Brewing 97, 133
copyright 121–127, 392
Copyright 392
corporation 5, 9, 17, 21–33, 46, 55, 83, 111, 205, 317, 323, 346, 389, 390
Criminal law 370
crowdfunding 75–77

D

damages 6, 44, 90, 163, 371
debt 10, 13, 38, 69, 71, 73, 325
distributor 79, 103, 140, 145, 186, 191, 198, 235, 263, 277, 279, 281, 285, 293, 295, 301, 394

E

Eighteenth Amendment 229
equity viii, 8, 26, 34, 38, 56, 69, 71, 72, 90, 118, 388, 393, 396
excise tax 98–213, 238, 299–310

F

Federal Alcohol Administration 188–201, 252, 266, 393, 395
Food and Drug Administration 199, 220, 258, 375
formula 14, 123, 128, 163, 199, 203, 222, 251

I

Immigration 333, 360–367
independent contractor 310, 334–346, 394
infrastructure 80, 108, 115, 279, 295, 296, 384, 386
Insurance 43, 59, 62, 339, 380
intern 334, 352–355, 394
Intrastate 70
IRS 18, 25, 38, 344, 390, 391

L

Lease 88, 100–106, 133, 206, 287, 317, 321, 329, 378, 394
liability shield 21, 29, 46, 47, 56
licensing 98, 103, 191, 197, 203, 229, 236, 238
Limited Liability Company 21, 46, 205, 390, 394

M

Manufacturer 192
mark 146
Meetings 11, 34, 51
Merger 37, 113, 289, 320
Minutes 35

N

Non-compete agreement 59, 138
Non-disclosure agreement 59, 135–137

O

Officer 31, 32
Operating Agreement 11, 21, 29, 30, 42, 394, 395

P

Partnership 395

   General Partnership 13
   Limited Liability Partnership 23
   Limited Partnership 15
   Sole Partnership 13
patent 121, 122, 396
Piercing the Corporate Veil 25, 49

R

recipe 129, 130, 142
Recycling 244
refrigeration 183
retailer 67, 181, 194, 195
risk 56, 60, 327

S

Securities 67
Social Media 271, 351
Sole Proprietorship 12
Supplier 101

T

Taproom 100, 107, 224
tasting room 100, 107, 224, 303
three-tier system 110, 181–196, 278
Tied House 183, 186
title 329, 380
Trademark
   Common Law Trademark 162
   Intent to Use 155
   In Use 155
   Likelihood of Confusion 155
   registration 27, 127, 128, 151, 157, 159
   Tax and Trade Bureau 27, 188
   trade dress 124, 156
   Trademark Dispute 164, 169
   TTB application 204, 208
   TTB Specialist 208, 211
   use in commerce 156

U

Uniform Trade Secret Act 128
United States Patent and Trademark Office 123, 124, 149, 151, 155
U.S. Copyright Office 128
Use Tax 312

V

Venture Capital 74
Visa 361, 363

W

Wastewater 246
wholesaler 190, 194

Z

zoning 115, 244, 377

Made in the USA
Lexington, KY
14 February 2018